RAILWAY DAY TRIPS

150 classic train journeys from around Britain

JULIAN HOLLAND

Collins

An imprint of HarperCollins Publishers
Westerhill Road, Bishopbriggs, Glasgow G64 2QT

Copyright © HarperCollins Publishers Ltd 2014
Text © Julian Holland
Maps © Collins Bartholomew Ltd 2014
Photographs © as per credits on page 192

First Edition 2014

PB ISBN 978 0 00 749715 7
EB ISBN 978 0 00 754969 6

10 9 8 7 6 5 4 3 2

British Library Cataloguing in Publication Data
A catalogue record for this book is available from the British Library

Printed in China

All mapping in this atlas is generated from Collins Bartholomew digital
databases. Collins Bartholomew, the UK's leading independent
geographical information supplier, can provide a digital, custom,
and premium mapping service to a variety of markets.
For further information:
Tel: +44 (0) 208 307 4515
e-mail: collinsbartholomew@harpercollins.co.uk

If you would like to comment on any aspect of this publication, please write to:
Collins Maps, HarperCollins Publishers, Westerhill Road, Bishopbriggs, Glasgow G64 2QT
e-mail: **collinsmaps@harpercollins.co.uk**
or visit our website at: **www.harpercollins.co.uk**

 facebook.com/collinsmaps

 @collinsmaps

The scenic railway line between Folkestone and Dover burrows through Shakespeare Cliff in a twin-bore tunnel.

₄ CONTENTS

*Empty deckchairs await
new customers on the
beach at Bognor Regis.*

For as long as I can remember, I've enjoyed taking railway day trips. As a young child I went nearly everywhere by train and the smells, sounds and sights are still vivid in my mind. The musty, stale-smoke smell of carriage compartments coupled with the rhythmic clickety-clack of the wheels on the rail joints, the whistling of the steam locomotive as we rushed through sleepy country stations and the stifling roar as we burrowed through dank and dripping tunnels will be with me forever. As I grew older, my interest in railways led me into the wonderful world of trainspotting and consequently my forays took me to some pretty amazing places all around Britain – my knowledge of the geography of our country has stood me in good stead ever since.

However, as we can't turn the clock back, it is heartening to know, despite the best efforts of certain politicians and dear old Dr Beeching, that railway travel is not a thing of the past. In recent years our railways have enjoyed a renaissance that would have seemed like a pipe dream back in the 1960s – closed railways and stations are being reopened and a vast amount of taxpayers' money is being invested in a transport system that was nearly killed off by the powerful road transport lobby 50 years ago. Passenger numbers are at their highest since the 1920s and, suddenly, Britain's love affair with the car and lorry seems to be on the wane – increasing road congestion and huge hikes in fuel prices have put paid to that. As the Father of Railways, George Stephenson, prophesied in 1825:

BELOW: *A steam train on the North Yorkshire Moors Railway between Goathland and Pickering.*

I think you will live to see the day, though I may not live so long, when railways will come to supersede almost all other methods of conveyance in this country … what I have said will come to pass as sure as we live.

Despite a few hiccups along the way, it looks as if he may have been right.

This book is not just aimed at die-hard railway enthusiasts – there are already enough books on the subject to sink the Titanic – but at a much wider audience who are now discovering the joy of leaving the car at home, sitting back, relaxing and watching Britain's ever-changing landscape unfold instead of hurtling to oblivion, stressed out along our multi-lane highways. While, in my mind anyway, a railway journey is in itself a voyage of discovery, the destination at the end is often the icing on the cake. For such a small country, Britain probably has more to offer the traveller or visitor, whether from home or abroad, than any other place on Earth – admittedly the weather can sometimes be inclement but that one factor surely gives the British so much of their resilient character.

The list of fascinating destinations that can be reached on a day trip by train in Britain is practically endless. In this book I have put together 150 of these trips, chosen with one eye on the journey itself and the other on the cities, towns or villages that are visited. From major historical sites, architectural gems, museums, gardens, historic pubs, boat trips and country walks to film and TV locations, seaside resorts, rides on heritage railways, festivals and markets there is something for everyone. A few of the trips also involve using a bus, ferry, catamaran or Shanks's Pony to complete the journey, but it is well worth the effort. It doesn't take a major leap in imagination to string some of these day trips together to make a long weekend break or even a week's railway holiday – the permutations are simply endless.

Each route featured in the book is illustrated by a location map and a route diagram:

- START/DESTINATION
- Interchange station
- Other town

- ● GLASGOW CENTRAL
- ○ PAISLEY GILMOUR ST
- ○ INVERKIP
- ● WEMYSS BAY
- ■ ROTHESAY
  (ISLE OF BUTE)

- ● START/DESTINATION/
  INTERCHANGE STATION
- ○ OTHER STATION
- ■ DESTINATION
  (NOT ON RAIL NETWORK)

NB minor stations have been omitted from some routes, especially those starting from London.

Each route also has the following information:

DESTINATION HIGHLIGHTS
give ideas of things to see and do at the journey's end

FREQUENCY OF TRAINS
indicates how often services run – but please check with the operator before travel

DISTANCE

JOURNEY TIME
one-way; includes time for connections, unless journey legs are shown separately, e.g. 5+10 mins

OPPOSITE: *Vintage luggage cases at the restored Sheringham station on the North Norfolk Railway.*

BELOW: *The spacious modern passenger departure concourse at King's Cross station was opened in 2012.*

Now to more practical matters. Do your homework and always plan your journey in advance, and if you are of a certain age take advantage of the Senior Railcard (over 60s) or, if in Scotland, ScotRail's Club 55, both of which offer amazing savings on rail fares. While many of the routes featured in this book are served by a frequent service of trains, some, in more rural or remote areas, see only a few trains each day. Trips along scenic routes such as the Esk Valley to Whitby in North Yorkshire, the Heart of Wales Line in Central Wales and in the more remote parts of Scotland need to be planned well so that the last train home is not missed. Although there are several online timetables with a ticket and seat booking service such as National Rail and the Train Line, these are computer generated and can often produce some mind-boggling results culminating in much lengthier journeys from A to B via X, Y and Z. While traditional printed timetables were once a thing of the past, the Stationery Office now publishes a paperback version (over 3,500 pages) – its GB Rail Timetable is updated usually twice a year. Sadly, on-train catering is not what it used to be. Apart from a handful of long-distance train journeys where silver service is still offered, passengers now have to put up with a budget airline-style trolley which is trundled up and down the train offering not very much for rather a lot of money – my advice is simple, take your own picnic with you.

In conclusion, when you are next planning on a day out, please remember to leave your car at home or at the station car park, catch a train and go out there to discover this wonderful country of ours.

WEST COUNTRY

PENZANCE ●
ST ERTH ●
LELANT SALTINGS ○
LELANT ○
CARBIS BAY ○
ST IVES ●

This is a great trip to explore one of Cornwall's (and Britain's) premier seaside resorts and avoid traffic queues in the busy summer months. Penzance's overall roofed station, 305 miles from Paddington, is the end of the line in the West Country. It was first reached by Brunel's West Cornwall Railway in 1852 but was not linked to the rest of Britain's rail network until 1859, with the opening of the Cornwall Railway between Truro and Plymouth. The short railway journey from Penzance to St Erth gives fine views of Mount's Bay and St Michael's Mount before turning inland at Marazion to cross this narrow point of the Cornish Peninsula. Passengers for St Ives must change trains at St Erth.

From St Erth, the 4¼-mile single-track branch line to St Ives hugs the west bank of the Hayle Estuary, passing through Lelant Saltings station where a park-and-ride scheme operates. Lelant station follows shortly after, where passengers are treated to stunning vistas across St Ives Bay to Hayle Sands. Opened in 1877, this branch line once carried thousands of holidaymakers from far-flung corners of Britain and even had its own through coach from Paddington on the GWR's 'Cornish Riviera Express'. Although listed for closure in the 'Beeching Report' of 1963, this scenic railway was reprieved and in recent years has seen buoyant growth in passenger numbers.

Following the coastline above Carbis Bay, the railway skirts Porthminster Beach before ending at the minimal, modern station of St Ives. From here it is but a short walk to the beaches, harbour, quaint streets and world-famous art galleries including the Leach Pottery, Tate St Ives and Barbara Hepworth Museum.

DESTINATION HIGHLIGHTS
14th-century Sloop Inn; harbour; beaches; shark fishing; Leach Pottery; Tate St Ives; Barbara Hepworth Museum and Sculpture Garden; St Ives Museum; St Ives September Festival; South West Coast Path

FREQUENCY OF TRAINS
1-2 per hour

10 MILES
40 MINUTES

Sandwiched between a golf course and sand dunes, a train for St Ives heads away from Lelant station.

Marketed today as the Maritime Line, this single-track branch was opened as a broad-gauge line by the Cornwall Railway in 1863. Engineered by Brunel, it was originally built to serve the international shippers that operated out of Falmouth but by the time the railway arrived the business had gone elsewhere. The branch was converted to standard gauge by the GWR in 1892. Our journey starts at Truro station which is well-served by trains on the Cornish main line between Plymouth and Penzance, with Falmouth trains plunging through Higher Town Tunnel before branching off at Penwithers Junction and heading off in a southwesterly direction. En route it passes through Sparnick Tunnel before crossing Restronguet Creek on the imposing 11-arch Carnon Viaduct. This is one of eight viaducts on the line, all originally built of timber on stone piers but later replaced by new stone structures. Carnon was rebuilt in 1933 and stands at nearly 100 ft high.

Perranwell station is soon reached before the railway dives into Perran Tunnel and crosses the 5-arch Perran Viaduct followed by the 9-arch Ponsanooth Viaduct – at 139 ft high this is the tallest on the line – then 6-arch Pascoe Viaduct and 5-arch Penryn Viaduct. From here there are panoramic views across the historic town of Penryn, which is set at the head of the Penryn Estuary and was once a thriving port with trade in fish, copper and tin. A recently installed passing loop at Penryn station has allowed a more frequent service of trains on the branch which in turn has led to a massive increase in passenger numbers.

Leaving Penryn, the railway crosses the imposing 14-arch Collegewood Viaduct before pausing at the renovated Penmere station. Next stop is Falmouth Town station, which is convenient for visitors to the National Maritime Museum. Our journey ends at Falmouth Docks station, set on a hillside overlooking the docks, Pendennis Castle and Gyllyngvase Beach.

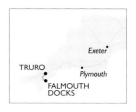

- **TRURO**
- PERRANWELL
- PENRYN
- PENMERE
- FALMOUTH TOWN
- **FALMOUTH DOCKS**

DESTINATION HIGHLIGHTS
harbour; 3 beaches; Pendennis Castle; National Maritime Museum Cornwall; Falmouth Art Gallery; South West Coast Path; passenger ferry to St Mawes (for walks on Roseland Peninsula)

FREQUENCY OF TRAINS
2 per hour (Mon-Sat)
1 per hour (Sun)

11¾ MILES
24 MINUTES

A sunny day on Swanpool Beach, close to the Swanpool Lake Nature Reserve in Falmouth.

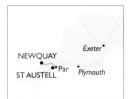

NEWQUAY
Exeter•
ST AUSTELL •Par Plymouth

ST AUSTELL ●
PAR ●
LUXULYAN ○
BUGLE ○
ROCHE ○
ST COLUMB ROAD ○
QUINTRELL DOWNS ○
NEWQUAY ●

The first 4½ miles of this railway trip to the surfing capital of Britain follow the Cornish main line from the town of St Austell to the china clay harbour town of Par. Soon after leaving St Austell the railway heads towards Carlyon Bay, where there are views across St Austell Bay to Gribbin Head. Passengers change trains at Par station before resuming their journey on what is now marketed as the 'Atlantic Coast Line' to Newquay.

Trains for Newquay take a 180-degree turn from Par station before joining the route of the former Cornwall Minerals Railway near St Blazey. The railway was opened in 1874 and followed the route of earlier horse-drawn tramways built alongside the Par Canal to carry china clay down to Par Harbour for onward shipment. Modern china clay trains still use this route from Goonbarrow Junction.

North of St Blazey, the railway threads through the heavily wooded Luxulyan Valley, now designated a World Heritage Site for its early 19th-century industrial remains, before passing under Treffry Viaduct. Built in 1844 this historic structure carried an aqueduct and a horsedrawn tramway serving local mines. West of tiny Luxulyan station – now a request stop, as are all the other intermediate stations on the line – Goonbarrow Junction is the limit of the china clay service and also the site of the only passing loop (still controlled by semaphore signals) on this single-track branch line. After Bugle and Roche stations the railway crosses a nature reserve on Goss Moor before reaching St Columb Road station. The view to the south along this stretch is dominated by huge china clay workings, which have the surreal appearance of a lunar landscape. A freight-only branch from Burngullow (west of St Austell) to Parkandillack still serves the china clay industry. Quintrell Downs is the penultimate station, followed by our journey's end at Newquay station. The current single-platform affair here is in marked contrast to the original 3-platform structure that was also served by trains from Chacewater and Perranport until the line's closure in 1963. The world-famous surfing beaches of Newquay are but a short walk from the station.

DESTINATION HIGHLIGHTS
harbour; Discovery Trail;
9 beaches; surfing from Fistral
Beach; Trenance Gardens;
South West Coast Path

FREQUENCY OF TRAINS
6 per day (Mon-Sat)
5 per day (Sun)

25¼ MILES
1 HOUR 20 MINUTES

Fistral Beach in Newquay is
one of the premier surfing
locations in Britain.

For the first 17¾ miles of this scenic rail journey trains from Plymouth travel along the route of Brunel's heavily engineered former broad-gauge Cornwall Railway, which opened in 1859 and still links Cornwall with the rest of Britain's rail network via the magnificent Royal Albert Bridge over the River Tamar. After crossing the wrought-iron single-track bridge from which there are fine views of the Tamar Estuary and the distant Devonport Royal Naval Dockyard, the railway heads through Saltash and St Germans stations, crossing creeks and rivers on the first of many viaducts that span the narrow valleys along this route. Winding its way through low hills past Menheniot station, the railway then approaches the historic market town of Liskeard over the 720-ft-long Liskeard Viaduct from where the single-track branch line to Looe can be seen 150 ft below.

At Liskeard, trains for Looe depart from a separate platform set at a right angle to the main line before descending a steeply graded 180-degree loop, which was opened by the Great Western Railway in 1901, to remote Coombe Junction. Here the guard changes the points before the train reverses direction to head south down the picturesque wooded valley of the East Looe River along the route of the Liskeard & Looe Railway that opened alongside the Liskeard & Looe Union Canal in 1860 – both canal and railway were originally built to carry minerals from mines and quarries on Bodmin Moor down to Looe Harbour. Keeping company with the river and disused canal, the railway passes through request stops at St Keyne Wishing Well, Causeland and Sandplace before slowing for a riverside road crossing at Terras Crossing. The journey ends at the modern minimal station at Looe from where it is but a short walk to the harbour, fish market, beach and quaint narrow streets of East Looe.

- PLYMOUTH
- DEVONPORT
- DOCKYARD
- KEYHAM
- ST BUDEAUX FERRY ROAD
- SALTASH
- ST GERMANS
- MENHENIOT
- LISKEARD
- COOMBE JUNCTION HALT
- ST KEYNE WISHING WELL HALT
- CAUSELAND
- SANDPLACE
- LOOE

DESTINATION HIGHLIGHTS
beach; harbour; fish market; quaint streets (East Looe); boat hire on West Looe River; boat trips to Looe Island; shark fishing; Old Guildhall Museum; South West Coast Path

FREQUENCY OF TRAINS
1 per hour

26½ MILES
1 HOUR 10 MINUTES

The picturesque harbour at Looe is the jumping-off point for boat trips up the West Looe River and to St George's Island.

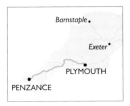

Barnstaple.

Exeter•

PLYMOUTH

•
PENZANCE

PLYMOUTH ●
DEVONPORT ○
DOCKYARD ○
KEYHAM ○
ST BUDEAUX FERRY ROAD ○
SALTASH ○
ST GERMANS ○
MENHENIOT ○
LISKEARD ○
BODMIN PARKWAY ○
LOSTWITHIEL ○
PAR ○
ST AUSTELL ○
TRURO ○
REDRUTH ○
CAMBORNE ○
HAYLE ○
ST ERTH ○
PENZANCE ●

DESTINATION HIGHLIGHTS
Art Deco Jubilee Bathing Pool;
Morrab Gardens; Golowan
Festival (June); Newlyn Art
Gallery; Penlee House Art
Gallery & Museum;
St Michael's Mount
(by bus to Marazion)

FREQUENCY OF TRAINS
1 per hour

79½ MILES
2 HOURS

Diesel trains for the scenic, switchback line to Penzance follow the same route as the day trip to Looe (see page 15) as far as Liskeard. Trains leave Liskeard in a westerly direction to cross the valley of the East Looe River on the imposing Moorswater Viaduct (147 ft high and 954 ft long). To the north lie the former granite quarries on Bodmin Moor while to the south the single-track branch line wends its way down the valley to Looe. After climbing to Doublebois, trains begin their descent of the wooded Fowey Valley to call at Bodmin Parkway station, junction for the steam-operated Bodmin & Wenford Railway. The heavily engineered section from Doublebois to Bodmin Parkway features no less than 7 viaducts. Originally designed by Isambard Kingdom Brunel in the 1850s with timber spans supported on masonry piers, the timber spans were later replaced by masonry arches. From here, the line heads south, continuing down the valley to Lostwithiel, junction for the freight-only line to Carne Point, near Fowey.

From Lostwithiel, the railway climbs away from the valley to pass through Treverran Tunnel before descending to Par station, junction for the Newquay branch line (see page 14). Leaving Par behind, the line heads along the Carlyon Bay coastline before climbing inland to St Austell, Cornwall's largest town and centre of the china clay industry. Westwards from here, the railway follows a switchback route to Truro, crossing steep-sided river valleys on 8 viaducts and boring through the hills in two tunnels. West of Truro (junction for Falmouth), it climbs steadily up through the hills to Redruth before descending to call at Camborne, Hayle and St Erth (junction for St Ives). The line then cuts across the Cornish peninsula to follow the shore of Mount's Bay past Long Rock depot to reach Penzance station.

Owned by the National Trust, St Michael's Mount near Penzance can be reached via an ancient causeway at low tide.

The rail journey from the maritime city of Plymouth to the cathedral city of Exeter is undoubtedly one of the most scenic in England. Trains leave Plymouth's 1960s station along the route of the original South Devon Railway that opened to the city in 1848. The planned extension of the disastrous atmospheric railway from Totnes never materialized and Brunel's eccentric but innovative system was replaced by a more conventional railway in the same year.

Today's modern trains make light work of the steeply graded section around the southern edge of Dartmoor but in steam days most trains needed to be double-headed up the 1-in-42 Hemerdon Bank to Ivybridge station before reaching the summit of the line at Wrangaton. From here it is downhill all the way through Brent and Rattery Bank to the historic riverside town of Totnes. After a brief stop at Totnes, trains continue on their switchback route with the steep climb up to Dainton Tunnel and a similarly steep descent down to Newton Abbot. In steam days the town was an important railway centre with workshops and large engine sheds, while today the station is still the junction for the line to Paignton (see page 20).

From Newton Abbot, the railway follows a fairly level route firstly alongside the Teign Estuary and then hugging the coastline, tunnelling through red sandstone cliffs between Teignmouth and Dawlish. This coastal route is often at the mercy of winter storms, which cause havoc with train services. The penultimate leg of this scenic route follows the west bank of the Exe Estuary from Dawlish Warren and through Starcross to end at Exeter's busy St Davids station where trains to London can still be seen departing in opposite directions. Here a change of train is necessary to complete the short journey up to Exeter Central station from where the delights of this historic city can be explored on foot.

EXETER CENTRAL
Exeter St Davids
PLYMOUTH
Penzance

- **PLYMOUTH**
- IVYBRIDGE
- TOTNES
- NEWTON ABBOT
- TEIGNMOUTH
- DAWLISH
- DAWLISH WARREN
- STARCROSS
- EXETER ST THOMAS
- **EXETER ST DAVIDS**
- **EXETER CENTRAL**

DESTINATION HIGHLIGHTS
12th-century cathedral; 11th-century Rougemont Castle; Danes Castle; St Nicholas Priory and Garden; Exeter Canal basin and riverside walks; 17th-century Butts Ferry; Royal Albert Memorial Museum; Spacex art gallery

FREQUENCY OF TRAINS
2 per hour (Mon–Sat)
1+ per hour (Sun)

52 MILES
1 HOUR 20 MINUTES

The journey from Plymouth to Exeter takes in this wave-swept coastal stretch of railway at Dawlish.

PLYMOUTH	●
DEVONPORT	○
DOCKYARD	○
KEYHAM	○
ST BUDEAUX VICTORIA ROAD	○
BERE FERRERS	○
BERE ALSTON	○
CALSTOCK	○
GUNNISLAKE	●

Set astride the Devon/Cornwall border, this highly scenic single-track branch line serves a string of villages along the valley of the River Tamar – hence its marketing title of the Tamar Valley Line. From Plymouth station, trains call at Devonport, Dockyard, Keyham and St Budeaux Victoria Road before diving under the road and rail bridges that cross the Tamar, while closely following its eastern shore along what was once the London & South Western Railway's main line to Exeter and Waterloo. This line opened in 1890 and, along with the branch line to Gunnislake and Callington, was listed for closure in the 'Beeching Report'. Fortunately the section from Plymouth to Bere Alston and the branch as far as Gunnislake were reprieved because of poor road connections and there are currently plans to reopen the line from Bere Alston to Tavistock.

After following the east bank of the Tamar, the railway crosses its tributary, the River Tavy, on an attractive 8-span bowstring bridge to arrive at the isolated village of Bere Ferrers, where the privately owned station buildings and signal box have been lovingly restored to their former glory and are open to the public. From here, the railway continues north to Bere Alston station where the train reverses direction to take the winding route to Gunnislake.

Abounding in sharp curves and steep gradients, the railway soon crosses the Tamar high above on the spectacular concrete 12-arch Calstock Viaduct, which was completed in 1908. After crossing the viaduct, today's trains call at tiny Calstock station before meandering high above the river to end at the minimal station of Gunnislake. For centuries the village was at the heart of an important industrial and mining region and was also the lowest crossing point of the Tamar until the opening of the Tamar Bridge near Plymouth in 1961. The mining and quarrying ended in the late 19th century and Gunnislake now lies in an Area of Outstanding Natural Beauty.

DESTINATION HIGHLIGHTS
walks in Tamar Valley (Area of Outstanding Natural Beauty) from Gunnislake station; Rising Sun Inn (real ale pub in Gunnislake); Cotehele House and Gardens (Calstock); Bere Alston station museum

FREQUENCY OF TRAINS
1 every 2 hours

15¼ MILES
45 MINUTES

A Plymouth to Gunnislake train slowly crosses the River Tamar on the impressive viaduct at Calstock.

The 9½-mile broad-gauge single-track branch line from Totnes to Ashburton was opened in 1872. It was converted to standard gauge in 1892 and became part of the Great Western Railway five years later. Serving small villages and farming communities on the edge of Dartmoor, the line led a fairly quiet life and was closed to passengers in 1958 and to goods in 1962. Lord Beeching reopened it as the South Devon Railway in 1969, but 'improvements' to the A38 trunk road led to the section between Buckfastleigh and Ashburton closing in 1971.

Steam-hauled trains now carry visitors on a delightful journey alongside the River Dart from the new terminus at Totnes (Littlehempston) – the station is accessible via a footbridge over the Dart from the national rail network station in the town. Leaving Totnes, the railway winds its way northwards up the meandering Dart Valley and past the parkland grounds of Dartington Hall to reach the only intermediate station and passing loop at Staverton. From here, the railway continues up the wooded valley, occasionally passing farms and isolated cottages before ending at the lovingly restored Buckfastleigh station. Here, a small but fascinating railway museum, miniature railway and café are found while in the town (reached under the ugly concrete bridge of the A38 dual carriageway) there is a butterfly farm, otter sanctuary and Buckfast Abbey, famous (some say notorious) for its popular tonic wine.

Exeter •
BUCKFASTLEIGH
TOTNES
(LITTLEHEMPSTON)
Penzance •

**TOTNES
(LITTLEHEMPSTON)**

STAVERTON

BUCKFASTLEIGH

DESTINATION HIGHLIGHTS
railway museum; miniature railway; Buckfast Abbey; otter sanctuary; butterfly farm; Sea Trout Inn (Staverton)

FREQUENCY OF TRAINS
4-9 per day (Mar-Nov)

7 MILES
30 MINUTES

Hauled by a restored GWR locomotive, a passenger train makes its way along the idyllic Dart Valley to Buckfastleigh.

Our journey starts at Exeter St Davids station, from where Brunel opened his broad-gauge atmospheric South Devon Railway to Totnes in 1848. The intention was to reach Plymouth but the resounding failure of this eccentric system, which required no locomotives, soon saw it replaced by more conventional steam motive power. Heading south, the railway closely follows the west bank of the ever-widening Exe Estuary through Starcross (for the passenger ferry to Exmouth) and Dawlish Warren before tunnelling through the red sandstone cliffs on a dramatic coast-hugging route to Dawlish and Teignmouth. From here the railway heads inland along the shore of the Teign Estuary to Newton Abbot, once an important railway junction town. Leaving the town behind, the Paignton branch soon diverges from the main line to Plymouth, to head south through Torre and Torquay along the former broad-gauge route that opened between 1848 and 1859.

On arrival at the resort town of Paignton passengers must transfer the short distance to the terminus of the Dartmouth Steam Railway before continuing their journey to Kingswear. This 6½-mile single-track railway was originally opened in 1864 and survived threatened closure by Dr Beeching when it was seamlessly reopened as a heritage railway at the beginning of 1973. South of Paignton, the railway climbs along the coastline above Goodrington Sands to Churston station from where a short branch line to Brixham operated until closure in 1963. Descending from Churston, the railway emerges from Greenway Tunnel to closely follow the east bank of the tidal River Dart before ending at the picturesque overall-roofed terminus at Kingswear. A regular ferry service operates from here across the Dart to Dartmouth.

DESTINATION HIGHLIGHTS
ferry to Dartmouth; boat trips up River Dart to Totnes; Dartmouth Castle; medieval and Elizabethan streets and architecture (Dartmouth); Dartmouth Museum (Butterwalk); 14th-century Cherub Inn (Dartmouth)

FREQUENCY OF TRAINS
Exeter to Paignton: 2 per hour
Paignton to Kingswear: 4–9 per day (Feb–Nov)

35 MILES
1 HOUR 45 MINUTES

RIGHT: *Trains on the Dartmouth Steam Railway end their journey from Paignton along the shore of the picturesque Dart Estuary at Kingswear.*

OPPOSITE: *Historic Kingswear is reached via a ferry from Dartmouth.*

Marketed as the 'Tarka Line', this scenic railway winds its way along the unspoilt valleys of the Yeo and Taw rivers through rich farmland and wooded countryside, linking the cathedral city of Exeter with scattered small villages and the 'capital' of North Devon. Opened in stages between 1851 and 1854 this railway is the only survivor of a network of lines – collectively known as the 'Withered Arm' – that served resorts in North Devon and North Cornwall until the "Beeching Axe" of the 1960s. Today's trains depart from Exeter Central station and descend the 1-in-37 gradient to busy St Davids station, situated on the former Great Western Railway's main line between Paddington and Penzance. From here, Barnstaple-bound trains head north alongside the River Exe before branching off up the Yeo Valley, criss-crossing the river eight times to reach the town of Crediton.

West of Crediton, the railway passes through Yeoford station and at Coleford Junction, where it diverges from the little-used heritage line to Okehampton, heads northwest through Copplestone station to reach the summit of the line at Morchard Road. From here it is downhill to Lapford before joining the winding, wooded valley of the River Taw to Eggesford station where there is a passing loop. Here the 12th-century church and surrounding countryside attract walkers while the nearby pub, and several others along the line, attract real ale aficionados. The railway continues its descent along the peaceful and heavily wooded Taw Valley through King's Nympton, Portsmouth Arms, Umberleigh and Chapelton stations (all request stops). North of Chapelton the valley broadens out through dairy farmland before the railway terminates at Barnstaple station. With its famous pannier market, unspoilt town centre and attractive riverside location Barnstaple is worthy of exploration and also makes a good starting point for walkers and cyclists along several closed railway lines that make up the Tarka Trail northwards to Braunton and southwards to Bideford and Torrington.

DESTINATION HIGHLIGHTS
cycle hire; Tarka Trail railway path to Bideford and Torrington; riverside railway path to Braunton; Queen Anne's Walk; Pannier Market and Butchers' Row; Barnstaple Castle Mound; Museum of Barnstaple and North Devon; Heritage Trail; South West Coast Path

FREQUENCY OF TRAINS
1 per hour (Mon-Sat)
1 every 2 hours (Sun)

39 MILES
1 HOUR 15 MINUTES

A colourful Tarka Line train from Exeter makes its way through rolling Devon farmland en route to Barnstaple.

This day trip is currently only possible on summer Sundays in conjunction with the Dartmoor Sunday Rover Network. Trains from Exeter St Davids station follow the same route as the 'Tarka Line' (see page 22) as far as Coleford Junction and then branch off along the route of the former London & South Western Railway's main line to Plymouth which opened throughout in 1890. This was effectively closed in 1968 with the ending of services between Bere Alston (see page 18) and Okehampton although the latter continued to be served by passenger trains from Exeter until 1972. Fortunately, a single track was retained for ballast traffic from Meldon Quarry and in recent years it has also seen the Dartmoor Railway operating a limited heritage service over a section of the line.

From Coleford Junction the railway skirts around the northern edge of Dartmoor for 16½ miles, passing through Sampford Courtenay station before terminating at the superbly restored Okehampton station, set high above the town. There is a café here, and a Youth Hostel is located in the former goods shed. From the station, the 11-mile Granite Way footpath and cycleway parallels the railway to Meldon before crossing the magnificent wrought- and cast-iron Meldon Viaduct to follow the trackbed of the closed railway around Dartmoor, over Lake Viaduct, to end at Lydford.

- **EXETER ST DAVIDS**
- NEWTON ST CYRES
- CREDITON
- SAMPFORD COURTENAY
- **OKEHAMPTON**

DESTINATION HIGHLIGHTS
walking and cycling on Granite Way to Meldon Viaduct, Lake and Lydford; Dartmoor Railway to Meldon; restored Okehampton station; Okehampton Castle; Museum of Dartmoor Life

FREQUENCY OF TRAINS
1 every 2 hours (Sun, summer)

25¼ MILES
45 MINUTES

The tastefully restored station at Okehampton is served by trains from Exeter on summer Sundays.

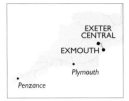

EXETER CENTRAL ●
ST JAMES PARK ○
POLSLOE BRIDGE ○
DIGBY & SOWTON ○
TOPSHAM ○
EXTON ○
LYMPSTONE COMMANDO ○
LYMPSTONE VILLAGE ○
EXMOUTH ●

This scenic seaside branch line that runs alongside the east shore of the Exe Estuary was opened in 1861. An extension from Exmouth to Budleigh Salterton and Sidmouth Junction was opened in 1903 but this route became a victim of the "Beeching Axe" in 1967. Trains for Exmouth depart from Exeter Central station and follow the route of the main line to Salisbury as far as Exmouth Junction. Here the Exmouth branch diverges southwards through Polsloe Bridge and Digby & Sowton stations before meeting the coast at Topsham. The line is marketed as the 'Avocet Line', so named after the pied avocet that live on the estuary, and has seen large increases in passenger usage in recent years, with Exmouth station being the fifth busiest in Devon.

At Topsham station there is a passing loop, which enables trains to run at 30-minute intervals. From here the coast-hugging line passes through Exton and Lympstone Commando stations, both request stops, and after halting at Lympstone Village station continues down the coast to terminate at Exmouth. With a population of over 35,000 this seaside resort town has much to offer the day tripper, from its fascinating architecture and promenade to beaches and water-sports facilities. A passenger ferry operates from Easter to October across the Exe Estuary – a Site of Special Scientific Interest noted for its migrating and wading birds – to Starcross, where a train can be caught back to Exeter.

DESTINATION HIGHLIGHTS
passenger ferry to Starcross; promenade and 2-mile sandy beach; water sports; South West Coast Path; bird watching on Exe Estuary; 18th-century A La Ronde (NT); railway path to Knowle

FREQUENCY OF TRAINS
2 per hour

10½ MILES
25 MINUTES

Colourful modern apartments overlook the harbour in the popular seaside resort of Exmouth.

This is a lovely day trip along the former London & South Western Railway's switchback main line (opened in 1860) through the rolling East Devon, Dorset and Wiltshire countryside to the historic cathedral city of Salisbury. Trains leave Exeter Central station and head east to Pinhoe from where the railway is single track as far as Yeovil Junction. Trains call at Whimple and Feniton en route before arriving at the picturesque market town of Honiton, once a centre of the lace-making industry. Here there is a passing loop, and a short distance to the east the railway reaches its first summit before plunging into 1,345-yd Honiton Tunnel to race downhill to the former carpet-making town of Axminster and another passing loop. Here, branch line trains used to wend their way up to Lyme Regis station until closure in 1965. Beyond Axminster the railway heads through the closed Chard Junction station, where there is a further passing loop, and up to Hewish Summit and the 206-yd Crewkerne Tunnel before arriving at Crewkerne station which, like many of the stations along this route, is some distance from the town centre. At Yeovil Junction the railway becomes double track again as far as Templecombe, with an intermediate stop at Sherborne.

Templecombe station closed in 1966 along with the Somerset & Dorset Joint Railway from Bath to Bournemouth but reopened following strong local community pressure in 1983 and is now used by around 100,000 passengers each year. East of Templecombe the single-track railway heads through Buckhorn Weston Tunnel, Gillingham and Tisbury stations (where there are passing loops) before joining the ex-GWR line from Westbury at Wilton Junction. From here it is but a short ride into Salisbury station from where the city's famous sites such as the magnificent cathedral with its 404-ft-high spire, the 14th-century city walls with their 5 gates and the landscaped water meadows alongside the River Avon can all be explored on foot.

- **EXETER CENTRAL**
- PINHOE
- WHIMPLE
- FENITON
- HONITON
- AXMINSTER
- CREWKERNE
- YEOVIL JUNCTION
- SHERBORNE
- TEMPLECOMBE
- GILLINGHAM
- TISBURY
- **SALISBURY**

DESTINATION HIGHLIGHTS
13th-century cathedral and Britain's oldest working clock; city walls and 5 gates; riverside walks; Queen Elizabeth Gardens; Poultry Cross Market (Tues and Sat); Salisbury and South Wiltshire Museum inc Pitt Rivers Collection

FREQUENCY OF TRAINS
1 per hour

88 MILES
1 HOUR 50 MINUTES

One of the finest medieval buildings in Britain, Salisbury Cathedral also has the highest spire of any church in the country.

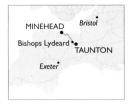

TAUNTON ●

BISHOPS LYDEARD ●

CROWCOMBE HEATHFIELD ○

STOGUMBER ○

WILLITON ○

DONIFORD BEACH HALT ○

WATCHET ○

WASHFORD ○

BLUE ANCHOR ○

DUNSTER ○

MINEHEAD ●

DESTINATION HIGHLIGHTS
railway museums (Bishops
Lydeard and Blue Anchor);
Watchet Harbour; Somerset
& Dorset Railway Trust
(Washford); Dunster Castle
and village; Minehead
Harbour; open-top bus trips
to Exmoor (Minehead,
summer); South West
Coast Path

FREQUENCY
Taunton to Bishops Lydeard:
2 buses per hour (Mon-Sat)
1 bus per hour (Sun)
Bishops Lydeard to Minehead:
4-7 trains per day (Feb-Nov)

24 MILES
20 MINUTES (BUS) +
1 HOUR 20 MINUTES (TRAIN)

*A restored GWR small prairie
tank steams towards Roebuck
Lane level crossing on the West
Somerset Railway with a train
for Minehead.*

Opened between 1862 and 1874, the long branch line from Taunton to Minehead became a victim of Dr Beeching's Axe when it was closed in 1971. However, with the support of Somerset County Council and hundreds, if not thousands, of volunteers and well-wishers the majority of this picturesque line, with its ten delightfully restored stations, was reopened as a heritage railway between 1976 and 1979. Today the West Somerset Railway (WSR) is Britain's longest and one of the most successful standard-gauge heritage lines, with hundreds of thousands of visitors bringing a much-needed boost to the local tourist industry.

While restored vintage steam and diesel trains operate for much of the year between Minehead and Bishops Lydeard, the section south of here to the former junction with the ex-Great Western Railway's Taunton to Exeter main line at Norton Fitzwarren sees only occasional use, and beyond here WSR trains are unable to reach Taunton. However, a connecting bus service operates between Taunton station and Bishops Lydeard station thus allowing this particular trip to be made without reverting to car travel.

From Bishops Lydeard station the WSR climbs up through the bucolic Somerset countryside, overlooked from the west by the Brendon Hills and from the east by the Quantocks. Occasional thatched cottages and burbling streams are glimpsed from the train as it proceeds slowly on its journey, pausing at Crowcombe Heathfield and Stogumber stations, to Williton where the railway has its restoration workshops. North of here the Bristol Channel is first glimpsed at Doniford Beach Halt before the line swings west to the historic harbour town of Watchet. It then climbs inland via Washford, where there is a railway museum, before rejoining the coastline at Blue Anchor, a favourite haunt of mobile holiday homes and caravans. The final leg of this superb trip offers fine views over the Channel to South Wales and inland to Dunster Castle and the wooded Brendon Hills, before ending close to the seafront at the popular seaside resort of Minehead.

Engineered by Brunel, the main line between Taunton and Exeter was opened by the broad-gauge Bristol & Exeter Railway in 1844. The line was rebuilt with mixed-gauge track in 1876 when the company was also amalgamated with the Great Western Railway – the broad gauge was eliminated in 1892. Today trains can operate along this route up to a maximum speed of 100 mph and as there is only one intermediate station at Tiverton Parkway journey times are fairly rapid. Prior to the wholesale closures of the 1960s there were 9 intermediate stations and 5 branch lines (to Minehead, Barnstaple, Hemyock, Tiverton and Dulverton) along this stretch.

Trains for Exeter head off in a southwesterly direction from Taunton station and soon pass the new triangular junction laid at Norton Fitzwarren for the West Somerset Railway (see page 26). The railway then climbs up the 1-in-80 gradient of Wellington Bank to the 1,092-yd Whiteball Tunnel and the summit of the line – it was down this bank that GWR 4-4-0 No. 3440 'City of Truro' was apparently timed at 100 mph while hauling an 'Ocean Mails' special from Plymouth to London in 1904. Although there has been much debate about this feat it is highly likely that this was the first time that a steam train achieved this speed anywhere in the world.

From Whiteball Summit trains coast down to a stop at Tiverton Parkway station before descending into the lush valley of the River Exe to Cowley Bridge Junction. This infamous spot, the junction for the 'Tarka Line' to Barnstaple (see page 22), is regularly flooded during periods of heavy rainfall, causing major disruption to services into Devon and Cornwall. Exeter St Davids station follows soon afterwards, from where visitors to the city centre can catch a connecting train up to Central station.

● **TAUNTON**
○ TIVERTON PARKWAY
● **EXETER ST DAVIDS**
● **EXETER CENTRAL**

DESTINATION HIGHLIGHTS
12th-century cathedral; 11th-century Rougemont Castle; Danes Castle; St Nicholas Priory and Garden; Exeter Canal basin and riverside walks; 17th-century Butts Ferry; Royal Albert Memorial Museum; Spacex art gallery

FREQUENCY OF TRAINS
1+ per hour (Mon-Sat)
1 per hour (Sun)

30¾ MILES
45 MINUTES

The restored Exeter Canal in Exeter. Beyond is Exeter Cathedral which was completed in 1400.

The first section of Brunel's broad-gauge Bristol & Exeter Railway opened from Bristol to Taunton in 1842 and until the opening of the cut-off line through Castle Cary and Langport in 1906 was the only railway route between London (Paddington) and the southwest. The original route via Bristol was nicknamed the 'Great Way Round' (using the initials of the Great Western Railway) that had taken over the B&ER in 1876. Broad-gauge trains ceased to run in 1892 when the whole route was converted to standard gauge.

Today's trains head eastward out of Taunton's busy main-line station and soon pass Cogload Junction, where there is a flyover for trains to and from the Castle Cary line. The first intermediate station on this trip is at Bridgwater and from here the main line heads north in a straight line for 13 miles across the Somerset Levels through Highbridge & Burnham station to Uphill Junction. Here, local stopping trains diverge to take the longer single-track loop line via the resort of Weston-super-Mare before rejoining the main line at Worle Junction. They then head inland through a gap in the Mendip Hills through Worle, Yatton, Nailsea & Backwell and Parson Street stations before ending their journey at the imposing overall-roofed 13-platform Bristol Temple Meads station. Brunel's original train shed, once the terminus of his broad-gauge line from Paddington, still survives and is currently used as a car park. A good bus service connects the station with Bristol's many attractions including the new city-centre shopping mall, historic docks, zoo and Clifton Gorge with its magnificent suspension bridge.

TAUNTON
BRIDGWATER
HIGHBRIDGE & BURNHAM

WESTON-SUPER-MARE
WESTON MILTON

WORLE
YATTON
NAILSEA & BACKWELL
PARSON STREET
BEDMINSTER
BRISTOL TEMPLE MEADS

DESTINATION HIGHLIGHTS
Bristol Zoo; Clifton Suspension Bridge; boat trips; 'SS Great Britain'; Bristol Harbour Railway; Cabot Tower; Bristol Cathedral; St Nicholas Church Museum; Bristol Harbour Festival (end July/early August); International Balloon Festival (August); Industrial Museum; Museum & Art Gallery; Banksy street art; 17th-century Llandoger Trow pub; jazz and blues at the 18th-century The Old Duke pub

FREQUENCY OF TRAINS
3 per hour (Mon-Sat)
2 per hour (Sun)

45 MILES
32 MINUTES (DIRECT)
1 HOUR 5 MINUTES

Overlooked by the colourful terraced house of Clifton, Brunel's restored 'SS Great Britain' is a major tourist attraction in Bristol.

Considered by some to be one of the most scenic railway lines in Europe, the branch from Bristol to Severn Beach certainly boasts a variety of scenery (some man-made) along its route. It was opened in stages between 1863 and 1922 and today's service consists of half-hourly trains between Temple Meads station and Avonmouth, with services extended to and from Severn Beach every 2 hours

Trains leave Temple Meads station in a northerly direction, taking the main line through Lawrence Hill and Stapleton Road stations before diverging at Narroways Junction. Here the line, now single track, heads west through suburban woodland and the short Montpelier Tunnel before calling at Montpelier station. Redland station follows, while at Clifton Down station there is a passing loop before trains plunge into the gloomy depths of mile-long Clifton Down Tunnel. Emerging high above the Clifton Gorge, trains run alongside this winding and tidal stretch of the River Avon through Sea Mills and Shirehampton stations before reaching Avonmouth.

From Avonmouth the scenery becomes more spectacularly man-made in the shape of chemical factories, an LPG terminal and the gigantic coal discharging plant close to St Andrews Road station. Looking more like a giant Anthony Caro sculpture, this brightly coloured structure is used for loading imported coal onto merry-go-round coal trains destined for distant power stations. To the north, freight trains take the Henbury Loop Line at Hallen Marsh Junction while our diesel railcar rattles along the last lonely 3 miles alongside the Severn Estuary. Disused chemical works punctuate the flat landscape before the train ends its journey at the minimal station of Severn Beach. Across the road are massive flood defence walls from which there is a panoramic view across the muddy estuary to South Wales and upstream to the new Severn Crossing. After gulping in the bracing sea air, taking a riverside walk and enjoying an ice cream it is time to retrace our steps back to Temple Meads.

- **BRISTOL TEMPLE MEADS**
- LAWRENCE HILL
- STAPLETON ROAD
- MONTPELIER
- REDLAND
- CLIFTON DOWN
- SEA MILLS
- SHIREHAMPTON
- AVONMOUTH
- ST ANDREWS ROAD
- **SEVERN BEACH**

DESTINATION HIGHLIGHTS
bird watching; conger fishing; views of Severn Crossing road bridge; Severn Way long-distance path

FREQUENCY OF TRAINS
1 every 2 hours (Mon-Sat)
1 per hour (Sun)

13½ MILES
37 MINUTES

Passengers travelling by train to Severn Beach are treated to fine views across the Severn Estuary to Wales.

Oxford

BATH SPA

Taunton   SALISBURY

SALISBURY
WARMINSTER
DILTON MARSH
WESTBURY
TROWBRIDGE
BRADFORD-ON-AVON
AVONCLIFF
FRESHFORD
BATH SPA

Our scenic journey to the UNESCO World Heritage city of Bath starts at Salisbury's busy junction station. From here trains head west to Wilton Junction where the line divides – the West of England main line from Waterloo to Exeter continues west while Bath-bound trains take a northwesterly route along the Wylye Valley, skirting round Salisbury Plain to Warminster. Trains pass a string of picturesque and peaceful villages en route, such as Wylye, Codford and Heytesbury, which lost their stations nearly 60 years ago. Warminster station is located on a sharp curve and its short platforms are a problem for long modern trains. The nearby town is famous not only for its military connections but also for sightings of UFOs in the 1960s and 1970s. From Warminster trains continue to skirt around Salisbury Plain before heading north to the important junction station of Westbury.

With the famous White Horse visible on the hillside to the east, trains leave Westbury in a northerly direction across the Wiltshire Plains before calling at the market and brewing town of Trowbridge. A short distance north of the station, Bath-bound trains branch off westwards at Bradford South Junction – here the single-track line to Melksham and Thingley Junction continues northwards – before reaching Bradford-on-Avon's attractive station. From here the railway keeps company with the River Avon and the Kennet & Avon Canal along the winding, wooded valley to Bath. Trains serve Avoncliff station (a request stop), where the canal crosses the river and railway on one of John Rennie's fine aqueducts, and Freshford en route. Now heading north up the valley, the railway passes under Rennie's graceful Dundas Aqueduct that carries the canal over river and railway. Bathampton Junction is soon reached, where trains join Brunel's former broad-gauge Great Western Railway as far as Bath. On the final approach, passengers are treated to fine views across this historic city before the railway crosses the River Avon to deposit visitors at the conveniently located station. From here it is but a short walk into the city centre.

DESTINATION HIGHLIGHTS
Abbey; Roman Baths; Thermae Bath Spa; American Museum (free shuttle bus); Georgian architecture (Royal Crescent); Sydney Gardens; Victoria Art Gallery; Green Park station (for Saturday farmers' market); Kennet & Avon Canal; Pump Room; Pulteney Bridge; Two Tunnels Greenway

FREQUENCY OF TRAINS
1-2 per hour (Mon-Sat)
1 per hour (Sun)

41½ MILES
1 HOUR

Pulteney Bridge and the River Avon in Bath.

A day trip to the seaside beckons and what better way to travel than by rail to Weymouth, on the Heart of Wessex Line. Our journey starts at Yeovil's Pen Mill station, opened in 1854, which features an island platform, passing loop, signal box and semaphore signals. Heading south along the Yeo Valley, the single-track railway soon passes under the Waterloo to Exeter main line before starting its 10-mile climb to cross the South Dorset Downs through Evershot Tunnel, passing through the tiny rural request stop stations of Thornford, Yetminster and Chetnole en route. The last 2 miles up to the tunnel feature a 1-in-51 gradient which severely tests the steam-hauled excursion trains from Bristol that still run along this route on Sundays in the summer months.

Reaching the summit of the line, trains emerge from Evershot Tunnel and head downhill into the valley of the River Frome before halting at Maiden Newton station, which until 1975 was the junction for the branch line to Bridport. From here the railway continues its descent down the valley, criss-crossing the river, to the historic town of Dorchester. After pausing at Dorchester West station, trains soon join the Bournemouth to Weymouth electrified main line and head uphill for 2 miles, past the Iron Age hill fort of Maiden Castle to Bincombe Tunnel. Then it is downhill all the way, through Upwey Wishing Well, before trains terminate at Weymouth station. From here it is but a short walk to the town's superb sandy beaches, Punch and Judy stall, renowned fish and chip shops and bustling harbour.

YEOVIL PEN MILL
THORNFORD
YETMINSTER
CHETNOLE
MAIDEN NEWTON
DORCHESTER WEST
UPWEY
WEYMOUTH

Holidaymakers sit on the beach at Weymouth to enjoy a traditional Punch and Judy Show.

DESTINATION HIGHLIGHTS
sandy beaches; water sports; Punch & Judy; busy harbour; sea-fishing trips; Rodwell Trail (railway walk to Isle of Portland)

FREQUENCY OF TRAINS
8 per day (Mon-Sat)
5 per day (Sun)

27½ MILES
50 MINUTES

SOUTH & SOUTHEAST ENGLAND

DESTINATION HIGHLIGHTS
sandy beaches; water sports;
Punch & Judy; busy harbour;
sea fishing trips;
Rodwell Trail (railway walk
to Isle of Portland)

FREQUENCY OF TRAINS
2-3 per hour (Mon-Sat)
1 per hour (Sun)

63½ MILES
1 HOUR 30 MINUTES

*Fishing boats and trawlers
moored in the busy harbour
at Weymouth.*

The railway journey from one of Europe's most important commercial sea ports to one of Britain's premier seaside resorts first follows the shore of the Test Estuary before entering the former royal hunting ground of the New Forest at Ashurst. For the next 10 miles the railway meanders through forest and heathland, with trains calling at Beaulieu Road and Brockenhurst stations – the latter is the junction for the branch line to Lymington with its ferry service to the Isle of Wight. At Sway the railway leaves the forest behind and heads towards the coast to serve the continuous ribbon development of the resort towns of Christchurch, Bournemouth and Poole that grew up following the coming of the railway in the late 19th century.

From Poole the railway heads across Holes Bay to Hamworthy before skirting around Poole Harbour to reach the historic town of Wareham. Here, in the not-too-distant future, travellers will once again be able to change trains for the journey down to the seaside resort of Swanage. Beyond Wareham the railway heads west along the broad, lush valley of the River Frome to Dorchester, calling at Wool and passing the decommissioned nuclear power station at Winfrith en route. This countryside was not only immortalized in Thomas Hardy's novels but has, in more recent times, been home to several large army-tank training grounds. From the county town of Dorchester the railway swings south to cross over and under the South Dorset Downs before finally descending to the seaside resort of Weymouth, host of the sailing events for the 2012 Olympic Games.

A great day out for all the family to the city of Portsmouth, for a chance to visit its historic naval ships and take a trip to the top of the 560-ft Spinnaker Tower with its far-reaching views across the harbour and the Solent. Trains leave Basingstoke in a westerly direction to Worting Junction before heading south through Micheldever to the historic cathedral city of Winchester. Leaving the city behind, the railway follows the course of the lush Itchen Valley through Shawford before arriving at the railway junction town of Eastleigh. The railway works here still clings to life but is a shadow of its former self which built thousands of steam locomotives for the London & South Western Railway, Southern Railway and British Railways.

At Eastleigh, trains for Portsmouth branch off the mainline to Southampton and head southeast through Hedge End to Botley. Here the line becomes single track for the next 5¼ miles to Fareham, passing through Tapnage and Fareham No. 2 tunnels en route. At Fareham, trains join the West Coastway Line and head east through Portchester and Cosham before branching off in a southerly direction to Portsmouth. Journey's end is at Portsmouth Harbour station. Built on a wooden pier alongside the city's harbour and opened in 1876, the station is still an important interchange for bus, ferry and railway passengers. From here it is but a short walk to the city's famous maritime attractions and the Spinnaker Tower.

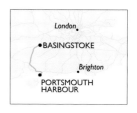

London

•BASINGSTOKE

Brighton

PORTSMOUTH HARBOUR

- **BASINGSTOKE**
- MICHELDEVER
- WINCHESTER
- SHAWFORD
- EASTLEIGH
- HEDGE END
- BOTLEY
- FAREHAM
- PORTCHESTER
- COSHAM
- HILSEA
- FRATTON
- PORTSMOUTH & SOUTHSEA
- **PORTSMOUTH HARBOUR**

DESTINATION HIGHLIGHTS
Mary Rose exhibition; *HMS Victory*; *HMS Conqueror*; D-Day Museum; Royal Marines Museum; Spinnaker Tower; boat trips around harbour and to Gosport for Royal Navy Submarine Museum

FREQUENCY OF TRAINS
1 per hour

37¼ MILES
1 HOUR 20 MINUTES

The historic Gunwharf Quay at Portsmouth is dominated by the modern 560-ft-high Spinnaker Tower.

Our journey westwards from Basingstoke to Salisbury follows the same route as the celebrated 'Atlantic Coast Express' which ran between London Waterloo and seaside resorts in North Devon and North Cornwall until 1964. The magnificent Bulleid 'Merchant Navy' Pacifics which once thundered along the track with their trainloads of holidaymakers are now just a distant memory. Today's travellers are carried in air-conditioned comfort in South West Trains' diesel multiple units with trains stopping at the intermediate stations of Overton, Whitchurch, Andover and Grateley. At Andover the remaining stub of the long-closed Midland & South Western Junction Railway can be seen trailing in from the north – this little-used branch line still serves the MOD Depot at Tidworth.

The entire journey is through rolling Hampshire and Wiltshire farmland, with the last 6 miles following the valley of the River Bourne through the quaint-sounding villages of the Winterbournes. On the approach to Salisbury, trains take the northern curve of the triangular Tunnel Junction before entering Fisherton Tunnel and arriving at the city's busy junction station. Salisbury's attractions are but a short walk from here.

DESTINATION HIGHLIGHTS
Salisbury cathedral with its 404-ft-high spire and oldest working clock in the world; 14th-century city walls and their five gates; ancient market at Poultry Cross; ghost tours; landscaped water meadows alongside the River Avon

FREQUENCY OF TRAINS
2 per hour (Mon-Sat)
1 per hour (Sun)

36 MILES
40 MINUTES

RIGHT: *New-build Class 'A1' 4-6-2 No. 60163 'Tornado' speeds across Hurstbourne Viaduct on the Basingstoke to Salisbury line with an enthusiasts' special train in 2009.*

OPPOSITE: *The beautiful Gothic nave in Salisbury Cathedral.*

READING	●
EARLEY	○
WINNERSH TRIANGLE	○
WINNERSH	○
WOKINGHAM	○
CROWTHORNE	○
SANDHURST	○
BLACKWATER	○
FARNBOROUGH NORTH	○
NORTH CAMP	○
ASH	○
WANBOROUGH	○
GUILDFORD	●

Diesel trains for the North Downs Line leave Reading's sparkling new modern station in an easterly direction, immediately diverging from the former GWR main line to Paddington, to head off along the former South Eastern & Chatham Railway's cross-country route to Guildford. Until the 1960s this was also the route taken by inter-regional holiday and excursion trains from the West Midlands to South Coast resorts. After calling at the intermediate stations of Earley, Winnersh Triangle and Winnersh, trains arrive at the market town of Wokingham, where the electrified line to Virginia Water and Waterloo branches off to the east.

From Wokingham the North Downs Line heads southeast to Crowthorne (home of Broadmoor Hospital), Sandhurst (home to the Royal Military Academy), Blackwater and Farnborough North. Immediately south of the latter the railway dives under the Waterloo to Basingstoke main line before calling at North Camp station. Passengers wishing to change trains here for the Alton or Ascot lines have a ½-mile walk to Ash Vale station – no interchange station was provided despite the lines crossing south of North Camp. From here the railway turns eastward through Ash and Wanborough stations before arriving at Guildford's busy 7-platform junction station.

DESTINATION HIGHLIGHTS
Guildford Castle; Tuesday farmers' market; Friday and Saturday street market; historic High Street; art gallery; National Trust boat trips along Wey Navigation; Guildford Lido (May to September); Yvonne Arnaud Theatre; Electric Theatre; modern cathedral

FREQUENCY OF TRAINS
2 per hour (Mon-Sat)
1 per hour (Sun)

25¾ MILES
45 MINUTES

This ornate 17th-century clock on the wall of the Guildhall is a well-known landmark in Guildford's High Street.

This day trip starts with a railway journey along the former London & South Western Railway's Portsmouth-direct main line from Guildford, cutting through the North Downs to the historic towns of Godalming and Haslemere en route before crossing into the heathlands of Hampshire just to the west of Liphook. Continuing in a southwesterly direction the railway passes through Liss (once the junction for the Longmoor Military Railway) to arrive at the pretty market town of Petersfield. South of here the railway soon dives under the South Downs National Park through Buriton Tunnel to reach the summit of the line and then descends through the Queen Elizabeth Country Park to reach Rowlands Castle station. The Fountain Inn in the village, run by guitarist Herbie Armstrong, is famous for its live music evenings. Havant station is soon reached and it is here that we leave the train to join the railway path for the 4½-mile level walk to Hayling Island.

Very popular with day trippers in the summer months, the Hayling Island branch line became an early victim of Dr Beeching's Axe when it closed in November 1963. Since then it has been reopened as a footpath and cycleway, although a diversion via the road bridge at Langstone is now necessary as the wooden railway lifting bridge that once crossed the harbour was demolished soon after the line's closure. South of here, the railway path, known as the Hayling Billy Trail, closely follows the east shore of Langstone Harbour – internationally recognized as a nature reserve for its abundant wildlife – before reaching the site of Hayling Island station. Here, the former goods shed is now a theatre, and Hayling's seafront delights are but a short walk away.

- ● **GUILDFORD**
- ○ FARNCOMBE
- ○ GODALMING
- ○ MILFORD
- ○ WITLEY
- ○ HASLEMERE
- ○ LIPHOOK
- ○ LISS
- ○ PETERSFIELD
- ○ ROWLANDS CASTLE
- ● **HAVANT**
- ▪ **HAYLING ISLAND**

DESTINATION HIGHLIGHTS
Hayling Billy Trail railway path; beach; funfair; narrow-gauge Hayling Seaside Railway; passenger ferry West Hayling to Fort Cumberland

FREQUENCY OF TRAINS
3 per hour (Mon-Sat)
2 per hour (Sun)

36¼ MILES (TRAIN) +
4½ MILES (ON FOOT)
2½ HOURS

The remains of a railway signal marks the beginning of the Hayling Billy Trail along the east shore of Langstone Harbour to Hayling Island.

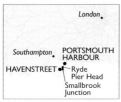

London

Southampton PORTSMOUTH
HARBOUR
HAVENSTREET Ryde
Pier Head
Smallbrook
Junction

PORTSMOUTH HARBOUR ●

RYDE PIER HEAD ●

RYDE ESPLANADE ○

RYDE ST JOHNS ROAD ○

SMALLBROOK JUNCTION ●

ASHEY ○

HAVENSTREET ●

WOOTTON ○

DESTINATION HIGHLIGHTS
Award-winning Victorian
steam railway; railway
museum; carriage and wagon
workshop; children's play
area; woodland walk;
Haven Falconry

FREQUENCY
Wight Link Catamaran:
2 per hour (Mon-Sat)
1 per hour (Sun)
Island Line:
1 per hour
Isle of Wight Steam Railway:
5-9 per day (Mar-Oct)

10 MILES
22 + 8 + 35 MINUTES

Despite its short length, this trip includes a journey in a catamaran ferry across the Solent, a short ride in an old London Underground train and a trip along a steam railway. Wight Link catamarans for Ryde depart from Portsmouth Harbour close to the national rail network station of the same name. Journey time across the Solent is 22 minutes and on arrival at Ryde Pier Head passengers transfer to an Island Line train on the electrified line to Shanklin. The line was electrified on the third-rail principle and opened in March 1967, replacing former Southern Railway Class '02' 0-4-4Ts and vintage rolling stock. The trains in use today were introduced in 1938 for use on the London Underground and are the oldest type in Britain to remain in regular service.

En route from Ryde Pier Head, trains call at Ryde Esplanade and Ryde St Johns Road – where Island Line trains have their depot – before arriving at Smallbrook Junction station. With no public access, this station was opened in 1991 to provide an interchange between the Island Line and the Isle of Wight Steam Railway. Passengers transfer to the latter for a trip to the railway's headquarters at Havenstreet. Steam trains call at Ashey and Havenstreet before continuing on to Wootton, and it is recommended that passengers stay on the train to Wootton before returning to Havenstreet to enjoy this delightful location.

Restored Southern Railway Class '02' 0-4-4T No. W24 'Calbourne' heads a vintage train on the Isle of Wight Steam Railway.

Marketed today as the West Coastway Line, the railway along the south coast of England between Brighton and Southampton has a complicated history, having been built by 5 different companies between 1840 and 1889. The Southern Railway electrified it using third rail in the 1930s. A regular interval service is currently operated by Southern.

Trains for Chichester depart from Brighton's 19th-century Italianate-style overall-roofed terminus and immediately head to the west through Hove Tunnel to call at Hove station, originally named Cliftonville and conveniently located close to the Sussex County Cricket Club's ground. Never far from the sea, the railway continues westward calling at Aldrington, Portslade (once the junction for the Devil's Dyke branch), Fishergate, Southwick and Shoreham-on-Sea, which until 1966 was the junction for the Steyning Valley line to Horsham. Beyond Shoreham trains cross the River Adur on a viaduct before calling at a string of 7 coastal towns and resorts, of which Worthing is by far the largest. At Arundel Junction the Arun Valley Line heads off northwards to London while the Littlehampton branch diverges to the south. At Barnham the Bognor Regis branch heads off to the coast, and in a short time Chichester station is reached. This stylish late-1950s building is conveniently located close to the unspoilt historic city centre.

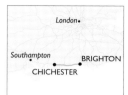

- **BRIGHTON**
- HOVE
- ALDRINGTON
- PORTSLADE
- FISHERSGATE
- SOUTHWICK
- SHOREHAM-BY-SEA
- LANCING
- EAST WORTHING
- WORTHING
- WEST WORTHING
- DURRINGTON-ON-SEA
- GORING-BY-SEA
- ANGMERING
- FORD
- BARNHAM
- **CHICHESTER**

DESTINATION HIGHLIGHTS
12th-century cathedral with separate bell tower and Roman mosaic pavement; Roman street plan; medieval city walls; Butter Market designed by John Nash; imposing Corn Exchange; 15th-century Chichester Cross; modern street art; Festival Theatre (Chichester Festival June/July); Fishbourne Roman Palace (next station)

FREQUENCY OF TRAINS
2 per hour

28¾ MILES
55 MINUTES

Founded in 1075, the Cathedral Church of the Holy Trinity in Chichester has fine architecture in both Norman and Gothic styles.

BRIGHTON
LONDON ROAD (BRIGHTON)
MOULSECOOMB
FALMER
LEWES
GLYNDE
BERWICK
POLEGATE
HAMPDEN PARK
EASTBOURNE
HAMPDEN PARK
PEVENSEY & WESTHAM
PEVENSEY BAY
NORMANS BAY
COODEN BEACH
COLLINGTON
BEXHILL
ST LEONARDS WARRIOR SQUARE
HASTINGS

DESTINATION HIGHLIGHTS
beach; harbour; sea-fishing trips; 1930s double-decker promenade; old town; Hastings Castle; West Hill Cliff Railway; East Hill Cliff Railway; St Clements Caves; Fishermen's Museum

FREQUENCY OF TRAINS
2 per hour (Mon-Sat)

34¼ MILES
1 HOUR 20 MINUTES

Completed in 1872, Eastbourne's elegant Victorian amusement pier is 1,000 ft long and features a restored camera obscura.

Marketed as the East Coastway Line, the railway from Brighton to Hastings is full of surprises. Trains leave Brighton's overall-roofed terminus and soon branch off to the east to cross the 28-arch London Road Viaduct from where there are panoramic views of the sprawling city. Climbing continuously towards the South Downs and the summit of the line at Falmer Tunnel, trains first call at London Road, Moulscomb and Falmer stations before descending towards the historic town of Lewes.

A busy railway crossroads, Lewes station platforms are set in a 'V' shape, with trains serving the Newhaven and Seaford branch, Brighton, the Plumpton line to Three Bridges and London, and Eastbourne. Plans to reopen the line to Uckfield are looking hopeful in the long term. Eastwards from Lewes, the East Coastway Line serves stations at Glynde, Berwick and Polegate (once the junction for the Cuckoo Line to Hailsham and Eridge) before ending at Eastbourne's terminus station, built in 1886 with an attractive lantern roof. Trains for Hastings reverse direction here and head back the way they came before branching off eastwards at Willingdon Junction. From here, the railway heads towards the coast across the Pevensey Levels, passing Pevensey Castle, through Normans Bay and Cooden Beach stations en route to Bexhill, where the Grade II station with its lantern roof has recently been restored. It is but a short distance from here to Bopeep Junction, where the line from Tunbridge Wells joins from the north, and through the long Bopeep Tunnel to St Leonards Warrior Square station. Built in 1851, the station is squeezed between Bopeep and Hastings Tunnel through which trains then pass to arrive at Hastings' ultra-modern station. The seafront and many other attractions are but a short walk from here.

This scenic train journey across the High Weald to the historic seaside resort of Hastings is a great day out for all the family. While the destination has much to offer, the railway journey is equally interesting, calling at historic towns and villages as it winds through forested valleys and burrows under the hard red sandstone hills via no less than seven tunnels. Trains leave Tunbridge Wells station in a southerly direction and immediately start the climb through Grove Tunnel and Strawberry Hill Tunnel before emerging into the lush High Wealden landscape. The railway follows the contours to reach the small town of Wadhurst and the summit of the line.

Leaving Wadhurst through the long Wadhurst Tunnel, the railway then weaves its way down into the valley of the River Rother, calling at Stonegate and Etchingham, before arriving at the picturesque village of Robertsbridge. From here, in the not too distant future, it will be possible to travel by steam train eastwards along the Rother Valley to Bodiam and Tenterden. From Robertsbridge, the railway climbs up through Mountfield Tunnel to reach the second summit of the line at Battle – this small town is so named after the Battle of Hastings, which took place here in 1066. From Battle, the railway meanders down through wooded hills to Crowhurst before joining the East Coastway Line at Bopeep Junction. Our journey's end is nigh but not before plunging through the long Bopeep Tunnel, calling at St Leonards Warrrior Square station and emerging from Hastings Tunnel into the ultra-modern Hastings station.

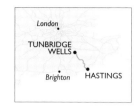

- ● **TUNBRIDGE WELLS**
- ○ FRANT
- ○ WADHURST
- ○ STONEGATE
- ○ ETCHINGHAM
- ○ ROBERTSBRIDGE
- ○ BATTLE
- ○ CROWHURST
- ○ WEST ST LEONARDS
- ○ ST LEONARDS WARRIOR SQUARE
- ● **HASTINGS**

Fishing boats high and dry on the beach at Hastings. In the background is the Victorian cliff railway.

DESTINATION HIGHLIGHTS
beach; harbour; sea fishing trips; 1930s double-decker promenade; old town; Hastings Castle; West Hill Cliff Railway; East Hill Cliff Railway; St Clements Caves; Fishermen's Museum

FREQUENCY OF TRAINS
2 per hour

28¼ MILES
45 MINUTES

TUNBRIDGE WELLS WEST	●
HIGH ROCKS HALT	○
GROOMBRIDGE	○
ERIDGE	●
ASHURST	○
COWDEN	○
HEVER	●

This delightfully short train journey can only be currently undertaken on Saturdays from April to October but the destination of Hever Castle is well worth the effort. The first part of our journey is along the Spa Valley Railway from Tunbridge Wells West station to Eridge – this section was closed by BR in 1985 and was completely reopened in 2011 as a heritage railway. Passenger services are either steam hauled or provided by a diesel multiple unit, with trains calling at High Rocks Halt and Groombridge before heading south to parallel the national rail network line from Hurst Green to Uckfield, as far as Eridge.

Passengers for Hever board a northbound train at Eridge for the 15-minute journey along the mainly single-track line to Hever, calling en route at Ashurst and Cowden then passing through Mark Beech Tunnel to arrive at their destination. The attractive village of Hever and its castle are about a 20-minute walk from the station via the signposted Eden Valley Walk.

Hever Castle has a fascinating history. It was built in the 13th century and from 1462 to 1539 was the seat of the Boleyn family. King Henry VIII's second wife, Ann Boleyn, spent her childhood there but following her execution in the tower of London in 1536 and the death of her father in 1539 the castle became the property of the king. He then bestowed it to his fourth wife, Anne of Cleves, as a settlement following the annulment of their marriage. After passing through several other owners the castle was bought in 1903 by American millionaire, William Waldorf Astor, who restored it to its former glory.

DESTINATION HIGHLIGHTS
15th-century Hever Castle (home of Ann Boleyn) with its mazes, lakes and gardens

FREQUENCY OF TRAINS
Tunbridge Wells West to Eridge
5 per day (Sat-Sun, Mar-Oct)
Eridge to Hever
1 per hour (Sat)

13¾ MILES
30 + 15 MINUTES

RIGHT: *Restored Southern Railway Class 'M7' 0-4-4T No. 53 makes a fine sight while heading a train on the Spa Valley Railway between Eridge and Groombridge.*

OPPOSITE: *The moated Tudor castle at Hever was the childhood home of Anne Boleyn, King Henry VIII's second wife.*

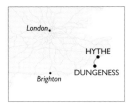

HYTHE ●
BURMARSH ROAD ○
DYMCHURCH ○
ST MARY'S BAY ○
WARREN HALT ○
NEW ROMNEY ○
ROMNEY SANDS ○
DUNGENESS ●

The world-famous Romney, Hythe & Dymchurch Railway runs for 13½ miles along the Kent coast from Hythe to the enormous shingle bank headland at Dungeness. Built to a gauge of 15 in, it was the creation of a wealthy racing driver and a miniature locomotive engineer and opened in 1927. It is a one-third scale, fully signalled, double-track main line (between Hythe and New Romney) with express trains operating at up to 25 mph, hauled by scale versions of LNER and Canadian steam engines. A single-track extension was opened between New Romney and Dungeness in 1928.

Trains depart from Hythe's overall-roofed station in a southwesterly direction along the double-track route between the expanse of Romney Marsh and the coastline. Serving the coastal ribbon development of bungalows, chalets and holiday camps, trains call at Burmarsh Road, Dymchurch, St Mary's Bay and Warren Halt before arriving at the railway's headquarters at New Romney. Here, workshops, engine shed, model railway and café are found. Beyond New Romney, trains on the single-track line negotiate a series of level crossings as they make their way through a landscape interspersed with fishermen's shacks and dominated by the lighthouses and nuclear power stations at Dungeness. After dropping off their passengers, trains take a 360-degree loop here before heading back to Hythe.

DESTINATION HIGHLIGHTS
Light Railway Café; National Nature Reserve; RSPB bird observatory; beach fishing; lighthouse open to public; 1930s concrete acoustic 'listening ears'; fishermen's wooden cottages

FREQUENCY OF TRAINS
3-9 per day (Apr-Sept)
NB Hythe can be reached by bus from Folkestone

13½ MILES
1 HOUR 20 MINUTES

Built in 1927, No. 8 'Hurricane' hauls a train near New Romney on the 15-in-gauge Romney Hythe & Dymchurch Railway.

This is an extremely pleasant day trip taking a leisurely journey in a vintage steam-hauled train to visit one of England's finest moated castles. With its headquarters today in Tenterden, the Kent & East Sussex Railway was originally built and owned by the legendary Colonel Holman F Stephens, and opened between Headcorn and Robertsbridge in 1905. This delightful rural line led a precarious existence until it was nationalized in 1948 and finally closed in 1961. Since then it has been gradually reopened westwards from Tenterden Town station, reaching Bodiam in 2000. The missing link from here to the national rail network at Robertsbridge is currently being rebuilt.

From Tenterden, trains descend in a westerly direction to Rolvenden station then head south, calling at Wittersham Road station towards the water meadows of the peaceful Rother Valley. After crossing the county border from Kent into East Sussex, trains call at Northiam (for Great Dixter House and Gardens) before following the valley westwards to Bodiam Station where the village, Castle Inn and National Trust castle are all within easy reach.

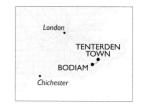

- **TENTERDEN TOWN**
- ROLVENDEN
- WITTERSHAM ROAD
- NORTHIAM
- **BODIAM**

DESTINATION HIGHLIGHTS
National Trust's 14th-century moated Bodiam Castle (NT); Castle Inn; Colonel Stephens Museum (Tenterden)

FREQUENCY OF TRAINS
4-8 per day
NB Tenterden can be reached by bus from Ashford

10½ MILES
50 MINUTES

A vintage steam train approaches Tenterden Town station on the Kent & East Sussex Railway.

HASTINGS ●
ORE ○
THREE OAKS ○
DOLEHAM ○
WINCHELSEA ○
RYE ○
APPLEDORE ○
HAM STREET ○
**ASHFORD
INTERNATIONAL** ●
WYE ○
CHILHAM ○
CHARTHAM ○
CANTERBURY WEST ○
STURRY ○
MINSTER ○
RAMSGATE ●

The first half of this railway trip follows the Marshlink Line from Hastings to Ashford, which survived a threatened closure in the 1963 'Beeching Report'. From Hastings' ultra modern station, diesel multiple units leave in a northeasterly direction, immediately passing through Mount Pleasant Tunnel to call at Ore. Here the third-rail double-track electrification ends and the single-track line begins, burrowing through Ore Tunnel before following the valley of the River Brede, calling at Three Oaks, Doleham and Winchelsea and arriving at Rye station, where there are staggered platforms and a passing loop. The most famous landmark here is the Grade II-listed white smock windmill that stands close to the railway. From Rye the railway heads across the Royal Military Canal to cross the vast expanse of Romney Marsh in a dead-straight line to Appledore station, where there is a freight-only branch line trailing in from Dungeness nuclear power station on the coast.

The single-track section ends at Appledore and trains soon cross the Royal Military Canal once more, calling at Ham Street, then paralleling the busy A4020 to the outskirts of Ashford. Passengers must change trains at Ashford International station to continue their journey to Ramsgate. From Ashford, electric trains head northeast along the Great Stour Valley, calling at Wye, Chilham and Chartham before diving under the Dover main line to arrive at Canterbury West. From here, the final part of this journey takes trains through Sturry to Minster, where the electrified line from Dover joins at a triangular junction. Ramsgate is but a short distance east of Minster and is also the end of the line for the Hitachi high-speed 'Javelin' service from London St Pancras (see page 67). A regular Thanet Loop bus service links the 1920s Grade II-listed brick-built station with the town centre and harbour.

The busy Royal Harbour and marina at Ramsgate.

Trains for Ramsgate depart from Folkestone's 1960s station and soon burrow through Martello Tunnel to start their scenic, coast-hugging journey to Dover. Set immediately below the world-famous White Cliffs, the railway passes through the long Abbotscliffe Tunnel, the shorter Shakespeare Tunnel and finally the even shorter Harbour Tunnel, to arrive at Dover Priory. This 1930s station is awkwardly sandwiched between two tunnels, and trains for Ramsgate head off through Priory Tunnel and Charlton Tunnel before branching off the Faversham line at Buckland Junction. From here, the railway follows a curving S-shape route to Guston Tunnel before heading off in a northeasterly direction through Martin Mill and Walmer to reach the seaside resort of Deal. Not far from the sea, the main station building here is the original structure built in 1847, while nearby Deal Castle was built for Henry VIII as an artillery fortress in the 16th century.

From Deal, trains head inland to the historic town of Sandwich. Located on the River Stour, Sandwich was made a Cinque Port in the 12th century but silting-up of the river and shifting sands have now left it two miles from the sea. Leaving Sandwich, trains head north to Minster Junction then turn east to Ramsgate. Here, passengers need to change trains for the short journey around the coast via the seaside resort of Broadstairs to Margate. The impressive 1920s Grade II-listed station building was designed by Edwin Maxwell Fry and is located just a short walk from the beach and Marine Terrace.

● **FOLKESTONE CENTRAL**
○ DOVER PRIORY
○ MARTIN MILL
○ WALMER
○ DEAL
○ SANDWICH
● **RAMSGATE**
○ DUMPTON PARK
○ BROADSTAIRS
● **MARGATE**

DESTINATION HIGHLIGHTS
harbour; beaches; amusement park; Shell Grotto; Turner Contemporary art gallery; Old Town

FREQUENCY OF TRAINS
1 per hour

34½ MILES
1 HOUR 15 MINUTES

The modern Turner Contemporary Art Gallery in Margate.

DAY TRIPS FROM LONDON

This day trip only became possible in March 2013 when the Bluebell Railway opened its extension northwards from Kingscote to East Grinstead, where it connects with the national rail network. The start of our journey is at London's Victoria station, once the jumping-off point for cross-Channel services such as the 'Golden Arrow' and the 'Night Ferry' and now the capital's second busiest station after Waterloo. Electric trains for East Grinstead thread their way through the South London suburbs en route for East Croydon and South Croydon. Trains diverge from the main line at South Croydon Junction to take the double-track Oxted line through Riddlesdown, Upper Warlingham and Woldingham before passing through the 1-mile 501 yd Oxted Tunnel to Oxted station. From here, trains pass through Limpsfield Tunnel before calling at Hurst Green station, the junction for the 25-mile branch line to Uckfield.

Heading due south, trains call at Lingfield and Dormans before terminating at East Grinstead, formerly known as Low Level station. The now-demolished High Level station was once served by trains on the Three Bridges to Tunbridge Wells route. The line westwards to Three Bridges is now a footpath and cycleway known as the Worth Way. Passengers change trains at East Grinstead to take an 11-mile steam-hauled trip in vintage carriages along the Bluebell Railway to Sheffield Park, calling at Kingscote and Horsted Keynes, the railway's headquarters, en route. Sheffield Park National Trust house and gardens are but a 10-minute stroll from the station.

LONDON VICTORIA ●
CLAPHAM JUNCTION ○
BALHAM ○
EAST CROYDON ○
SOUTH CROYDON ○
RIDDLESDOWN ○
UPPER WARLINGHAM ○
WOLDINGHAM ○
OXTED ○
HURST GREEN ○
LINGFIELD ○
DORMANS ○
EAST GRINSTEAD ●
KINGSCOTE ○
HORSTED KEYNES ○
SHEFFIELD PARK ●

DESTINATION HIGHLIGHTS
trip on an 11-mile steam heritage railway; railway museum; visitor centre; Sheffield Park and Garden (NT)

FREQUENCY OF TRAINS
Victoria to East Grinstead:
2 per hour
East Grinstead to Sheffield Park:
3-7 trains per day (Sat-Sun all year; daily Apr-Oct)

41¼ MILES
54 + 41 MINUTES

The first through train to reach Horsted Keynes, on the Bluebell Railway, from London for over 50 years arrives behind Class 66 diesel No. 66739 on 28 March 2013.

This trip follows the same route as the 'Brighton Belle' Pullman train in the BBC's famous 1952 film 'London to Brighton in 4 Minutes', but takes a while longer! On leaving Victoria Station, trains for Brighton wend their way through the sprawling South London suburbs, negotiating Clapham Junction – the busiest junction in the world – to East Croydon. After continuing southwards through Purley, the alternative Quarry Line and Redhill Line part company, both heading through tunnels and under the M23 before rejoining at Earlswood. From here, the Victorian railway builders had to conquer the North Downs, the Wealden Ridge and the South Downs, an immense feat that was completed in 1841 and involved excavating deep cuttings, high embankments, 7 tunnels and the 1,475-ft-long Ouse Valley Viaduct.

South of Earlswood the Brighton main line serves Gatwick Airport and Three Bridges before heading through Balcombe Tunnel to Balcombe and over the Ouse Valley Viaduct to Haywards Heath. The final stretch of our journey southwards is through Haywards Heath Tunnel to Wivelsfield, Keymer Junction – where the line to Lewes branches off to the east – Burgess Hill and Hassocks, before passing through Clayton and Patcham Tunnels and making its final approach to the city. The original part of Brighton's busy terminus station – the UK's 7th busiest outside London – was designed in the Italianate style in 1840 but the imposing double-spanned curved glass and iron roof was a late 19th-century addition. From here, the seafront is just a 10-minute walk away down West Street.

- **LONDON** VICTORIA
- CLAPHAM JUNCTION
- BALHAM
- EAST CROYDON
- PURLEY
- REDHILL
- EARLSWOOD
- GATWICK AIRPORT
- THREE BRIDGES
- BALCOMBE
- HAYWARDS HEATH
- WIVELSFIELD
- BURGESS HILL
- HASSOCKS
- **BRIGHTON**

DESTINATION HIGHLIGHTS
Royal Pavilion; Palace Pier; Volk's Electric Railway; 'The Lanes'; Brighton Wheel; naturist beach; museum and art gallery; Toy and Model Museum; Brighton Festival (May)

FREQUENCY OF TRAINS
4 per hour

50¾ MILES
1 HOUR

The Royal Pavilion at Brighton was built in three stages, beginning in 1787, as a seaside retreat for George, Prince of Wales.

Our journey to Bognor Regis begins by following the same route as the London Victoria to Brighton trip (see page 53) as far as Three Bridges. From here, Bognor electric trains branch off to the west along the Arun Valley Line, first calling at the modern town of Crawley before making the short run to Horsham. This route was electrified using the third-rail system by the Southern Railway as long ago as 1938 but many of the stations were not modernized, their short platforms creating difficulties for today's long trains. At the Grade II-listed 1930s station at Horsham, the Mole Valley Line from Leatherhead and Dorking joins from the north.

From Horsham, Arun Valley Line trains head off through the countryside in a southwesterly direction to Pulborough, calling at Billingshurst en route. Some trains also stop at Christ's Hospital station – once a busy junction for trains to Guildford and Shoreham-by-Sea but now a shadow of its former self. Billingshurst station is the original built by the Mid-Sussex Railway in 1859 and the signalbox, which controls a level crossing, is believed to be the oldest still working on the national rail network, having been built in 1868. Dating from 1859, Pulborough station is also the original building, and until 1955 was the junction for the branch line up the Rother Valley to Midhurst. From Pulborough the railway heads south down the Arun Valley, cutting through the South Downs at Amberley, home to the narrow-gauge collection of the Chalk Pits Museum, before burrowing through North Stoke Tunnel. Historic Arundel, with its castle, is the next stop followed by Arundel Junction, where Bognor trains head west through Ford (home to an Open Prison) to Barnham. Here, trains head off down the branch line to the coast before terminating at Bognor Regis's attractive early 20th-century station.

DESTINATION HIGHLIGHTS
East and West beaches; 2.7-mile promenade; Hotham Park boating lake and miniature railway; Butlin's indoor leisure park; museum; pier; International Birdman competition; seafront market

FREQUENCY OF TRAINS
2 per hour
(change at Ford on Sun)

66½ MILES
1 HOUR 46 MINUTES

The seafront at the popular resort of Bognor Regis.

This railway journey takes us to one of Britain's most visited cities, its historic legacy and buildings a magnet for visitors from around the world. Trains depart from Victoria station and take the former London, Chatham & Dover Railway's main line through London's southeastern suburbs to Bromley South, Rochester, Chatham, Gillingham, Sittingbourne (for the branch line to Sheerness and the Sittingbourne & Kemsley narrow-gauge railway) and Faversham. The station building at this important junction station was built in 1898 and is Grade II-listed (so is the old engine shed despite its poor state of repair). Third-rail electrification along this route was completed in 1959 and the station has also been served by high-speed services to and from St Pancras via Ebbsfleet International since 2009.

Immediately east of Faversham, trains for Whitstable, Herne Bay and Margate branch off towards the North Kent coast while trains heading for Canterbury and Dover head southeast, first calling at Selling then burrowing under the North Downs through Selling Tunnel to reach the Great Stour Valley – here the railway, main road and Ashford to Ramsgate line all head down the valley to Canterbury. The city centre is about a 10-minute walk from Canterbury East station.

- **LONDON** VICTORIA
- BRIXTON
- HERNE HILL
- BECKENHAM JUNCTION
- BROMLEY SOUTH
- ROCHESTER
- CHATHAM
- GILLINGHAM
- RAINHAM
- SITTINGBOURNE
- FAVERSHAM
- SELLING
- **CANTERBURY EAST**

DESTINATION HIGHLIGHTS
Canterbury Cathedral and ruins of St Augustine's Abbey (both within UNESCO World Heritage Site); ruins of Norman castle; Saxon church; city walls and gates; Huguenot weavers' houses; Roman Museum; Rupert Bear Museum; punt and boat hire on River Stour

FREQUENCY OF TRAINS
2 per hour

61¾ MILES
1 HOUR 36 MINUTES

Home to a museum and overlooking the River Stour, the 60-ft-high Westgate Towers in Canterbury is England's finest medieval fortified gatehouse.

DESTINATION HIGHLIGHTS
trip on steam heritage railway;
Georgian town centre
(conservation area);
art galleries; traditional shops;
tea rooms; Brandy Mount
House Gardens; fulling mill;
river walks; Watercress
Festival (May); Alresford Show
(September); Alresford
Fair (October)

FREQUENCY OF TRAINS
Waterloo to Alton:
2 per hour (Mon-Sat),
1 per hour (Sun, change
at Aldershot)
Alton to Alresford:
3-6 per day (selected days
Mar-Oct; daily July-Aug)

57 MILES
1 HOUR 15 MINUTES
+ 35 MINUTES

This pleasant day trip to the watercress meadows of the Itchen Valley includes a 10-mile ride in a steam train over the Hampshire hills. Electric trains for Alton leave London's Waterloo Station, the busiest station in Britain, and head off down the former London & South Western Railway's main line. Pausing at Clapham Junction (the busiest railway junction in the world), trains make their way through London's leafy southwestern suburbs and into wealthy commuter belt country via Wimbledon and Weybridge to arrive at Woking. Here, just before the station, the Shah Jahan Mosque (built in 1889) can be spotted to the south of the railway. At Woking the Portsmouth-direct line via Guildford branches off to the south while Alton-bound trains continue along the main line as far as Brookwood, where they branch off at Pirbright Junction. Brookwood is home to the vast (once rail-served) London Necropolis Cemetery, which even had its own separate railway station at Waterloo.

From Pirbright Junction the Alton branch winds through pine woods and heathland, calling at Ash Vale (for trains to Ascot), then crossing over the Reading to Guildford line before arriving at the military town of Aldershot. The picturesque town of Farnham is the next stop and just beyond here the line becomes single track through Bentley (once the junction for the Bordon branch) before terminating at Alton. Steam trains for Alresford leave from the island platform and head out past the site of Butts Junction, from where the Light Railway to Basingstoke ran until 1932 and the Meon Valley Line to Fareham ran until 1955, climbing steadily to the highest point of the line at Medstead & Four Marks station. From here it is downhill to Ropley, where the Mid-Hants Railway has its engine shed and the station platform is decorated with examples of topiary. Continuing westward past the watercress beds unique to this area, the railway ends at pretty Alresford station, located just a few minutes' walk from the town centre.

*'West Country' Class 4-6-2
No. 34007 'Wadebridge' enters
the restored Medstead & Four
Marks station with a train
on the Mid-Hants Railway.*

This short railway journey is by far the best way to visit one of London's premier historic attractions. Electric trains for Hampton Court leave Waterloo station which, with 94 million passenger entries and exits during 2011/12, is the busiest station in the UK, in a southerly direction, first calling at Vauxhall station before passing through Queenstown Road (Battersea) station to arrive at Clapham Junction. Each day around 2,000 trains, many stopping, pass through this station making it the busiest through station in Europe.

Beyond here, trains head through London's leafy southwestern suburbs, calling at Earlsfield then passing Durnsford Road electric depot and its tiny railway staff halt to reach Wimbledon. Next stop is Raynes Park, where the Chessington and Epsom line branches off to the south, followed by Berrylands and Surbiton, where the 1937 Grade II-listed art deco station building is considered to be one of the finest modernist stations in the country. Just over a mile beyond Surbiton, the Hampton Court branch leaves the main line by means of a flyover at Hampton Court Junction, then heads north to the only intermediate station of Thames Ditton before terminating at Hampton Court. Hampton Court Palace and gardens are but a short walk from the station via a bridge over the River Thames.

- **LONDON** WATERLOO
- VAUXHALL
- QUEENSTOWN ROAD (BATTERSEA)
- CLAPHAM JUNCTION
- EARLSFIELD
- WIMBLEDON
- RAYNES PARK
- BERRYLANDS
- SURBITON
- THAMES DITTON
- **HAMPTON COURT**

DESTINATION HIGHLIGHTS
16th/17th-century Hampton Court Palace and landscaped grounds, gardens, maze, Flower Show (early July)

FREQUENCY OF TRAINS
2 per hour

15 MILES
36 MINUTES

Hampton Court Palace was originally built for Cardinal Thomas Wolsey in the early 16th century. Now open to the public, its grounds are host to the annual Flower Show.

LONDON MARYLEBONE
WEMBLEY STADIUM
SUDBURY HILL HARROW
NORTHOLT PARK
SOUTH RUISLIP
WEST RUISLIP
HIGH WYCOMBE
SAUNDERTON
PRINCES RISBOROUGH
HADDENHAM & THAME PARKWAY
BICESTER NORTH
KINGS SUTTON
BANBURY
LEAMINGTON SPA
WARWICK
HATTON
CLAVERDON
BEARLEY
WILMCOTE
STRATFORD-UPON-AVON

DESTINATION HIGHLIGHTS
Royal Shakespeare Theatre;
Hall's Croft; Nash's House;
New Place; Holy Trinity
Church; historic town centre;
boat hire on River Avon;
Stratford-upon-Avon
Canal walks

FREQUENCY OF TRAINS
1 every 2 hours

104 MILES
2 HOURS 20 MINUTES

*Anne Hathaway's Cottage was
once home to the wife of
William Shakespeare. Located in
the village of Shottery, 1 mile
west of Stratford-upon-Avon,
it is now open to the public.*

Diesel trains for Stratford-upon-Avon depart from London's Marylebone station, which was opened by the Great Central Railway in 1899 as the southern terminus of its London Extension from Sheffield. Following the closure of this route in 1966, the station suffered years of neglect with threats of closure and conversion into a bus station in the 1980s. However, since then it has seen a renaissance with a major facelift and improved services to Birmingham. Trains depart in a northerly direction, crossing over the Regents Canal before burrowing through St John's Wood Tunnel to West Hampstead where the railway turns westward, paralleling the Metropolitan and Jubilee lines of London Underground as far as Neasden Junction. From here, trains for Stratford-upon-Avon branch off through Wembley, Sudbury Hill and Northolt Park to join the former GW & GC Joint Railway's route at Northolt Junction.

From Northolt Junction trains head northwest through the Buckinghamshire countryside, calling at High Wycombe and climbing to the summit of the line across the Chiltern Hills at Saunderton before reaching Princes Risborough station. Haddenham & Thame Parkway, Brill Tunnel, Bicester North (junction for Oxford), the flyover at Aynho Junction (also for Oxford) and Kings Sutton all follow before trains call at the market town of Banbury. From here they head north, passing the junction for the large rail-served Kineton MOD depot at Fenny Compton, to Leamington Spa, Warwick and Hatton, taking the single-track line through Claverdon and Bearley. At Bearley Junction the line from Birmingham, Tyseley and Henley-in-Arden is joined for the final few miles through Wilmcote to Stratford-upon-Avon.

This is a circular railway trip, heading through Buckinghamshire countryside and the Chiltern Hills via Princes Risborough on the outbound journey, and returning along the direct line from Aylesbury to Marylebone via Amersham.

As described on page 58, trains for Princes Risborough depart from London's reborn Marylebone station and after burrowing through St John's Wood Tunnel take the route from Neasden Junction to Northolt Junction, to join the former GW & GC Joint Railway. This railway was opened in 1906 and gave the Great Central Railway an alternative route to the north avoiding Aylesbury, via High Wycombe, Princes Risborough and Ashendon Junction, where the company's trains branched off to join its original main line at Grendon Underwood.

After calling at Princes Risborough (for the Chinnor & Princes Risborough heritage railway), trains for Aylesbury branch off northwards along the single-track line that skirts the northern scarp of the Chiltern Hills. Trains serve the picturesque, historic villages of Monks Risborough and Little Kimble en route before calling at Aylesbury station, where visitors to the town should alight. This was the terminus of the truncated route from Marylebone to the north from 1966 until 2008, when a further 2 miles was opened northwards to a new Aylesbury Vale Parkway station.

● **LONDON** MARYLEBONE

○ SOUTH RUISLIP
○ WEST RUISLIP
○ HIGH WYCOMBE
○ PRINCES RISBOROUGH
○ MONKS RISBOROUGH
○ LITTLE KIMBLE

● **AYLESBURY**

DESTINATION HIGHLIGHTS
historic market square; market (4 days per week); haunted 15th-century King's Head Inn (NT); grave of Marie-Antoinette; arts centre; Roald Dahl Children's Gallery; Waterside Theatre; canal walks

FREQUENCY OF TRAINS
1 per hour (Mon-Sat)
2 per hour (Sun)

43¼ MILES
1 HOUR 10 MINUTES
NB some services require a change at Princes Risborough

Celebrating its 50th operational anniversary, a Class 121 'Bubble Car' approaches Princes Risborough station from Aylesbury in January 2011.

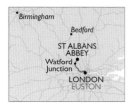

DESTINATION HIGHLIGHTS
11th-century abbey and cathedral (longest nave in Britain); Ye Olde Fighting Cocks pub (with 8th-century foundations, the oldest pub in England); Verulamium Park; Roman remains and museum; Kingsbury Watermill Museum; 15th-century Clock Tower; city streets used as film locations

FREQUENCY OF TRAINS
1 per hour

24 MILES
43 MINUTES

This day trip to one of England's most historic cities begins at London's modern Euston station – the demolition of the original 1837 building and famous Doric Arch in 1961–2 has quite rightly been described as an act of vandalism unparalleled in post-war Britain. Trains head off in a northwesterly direction along the route of Robert Stephenson's London & Birmingham Railway, with today's modern electric trains making light of the steep climb up to Camden, before heading west through Primrose Hill Tunnel to Queens Park, where the Bakerloo London Underground line joins on its parallel route. Our train continues through Kensal Green Tunnel, busy Willesden Junction and then past the modern Wembley European Freight Yard before calling at Wembley Central, Harrow & Wealdstone (site of the 1952 rail crash that claimed 112 lives) and Bushey before halting at Watford Junction.

Passengers for the St Albans Abbey branch change here and then proceed in a more leisurely fashion in a diesel train along the single-track line, calling at the minimal and unstaffed stations of Watford North, Garston, Brickett Wood, How Wood and Park Street to the basic terminus of St Albans Abbey. From here it is a 10-minute walk into the city centre. Visitors to the city can return to London via the St Albans City to St Pancras main line.

Founded as an abbey in AD 793, St Albans Cathedral has the longest nave of any cathedral in England.

This day trip to the world-famous university city of Cambridge begins at London's Liverpool Street station, which was opened by the Great Eastern Railway in 1874 on the site of the Bethlem Royal Hospital, more commonly known as 'Bedlam'. On leaving this busy station, electric trains immediately start the climb to Bethnal Green, from where they take a northerly route up the Lee Valley. This 10,000-acre Regional Park extends for 26 miles and includes numerous country parks, nature reserves, lakes and sports centres, with much of the southern half developed for the 2012 Olympic Games. Trains pass through Ponders End, Brimsdown, Enfield Lock and Cheshunt en route before arriving at Broxbourne, the junction for the Hertford East branch.

From Broxbourne, trains head into Essex for a short distance through Harlow New Town and then back into Hertfordshire to Bishops Stortford, once the junction for the Braintree branch. North of here the railway re-enters Essex, with stations at Stansted Mountfitchet (junction for Stansted Airport), Elsenham (summit of the line), Newport and Audley End (once the junction for Saffron Walden), and passes through Audley End and Littlebury tunnels to reach the valley of the River Cam. At Great Chesterford the railway enters Cambridgeshire for the final miles through Whittlesford and Shelford (once the junction for the line to Haverhill and Sudbury) to Shepreth Branch Junction, where it meets the electrified line from King's Cross via Hitchin. To the south of Cambridge station, the Varsity Line from Oxford once joined the line until its controversial closure at the beginning of 1968. Cambridge's busy station with its Grade II-listed main building has the third-longest railway platform in the UK and has recently been the subject of major improvements. It is but a short bus ride from here to the city centre.

- **LONDON** LIVERPOOL STREET
- BETHNAL GREEN
- TOTTENHAM HALE
- PONDERS END
- BRIMSDOWN
- ENFIELD LOCK
- WALTHAM CROSS
- CHESHUNT
- BROXBOURNE
- ROYDON
- HARLOW TOWN
- HARLOW MILL
- SAWBRIDGEWORTH
- BISHOPS STORTFORD
- STANSTED MOUNTFITCHET
- ELSENHAM
- NEWPORT
- AUDLEY END
- GREAT CHESTERFORD
- WHITTLESFORD PARKWAY
- SHELFORD
- **CAMBRIDGE**

DESTINATION HIGHLIGHTS
Saxon St Bene't's Church; Castle Hill; Parker's Piece (birthplace of Association Football); Midsummer Fair; Strawberry Fair (early June); Cambridge Beer Festival (May); Cambridge Folk Festival (late July); King's College Chapel; punt hire on River Cam; 14 museums; Kettle's Yard Gallery; walking tours of universities

FREQUENCY OF TRAINS
2 per hour

55¾ MILES
1 HOUR 15 MINUTES

Punts lined up on the River Cam in Cambridge await their next punter.

DESTINATION HIGHLIGHTS
11th-century cathedral; remains of city walls; medieval streets; Norwich Castle Museum; Strangers' Hall Museum; Bridewell Museum; Printing Museum; Dragon Hall Museum; Octagon Chapel; Royal Arcade; Colman's Mustard Shop; large 6-days-a-week open-air market; Sainsbury Centre for Visual Arts; Norfolk & Norwich Festival (May); 23 parks

FREQUENCY OF TRAINS
2 per hour (Mon–Sat)
1 per hour (Sun)

115 MILES
1 HOUR 55 MINUTES

RIGHT: *Norwich Castle was founded by William the Conqueror in the late 11th century.*

OPPOSITE: *Norwich Cathedral was begun in 1096 and is faced with cream-coloured Caen stone from northern France.*

Discover the delights of the most complete medieval city in England on this fantastic railway day trip. Fast electric trains for Norwich leave London's Liverpool Street station and thread their way through the suburbs to Romford and Brentwood before entering Essex countryside and the summit of the line at Ingrave. Beyond here is Chelmsford, Witham (junction for the Braintree branch) and Marks Tey (junction for the Sudbury branch) – both branch lines fortunate survivors of threatened closure in the 'Beeching Report'. The historic city of Colchester is next (junction for Clacton and Walton-on-the-Naze) followed by Manningtree (junction for Harwich) and then it is into Suffolk with a stop at Ipswich's busy station, from where trains leave for Cambridge, Ely, Felixstowe and along the East Suffolk Line (another Beeching survivor) to Lowestoft.

Our fast journey through the Suffolk and Norfolk countryside to Norwich takes us northwards up the Gipping Valley from Ipswich through Needham Market, Stowmarket and Haughley Junction (for Ely and Cambridge and once the junction for the Mid Suffolk Light Railway) to Diss. It was through here, just inside the Norfolk border, that 'Britannia' Class 4-6-2s once thundered through in the 1950s at the head of the 'East Anglian' express between Liverpool Street and Norwich. The famous Bressingham Steam Museum is located 2 miles east of here.

With no more intermediate stations, the final 20 miles through level Norfolk countryside to Norwich is completed in just 20 minutes. On the approach to Norwich station the railway first crosses over the Ely line before joining it at Trowse Junction for the final mile through Thorpe Junction (for Sheringham, Yarmouth and Lowestoft) to the city's terminus station. This magnificent Grade II-listed building was opened in 1886 and features an imposing 70-ft-high dome covered in zinc tiles. From here it is but a short walk across Foundry Bridge over the River Wensum to the city centre.

LONDON
LIVERPOOL STREET ●
STRATFORD ○
ROMFORD ○
BRENTWOOD ○
SHENFIELD ○
CHELMSFORD ○
WITHAM ○
MARKS TEY ●
CHAPPEL & WAKES COLNE ●

This day trip for railway enthusiasts to the East Anglian Railway Museum begins at London's Liverpool Street station, with electric trains following the same route as the trip to Norwich (see page 62) as far as Marks Tey. Changing trains here, passengers are conveyed in a diesel unit along the single-track Sudbury branch to Chappel & Wakes Colne station. Marketed as the Gainsborough Line for the area's links with the artist Thomas Gainsborough, this scenic branch line survived threatened closure in the 1960s and features a 1,066-ft-long viaduct, which carries the railway 75 ft above the Colne Valley on the approach to Chappel & Wakes Colne. Opened in 1849, the 32-arch viaduct was constructed of 7 million bricks and is the second-largest brick structure in England.

The East Anglian Railway Museum is located at Chappel & Wakes Colne station. This working museum features the restored late 19th-century Great Eastern Railway station building, a large collection of railway items and two restored, working signal boxes. Running days and events are held on various weekends throughout the year. For details visit: www.earm.co.uk

DESTINATION HIGHLIGHTS
East Anglian Railway Museum; restored Victorian station; Victorian viaduct (second-largest brick structure in England)

FREQUENCY OF TRAINS
1 per hour

32½ MILES
1 HOUR 5 MINUTES

This massive brick viaduct at Chappel & Wakes Colne carries the Marks Tey to Sudbury branch line over the Colne Valley.

Until the Second World War a day trip to Southend was one of the few enjoyments available to working class Londoners. Every weekend, thousands would climb aboard the steam train to escape the sweat shops and slums of the East End and enjoy a jolly day out at the seaside. Since then, Southend has reinvented itself and still offers plenty of entertainment for all the family.

Electric trains for Southend depart from London's small, lesser-known terminus of Fenchurch Street station, which was built in 1854. Today its attractive grey-brick façade and rounded gable roof are dwarfed by the glass-fronted high-rise offices of the City of London. In 1858 Fenchurch Street became the western terminus of the London, Tilbury & Southend Railway and part of the route was used by boat trains from St Pancras to Tilbury until the 1960s. Today's more direct route avoids Tilbury, instead taking the line from Barking to Pitsea via Upminster that was completed in 1888.

Much of this route passes through the East London suburbs and only reaches open country beyond Upminster, junction for the single-track line to Grays on the Tilbury Loop. The latter is rejoined at Pitsea from where the railway heads down to South Benfleet, the nearest station to Canvey Island (birthplace of Wilko Johnson of Dr Feelgood). From here the railway follows muddy tidal creeks along the shoreline of the Thames Estuary, passing through Leigh-on-Sea (for the Leigh Island National Nature Reserve) and along the coastal ribbon development through Chalkwell and Westcliff before arriving at the recently refurbished Southend Central station. It is just a short walk from the station to the cliff gardens along the Western Esplanade, the pier and the sea.

LONDON
FENCHURCH STREET

BARKING

UPMINSTER

BASILDON

PITSEA

BENFLEET

LEIGH-ON-SEA

CHALKWELL

WESTCLIFF

SOUTHEND CENTRAL

DESTINATION HIGHLIGHTS
3 Blue Flag beaches; world's longest pleasure pier and pier railway; cliff railway; seafront cliff gardens; promenade; amusement park; aquarium; farmers' market (2nd and 4th Saturday each month); airshow (May); carnival (August); art galleries and museums

FREQUENCY OF TRAINS
4 per hour (Mon–Sat)
2 per hour (Sun)

35¾ MILES
55 MINUTES

Completed in 1889, Southend Pier is the longest pleasure pier in the world. A railway runs along its 1.34-mile length over the Thames Estuary to Pier Head station

Our day trip to the historic city of Peterborough begins at London's recently refurbished King's Cross station. Designed by Lewis Cubitt and opened by the Great Northern Railway in 1852, this is the southern terminus of the electrified East Coast Main Line. Its platform numbers are interesting as there is a Platform 0 and a 'secret' Platform 9¾ which features in the Harry Potter films.

Trains head north from the station and immediately enter Gasworks Tunnel, followed by Copenhagen Tunnel, for the climb up Holloway Bank to Finsbury Park. Accelerating through the North London suburbs into Hertfordshire, trains encounter a further succession of tunnels at Wood Green, Barnet, Hadley Wood South and North, Potters Bar and Welwyn South and North, before speeding through Stevenage and Hitchin (junction for the Cambridge line). Leaving Hertfordshire to enter Bedfordshire, trains pass through Biggleswade and then Sandy – here the Varsity Line from Cambridge to Oxford crossed over the East Coast Main Line until the former's closure at the beginning of 1968.

North of Sandy, the ECML enters Huntingdonshire, passing through St Neots before reaching the historic market town of Huntingdon, famous as the birthplace of Oliver Cromwell and once the junction for the GN & GE Joint Railway to St Ives. Continuing their northward journey, trains flash through Abbots Ripton, scene of a major rail disaster in 1876 when the 'Special Scotch Express' (forerunner of the 'Flying Scotsman') collided with a coal train in a blizzard. A second express then ran into the wreckage and 13 passengers were killed – the subsequent inquiry led to major improvements in railway signalling practice. North of here lies Holme, once the junction for the Ramsay branch, and soon trains are slowing for the final approach to Peterborough. Just south of the station lies Fletton Junction, from where the single line to Longueville Junction has recently been purchased by the Nene Valley Railway. A major rail interchange, Peterborough station is a few minutes' walk from the city centre.

DESTINATION HIGHLIGHTS
12th-century cathedral; Minster Precincts; museum and art gallery; Nene Valley Railway; Ferry Meadows Park and miniature railway; Railworld Museum; Green Wheel Sculpture Trail

FREQUENCY OF TRAINS
3 per hour (Mon-Sat)

1 per hour (Sun)

76¼ MILES
50 MINUTES (MON-SAT)
1 HOUR 25 MINUTES (SUN)

A steam-hauled Travelling Post Office train at Wansford on the Nene Valley Railway.

Opened throughout in 2007, the High Speed 1 rail link from St Pancras International station to Ashford International and the Channel Tunnel has brought vastly improved passenger services between the capital and the Kent Coast. These domestic high-speed trains began operating in 2009 with a fleet of Class 395 'Javelin' electric multiple units built by Hitachi of Japan. Capable of 140 mph, their acceleration is even faster than the Eurostar trains to the Continent.

Our day trip to Ramsgate begins at London's Grade I-listed St Pancras International station, which was opened by the Midland Railway in 1868. Designed by William Barlow, the arched glass-and-iron roof was then the largest single-span roof in the world. This historic station was threatened with closure back in the 'enlightened' 1960s but a campaign led by Poet Laureate John Betjeman was successful in halting its demolition and it is now the railway gateway to the Continent. On leaving the station, trains for Ramsgate soon head east to enter a series of long tunnels, including one under the Thames, totalling 12½ miles in length, calling at Stratford International before reaching Ebbsfleet International station over a series of 3 viaducts. Now heading southeast, trains accelerate to their top permissible speed of 130 mph, crossing the Medway Valley on a long viaduct, burrowing under the North Downs and passing through a cut-and-cover tunnel to arrive at Ashford International. From here 'Javelin' trains for Ramsgate take the slower national rail network route via Canterbury West to Ramsgate (see page 48). A regular Thanet Loop bus service links the 1920s Grade II-listed brick-built station with the town centre and harbour.

LONDON ST PANCRAS INTERNATIONAL

STRATFORD INTERNATIONAL

EBBSFLEET INTERNATIONAL

ASHFORD INTERNATIONAL

CANTERBURY WEST

RAMSGATE

DESTINATION HIGHLIGHTS
trip along HS1; Blue Flag beach; marina; seafront parade with bars and restaurants; maritime museum; motor museum; Regency and Victorian architecture; cliff-top promenades; street market (Friday and Saturday)

FREQUENCY OF TRAINS
1 per hour

91 MILES
1 HOUR 17 MINUTES

A view of the Royal Harbour and seafront at Ramsgate.

LONDON ST PANCRAS
INTERNATIONAL
KENTISH TOWN
CRICKLEWOOD
ST ALBANS
HARPENDEN
LUTON
BEDFORD
WELLINGBOROUGH
KETTERING
MARKET
HARBOROUGH
LEICESTER
LOUGHBOROUGH
EAST MIDLANDS
PARKWAY
NOTTINGHAM

Diesel trains for Nottingham depart from London's historic St Pancras International station, which is also the terminus for the high-speed service to the Continent and the Kent Coast (see page 67). Trains head up the Midland main line through Kentish Town before heading west to burrow under Hampstead Heath to Cricklewood, where there is a major rail-freight depot. After speeding through the North London suburbs and burrowing through Elstree Tunnel, trains enter Hertfordshire to call at St Albans and Harpenden before entering Bedfordshire to call at Luton and Bedford. The latter's modern station was built to replace the original building that was badly damaged in the Second World War.

Still heading north, trains breast Sharnbrook Summit before entering Northamptonshire to serve the towns of Wellingborough and Kettering. North of here the line to Corby and Oakham branches off at Kettering North Junction while the Midland main line climbs to Desborough Summit before descending into Leicestershire at Market Harborough. Climbing once more, trains reach Kibworth Summit and clatter through the junctions at Wigston and Knighton to arrive at Leicester's grand Victorian station.

North of Leicester, trains head for Syston Junction (for Stamford and Peterborough), Loughborough (home to the Great Central Railway and Brush Traction) and East Midlands Parkway, before passing the enormous Ratcliffe-on-Soar coal-fired power station and the triangular junction at Trent to arrive at Nottingham's Midland station. Built in an Edwardian Baroque Revival style, it was opened in 1904 and is currently the subject of a major redevelopment project.

DESTINATION HIGHLIGHTS
Nottingham Castle, museum
and art gallery; Galleries
of Justice; Old Market Square;
City of Caves; Exchange Arcade;
19th-century Gothic Revival
cathedral; Lace Market; Ye Old
Trip to Jerusalem, The Bell Inn
and Ye Olde Salutation Inn;
Wollaton Hall for Industrial
and Natural History museums

FREQUENCY OF TRAINS
2 per hour (Mon-Sat)
1 per hour (Sun)

123½ MILES
1 HOUR 55 MINUTES (MON-SAT)
2 HOURS 15 MINUTES (SUN)

RIGHT: *The Nottingham Express
Transit system currently serves
lines to Hucknall and Phoenix
Park in the northern suburbs.*

OPPOSITE: *Dating from 1189,
Nottingham's Ye Olde Trip to
Jerusalem Inn is reputed to be
the oldest pub in England.*

LONDON PADDINGTON ●
EALING BROADWAY ○
HAYES & HARLINGTON ○
SLOUGH ○
BURNHAM ○
TAPLOW ○
MAIDENHEAD ○
TWYFORD ○
READING ○
PANGBOURNE ○
GORING & STREATLEY ○
CHOLSEY ○
DIDCOT PARKWAY ○
APPLEFORD ○
CULHAM ○
RADLEY ○
OXFORD ●

DESTINATION HIGHLIGHTS
Carfax Tower; Radcliffe
Camera; Bridge of Sighs;
Blackwell's Bookshop;
Ashmolean Museum;
Bodleian Library; Christ
Church Cathedral; Modern Art
Oxford; Headington Shark;
Botanic Garden; Museum of
Natural History; Pitt Rivers
Museum; Oxford Castle and
Prison; punt hire on Thames,
Isis and Cherwell rivers;
university parks; canal walks
along Oxford Canal

FREQUENCY OF TRAINS
2 per hour (Mon-Sat)
1 per hour (Sun)

63½ MILES
1 HOUR (MON-SAT)
1 HOUR 15 MINUTES (SUN)

This day trip to the 'city of dreaming spires' begins at Brunel's Paddington station, the London terminus of this famous engineer's former broad-gauge Great Western Railway to Bristol, which opened throughout in 1841. The present overall-roofed station at Paddington opened in 1854. Diesel trains depart in a westerly direction, soon accelerating through London's western suburbs past the site of Old Oak Common engine shed, which is now undergoing major redevelopment in connection with the Crossrail project.

Heading westward, our train passes through Slough (junction for Windsor), Burnham and Taplow before crossing the River Thames on Brunel's magnificent brick-arched bridge at Maidenhead, whose station is the junction for the single-track branch line to Bourne End and Marlow. Onwards to Twyford, junction for Henley-on-Thames, before trains enter Brunel's Sonning Cutting – over a mile long and 60 ft deep, it took hundreds of navvies using only pick axes, shovels and wheelbarrows 2 years to complete. The recently remodelled junction station at Reading soon follows before the railway heads northwest up the Thames Valley, through Pangbourne and Goring as far as Cholsey & Moulsford. Here, the river is left behind as the railway heads off to Didcot – fast trains to Oxford take the avoiding line here, passing the Great Western Society's steam-engine sheds, running lines and museum. Now heading north away from the Bristol main line, trains pass through Appleford and Culham before rejoining the Thames Valley for the final approach through Radley to Oxford. The city centre is a 15-minute walk from the station.

A bird's-eye view of All Souls College in Oxford – known as the 'City of Dreaming Spires'.

The first part of our journey to the UNESCO World Heritage city of Bath follows the same route as the day trip to Oxford (see page 70) as far as Didcot. From here, the level route of Brunel's broad-gauge line to Bristol is followed westwards along the Vale of White Horse through Steventon. After passing the sites of long-closed stations at Wantage Road and Challow, the famous Uffington White Horse can be seen on the northern slopes of Whitehorse Hill to the south before our diesel train speeds through Shrivenham on the approach to Swindon.

Immediately west of Swindon station (junction for Gloucester and Cheltenham, see page 90) the remains of the vast GWR railway works (now a shopping outlet and museum) can be seen to the north. At Royal Wootton Bassett the more direct route to the Severn Tunnel and South Wales continues westwards while the original Brunel route heads off in a southwesterly direction to Chippenham. Trains soon reach Thingley Junction (for Melksham and Trowbridge) before entering Box Tunnel – this Brunel masterpiece was opened in 1841 and at 1.83 miles in length was then the longest railway tunnel in the world. The shorter Middle Hill Tunnel soon follows before the railway descends to the Avon Valley at Bathampton Junction, where it is joined from the south by the scenic route along the valley to Bradford-on-Avon and Westbury. The approach to Bath extends along a low viaduct giving fine views of the city, before the railway finally crosses the River Avon at the eastern end of the station. From here it is but a short walk into the city centre.

- **LONDON** PADDINGTON
- EALING BROADWAY
- HAYES & HARLINGTON
- SLOUGH
- BURNHAM
- TAPLOW
- MAIDENHEAD
- TWYFORD
- READING
- PANGBOURNE
- GORING & STREATLEY
- CHOLSEY
- DIDCOT PARKWAY
- SWINDON
- CHIPPENHAM
- **BATH SPA**

DESTINATION HIGHLIGHTS
Abbey; Roman Baths; Thermae Bath Spa; American Museum (free shuttle bus); Georgian architecture (Royal Crescent); Sydney Gardens; Royal Victoria Park; Victoria Art Gallery; Green Park station (for Saturday farmers' market); Kennet & Avon Canal; Pump Room; Pulteney Bridge; Two Tunnels Greenway

FREQUENCY OF TRAINS
2 per hour (Mon-Sat)
1 per hour (Sun)

107 MILES
1 HOUR 30 MINUTES

Overlooked by the floodlit Abbey, the Roman Baths in the city of Bath are one of the most popular tourist destinations in Britain.

EASTERN ENGLAND

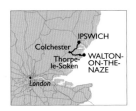

IPSWICH ●
MANNINGTREE ○
COLCHESTER ●
HYTHE ○
WIVENHOE ○
ALRESFORD ○
GREAT BENTLEY ○
WEELEY ○
THORPE-LE-SOKEN ●
KIRBY CROSS ○
FRINTON-ON-SEA ○
WALTON-ON-THE-NAZE ●

Our day trip to the seaside begins at Ipswich station, a busy junction with over 3 million passenger exits and entries during 2011/12. On leaving the station, electric trains immediately plunge into Stoke Tunnel before heading south into the Suffolk countryside – opened in 1846, the 361-yd curving tunnel is the only one on the Great Eastern main line. Our electric train speeds on, passing the site of Bentley station, once the junction for the Hadleigh branch, before crossing into Essex to call at Manningtree (junction for the Harwich branch). From here, trains head southwest before arriving at the historic town of Colchester, where we must change trains for the journey eastwards along the Sunshine Coast Line to Walton-on-the-Naze. Some journeys also require changing from a Clacton-bound train at Thorpe-le-Soken.

Colchester station is located some distance from the city centre and electric trains for Clacton/Walton-on-the-Naze depart in an easterly direction before burrowing under the Great Eastern main line – at East Gate Junction alternate trains take the single-line spur to Colchester Town station. Opened in 1866 by the Tendring Hundreds Railway, this single-platform terminus was originally named St Botolph's. From here trains reverse direction to Colne Junction before resuming their journey through Hythe, Wivenhoe (once the junction for Brightlingsea), Alresford, Great Bentley, Weeley and Thorpe-le-Soken. Here, a change of train is often necessary before continuing the journey along the single-line branch to Walton-on-the-Naze. All trains call at Kirby Cross, where there is a passing loop, and Frinton before arriving at Walton-on-the-Naze's modern single-platform terminus station. It is but a short walk from here to the seafront promenade and pier.

DESTINATION HIGHLIGHTS
pier (second longest in UK);
promenade; sea angling;
miles of sandy beaches;
Naze Tower; bird watching
on The Naze nature reserve

FREQUENCY OF TRAINS
2 per hour (Mon-Sat)
1 per hour (Sun)

36¾ MILES
57-64 MINUTES

Beach huts on stilts on the seafront at sunny Walton-on-the-Naze.

Although home to Britain's largest container port, the town of Felixstowe has a more genteel heritage as a fashionable Victorian seaside resort. Diesel trains for the seaside town leave Ipswich's busy junction station in a northerly direction, first following the Great Eastern main line then heading east along the East Suffolk Line at East Suffolk Junction. After a short distance Westerfield station is reached, where Felixstowe trains branch off southwards along the single-track branch line.

Incredibly, this line also serves Britain's largest container port and its heavy use by container trains has meant that passenger train frequency cannot be increased. The only crossing loop on the branch is at Derby Road station, although beyond here there is a proposal to double the track between Levington and the next station, Trimley. Opened in 1970, a direct loop line to Felixstowe Docks branches off here while passenger trains for the town continue eastwards through Felixstowe Beach Junction, where the line from the docks joins from the south, before terminating at the Town's single-platform station. Passenger facilities are now fairly minimal, with the original Grade II-listed red-brick station building, opened by the Great Eastern Railway in 1898, having been converted to a shopping centre. From here it is a 10-minute walk to the seafront.

● **IPSWICH**
○ WESTERFIELD
○ DERBY ROAD
○ TRIMLEY
● **FELIXSTOWE**

DESTINATION HIGHLIGHTS
pier; museum and Martello Towers; sandy beach; Victorian promenade; Landguard Fort and nature reserve; passenger ferry to Harwich (summer only); Sunday market; restored 1898 station building

FREQUENCY OF TRAINS
1 per hour

15¾ MILES
26 MINUTES

Although Felixstowe is now the largest container port in Britain, this Victorian seaside town was a fashionable resort until the outbreak of the Second World War.

Listed for closure in the 1963 'Beeching Report', the rural East Suffolk Line from Ipswich to Lowestoft was saved by the introduction of many cost-cutting measures including singling of much of the track, de-staffing stations and the introduction of pay trains. Many other doomed branch lines across the country could also have been saved if these measures had been more widely implemented.

Diesel trains for Lowestoft leave Ipswich station heading northwards along the Great Eastern main line before branching off eastwards at East Suffolk Junction. The line is double track through Westerfield station (for Felixstowe, see page 75) as far as the historic riverside town of Woodbridge – a popular spot for yachtsmen on the tidal River Deben – before becoming single track through the Suffolk countryside through Melton to Saxmundham, where a freight-only line branches off to serve Sizewell Nuclear Power Station near Aldeburgh.

IPSWICH
WESTERFIELD
WOODBRIDGE
MELTON
WICKHAM MARKET
SAXMUNDHAM
DARSHAM
HALESWORTH
BRAMPTON
BECCLES
OULTON BROAD SOUTH
LOWESTOFT

Heading northwards, the line is double track once more through Darsham to Halesworth, once the western terminus of the delightful narrow-gauge Southwold Railway until its closure in 1929. It then reverts to single track, with trains calling at Brampton and Beccles stations – the latter was once a busy railway crossroads with branches to Tivetshall and Great Yarmouth – where the East Suffolk Line turns sharply east before reaching Oulton Broad South station and crossing Oulton Broad via a swing bridge. After slowly crossing the bridge, trains join the double-track Wherry Line from Norwich before terminating at Lowestoft station. Much of the original station has fortunately survived despite modernization and the *pièce de résistance* is the large wall-mounted early British Railways' enamel sign proudly proclaiming 'British Railways – Lowestoft Central'. It is but a short walk from here to the seafront.

DESTINATION HIGHLIGHTS
harbour; Blue Flag sandy beaches; 'Mincarlo' floating trawler museum; two piers; Pleasurewood Hills Theme Park and miniature railway; museums; Ness Point wind turbine

FREQUENCY OF TRAINS
1 per hour (Mon-Sat)
1 every 2 hours (Sun)

49 MILES
1 HOUR 26 MINUTES

Colourful beach huts and grand terraced houses overlook the sandy beach at Lowestoft.

This day trip to the birthplace of 18th-century painter Thomas Gainsborough begins at Ipswich station and follows the same route to Colchester as the day trip to Walton-on-the-Naze (see page 74). From Colchester electric trains continue southwest to Mark Tey station, where a change of trains is required.

From Marks Tey, diesel trains head north to Sudbury on what is now marketed as the 'Gainsborough Line'. Single track with no passing loops, the railway slices through undulating farmland in a series of long cuttings before crossing the long brick-built viaduct across the Colne Valley on the approach to Chappel & Wakes Colne station. Here, the East Anglian Railway Museum has its collection of railway artefacts in the restored Victorian station building. Beyond, the railway climbs to enter a long cutting before joining the Stour Valley at Bures. North of the station the railway follows the meandering River Stour, crossing the border from Essex to Suffolk through a landscape made famous in the early 19th century by the artist John Constable. Trains terminate at Sudbury's minimal 1-platform station, from where it is a short walk into this historic market town or to the start of the railway walk to Long Melford.

- **IPSWICH**
- MANNINGTREE
- COLCHESTER
- **MARKS TEY**
- CHAPPEL & WAKES COLNE
- BURES
- **SUDBURY**

DESTINATION HIGHLIGHTS
Market Hill (market Thurs and Sat); Gainsborough's House; walks along River Stour and water meadows; railway walk to Long Melford; Heritage Centre and Museum; Weavers' Piece garden; Old Market Place

FREQUENCY OF TRAINS
1 per hour

33¾ MILES
1 HOUR 29 MINUTES

The pleasant railway path to Long Melford offers walkers and cyclists glimpses of the River Stour and converted warehouses in the town of Sudbury.

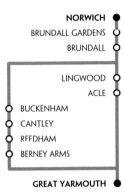

NORWICH ●
BRUNDALL GARDENS ○
BRUNDALL ○

LINGWOOD ○
ACLE ○
○ BUCKENHAM
○ CANTLEY
○ REEDHAM
○ BERNEY ARMS

GREAT YARMOUTH ●

This day trip along the 'Wherry Line' to the 'Golden Mile' at Great Yarmouth can be treated as a circular tour by travelling out via Acle or Berney Arms and returning on the alternative route. Trains leave Norwich's grand 19th-century Thorpe terminus and head eastwards through Thorpe Junction, Wensum Junction and Whitlingham Junction (for Sheringham). Never straying far from the meandering River Yare, we then call at Brundall Gardens and Brundall, where the line splits, with the single-track route via Acle continuing eastward and the double-track route to Reedham heading off in a southeasterly direction. Taking the first route, trains call at Lingwood and Acle, where there is a passing loop, before heading off across drained marshland to the south of the River Bure and rejoining the single-track line from Reedham on the approach to Great Yarmouth station.

Still following the River Yare, the alternative route leaves Brundall to call at Buckenham and Cantley – the giant sugar beet factory here was once rail served – before arriving at Reedham. Beyond the station the double-track line continues southeast over Reedham Swing Bridge to Lowestoft, while the now single-track route to Great Yarmouth strikes off northeast in a dead-straight line for 5 miles through Berney Arms station. Only accessible by train, boat or on foot, lonely Berney Arms is popular with birdwatchers and is served by two trains a day in each direction. This line joins the Acle route on the approach to Great Yarmouth station. South Quay is but a 5-minute walk from here while the 'Golden Mile', with its seafront entertainments and broad sandy beach, is a 20-minute walk away via the bridge over the River Bure.

DESTINATION HIGHLIGHTS
historic narrow streets; medieval town wall; Golden Mile seafront with beaches and amusement arcades; Britannia Pier; Wellington Pier; Grade II-listed Winter Gardens; Nelson Museum and Monument; Time and Tide Museum; 13th-century toll house and dungeons; historic market place; bird watching; river excursions on restored 1925 'Southern Belle' steamer

FREQUENCY OF TRAINS
1 per hour

20½ MILES
33 MINUTES (VIA ACLE)
38 MINUTES (VIA BERNEY ARMS)

The offshore wind farm at Scroby Sands, Great Yarmouth – on a windy day visitors to this popular seaside resort can witness renewable energy at work.

'Bittern Line' diesel trains for Sheringham leave Norwich's grand Victorian terminus and head east through Thorpe Junction and Wensum Junction before turning north away from the Yare Valley at Whitlingham Junction. Trains follow a straight and level route to the village of Salhouse before crossing the River Bure on the approach to Hoveton & Wroxham station. This is a popular spot for visitors to the Norfolk Broads and is also the interchange point for the 15-in-gauge Bure Valley Railway to Aylsham. Continuing northwards across flat farmland, trains call at Worstead before arriving at the market town of North Walsham – once an important centre of the Flemish weaving industry, the town also lies on the 56-mile Weavers' Way Long Distance Path, part of which follows the route of the long-closed Midland & Great Northern Joint Railway.

From North Walsham trains continue northwards, calling at Gunton – once used by royalty visiting Lord Suffield of Gunton Hall – then Roughton Road, before looping around the outskirts of Cromer and arriving at the town's small terminus station. Once named Cromer Beach, the original M&GNJR station building is now a pub. Trains reverse direction here and head west along the coast, calling at West Runton before terminating at Sheringham. The basic single-platform terminus is the smallest in Britain, while just across the road (and linked to the national rail network) is the original M&GNJR station, now used by the North Norfolk Railway at the start of its heritage line to Holt. The town and beach are but a short walk from the station.

- **NORWICH**
- SALHOUSE
- HOVETON & WROXHAM
- WORSTEAD
- NORTH WALSHAM
- GUNTON
- ROUGHTON ROAD
- CROMER
- WEST RUNTON
- **SHERINGHAM**

DESTINATION HIGHLIGHTS
steam-operated North Norfolk Railway to Holt; market (Saturdays); Mo Sheringham Museum; Sheringham Park (NT); Norfolk Coast Path to Beeston Bump; locally caught crab and lobster; Blue Flag beach (sandy at low tide)

FREQUENCY OF TRAINS
1 per hour

30½ MILES
1 HOUR

A short distance from the Norfolk coastline, preserved British Railways Class '9F' 2-10-0 No. 92203 hauls a train on the North Norfolk Railway between Sheringham and Holt.

NORWICH

WYMONDHAM

WYMONDHAM ABBEY

KIMBERLEY PARK

THUXTON

YAXHAM

DEREHAM

The first part of this day trip to the historic town of Dereham follows the same route as the trip to Ely as far as Wymondham (see page 82). Alighting at Wymondham station, travellers will need to make their way across town to the Mid-Norfolk Railway's Abbey station, about 1 mile away. The station is located close to the Grade I-listed 12th-century Wymondham Abbey which is also well worth a visit. This line once extended to Wells-next-the-Sea until closure beyond Dereham in 1964, while a line from Dereham to King's Lynn closed in 1968. Dereham lost its passenger service from Wymondham in 1969 although the line remained open for freight. The Mid-Norfolk Railway opened as a heritage line in 1997 and there are currently plans to extend it northwards from Dereham to County School and Fakenham.

Trains are normally diesel hauled although visiting steam locos also make an appearance. Intermediate stations are Yaxham, home to the 2-ft-gauge Yaxham Light Railway, Thuxton and Kimberley Park, and on the final approach to Dereham the town's Grade II*-listed maltings building is passed. The town centre is but a short walk from the station.

DESTINATION HIGHLIGHTS
Mid-Norfolk Railway; East Dereham Windmill; Norman church of St Nicholas; Georgian Market Place; Bishop Bonner's Cottage museum; St Withburga's Well

FREQUENCY OF TRAINS
Norwich to Wymondham:
1 per hour
Wymondham to Dereham:
3-5 per day (selected days, Apr-Oct)

21¾ MILES
11 + 35 MINUTES

RIGHT: *A Norwich to Ely train halts at Wymondham station. Passengers for Dereham have to alight here and make their own way across the town to the Mid-Norfolk Railway's station.*

OPPOSITE: *Famed for its curative properties, St Withburga's Well in Dereham forms part of a ruined tomb that contained the remains of Withburga, youngest daughter of Anna, King of the East Angles.*

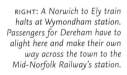

NORWICH	●
WYMONDHAM	○
SPOONER ROW	○
ATTLEBOROUGH	○
ECCLES ROAD	○
HARLING ROAD	○
THETFORD	○
BRANDON	○
LAKENHEATH	○
SHIPPEA HILL	○
ELY	●

This day trip from one historic cathedral city to another takes in miles and miles of glorious Norfolk countryside, two historic market towns and the gorse-covered sandy-heath region of Breckland from which this railway gets its name – the Breckland Line. Trains depart from Norwich's fine Victorian terminus, heading south to Trowse Junction where the Great Eastern main line continues on before taking a flyover across the westbound Ely line. First stop is at the historic market town of Wymondham (for the Mid-Norfolk Railway to Dereham), where the attractive station has received numerous awards over the past few years. Diminutive Spooner Row station is next, with one of the many automated level crossings that are a feature on this route, followed by Attleborough, which lost its unstaffed status in 2008 with the opening of a new ticket office. Little-used Eccles Road and Harling Road stations follow before trains arrive at the historic market town of Thetford (supposedly once the royal residence of Boudica), where the attractive 19th-century station was formerly the junction for branch lines to Swaffham and Bury St Edmunds.

Beyond Thetford the railway follows the winding Little Ouse River through Thetford Forest, the largest lowland pine forest in Britain, which was created after the First World War as a strategic reserve of timber. Leaving the forest behind, trains call at Brandon station, which has seen an enormous upsurge in passenger usage over the last ten years due to the introduction of a regular and frequent service. From here the railway heads westwards in a dead-straight line across the flat Fens, calling at Lakenheath before crossing into Cambridgeshire just before Shippea Hill station. Both stations have the dubious honour of being amongst the least-used in Britain! From here it is but a few minutes' travel before trains arrive at busy Ely station, junction for lines to King's Lynn, Peterborough, Cambridge and Ipswich. Built in 1845 on what was then a marshy swamp, the station is a 10-minute walk from the historic city centre.

DESTINATION HIGHLIGHTS
12th-century cathedral; Stained Glass Museum; Oliver Cromwell House Museum; Ely Museum; Bishop's Palace; motte and bailey castle; boat hire on Great Ouse River; riverside walks; fair (late June); four markets

FREQUENCY OF TRAINS
2 per hour

53½ MILES
55 MINUTES

The view up the Great Ouse River to Ely Cathedral, known as 'the ship of the Fens' because of its prominent shape which is visible from miles around.

Our day trip to the city of Leicester starts at Peterborough station, a major interchange point on the electrified East Coast Main Line. Trains to Leicester are diesel powered and head northwest, parallel to the main line as far as Helpston, from where they head east through Stamford Tunnel to arrive at the attractive town of Stamford. Recently refurbished, the Mock-Tudor style stone station building bears architectural similarities to nearby Burghley House. Beyond Stamford, the railway heads into Britain's smallest county of Rutland, joined at Manton Junction by the little-used line from Kettering. Now heading north through Manton Tunnel, the railway skirts the man-made expanse of Rutland Water before arriving at Oakham. Of interest to railway enthusiasts is the level crossing signal box here, which featured as the prototype for the famous Airfix kit of the 1960s.

From Oakham the railway follows a circuitous route northwards, winding through the Vale of Catmose and into the Leicestershire countryside before arriving at Melton Mowbray. The attractive 19th-century station, with its glass platform awnings, has recently been the subject of major refurbishment. Now heading east, trains to Leicester soon pass Melton Junction where the Old Dalby Test Track joins from the north. From here the line follows the Wreake Valley, sweeping southwards to join the Midland Main Line at the triangular Syston Junction before arriving at Leicester station, a late-Victorian building whose grand frontage has fortunately been preserved. The city centre with its diverse attractions is just a 10-minute walk away.

- **PETERBOROUGH**
- STAMFORD
- OAKHAM
- MELTON MOWBRAY
- SYSTON
- **LEICESTER**

DESTINATION HIGHLIGHTS

Jewry Wall and Roman Museum; Abbey ruins and Abbey Park; 14th-century Guildhall; War Memorial; National Space Centre; cathedral; castle; outdoor market (largest in Europe); Watermead Country Park; Botanic Gardens; Great Central Railway (Leicester North by bus in summer)

FREQUENCY OF TRAINS

1 per hour

52 MILES
55 MINUTES

A flashback to 1963 with BR Standard Class '4' 4-6-0 No. 75061 heading out of Stamford town station with a local train for Leicester.

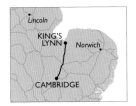

CAMBRIDGE ●
WATERBEACH ○
ELY ○
LITTLEPORT ○
DOWNHAM MARKET ○
WATLINGTON ○
KING'S LYNN ●

Known as the Fen Line, the electrified railway route from Cambridge to Kings Lynn heads northeast away from the university city and soon passes Coldham Lane Junction, where the single-track line to Newmarket and Ipswich branches off to the east. Waterbeach station, with its staggered platforms, is the first stop. Serving a large part of South Cambridgeshire this basic, unstaffed station has seen a huge upsurge in passenger usage over the last 10 years. From here the railway heads north, following the course of the River Cam in a dead-straight line across the flat landscape of the Fens to Ely, its magnificent cathedral a landmark for miles around. At Ely Dock Junction, just before Ely station is reached, the single line from Ipswich comes in from the southeast.

Travelling north from Ely, trains for Kings Lynn pass Ely North Junction (for Norwich) and Ely West Junction (for Peterborough), before arriving at the village of Littleport – this was the site of the infamous Littleport Riots by unemployed soldiers just home from the Battle of Waterloo in 1816. From here to the next station of Downham Market the line is reduced to single track and signalled for bi-directional working. Featuring tall and graceful chimneys, the Grade II-listed station building at Downham Market was opened by the Lynn & Ely Railway in 1846. The route northwards now reverts to double track to the next stop at Watlington – once named Magdalen Road, this station was the junction for the line to Wisbech and March until its closure in 1969. The railway becomes single track once more from here to Kings Lynn, where on the approach to the town the freight-only branch line from Middleton Towers joins from the east. Kings Lynn station is now but a shadow of its former self but it is hoped that one day the branch line northwards to the seaside resort of Hunstanton, once a favourite of John Betjeman, may reopen (optimistic author!). The station is well placed for the town centre and The Walks park.

DESTINATION HIGHLIGHTS
12th-century St Margaret's Church; Saturday market; Greyfriars Tower; 15th-century Guildhall and South Gate; 17th-century Custom House; Corn Exchange; 18th-century The Walks park and Red Mount Chapel; haunted Duke's Head Hotel; True's Yard Museum; Literature Festivals (March and September); Sandringham House (by No. 11 bus)

FREQUENCY OF TRAINS
1 per hour

41¼ MILES
45 MINUTES

RIGHT: *Sunset on the Great Ouse River at King's Lynn.*

OPPOSITE: *English naval officer and explorer Captain George Vancouver (1757-1798) was born in King's Lynn and is commemorated by this statue close to the Custom House in the town.*

LINCOLN CENTRAL	●
METHERINGHAM	○
RUSKINGTON	○
SLEAFORD	●
HECKINGTON	○
SWINESHEAD	○
HUBBERTS BRIDGE	○
BOSTON	○
THORPE CULVERT	○
WAINFLEET	○
HAVENHOUSE	○
SKEGNESS	●

Our day trip to the seaside resort made famous by the Great Northern Railway poster featuring the Jolly Fisherman exclaiming that 'Skegness is so Bracing' starts at the railway crossroads of Lincoln. There were once 7 routes converging on the city but over the years this has been reduced to 4. Diesel trains for Sleaford and Spalding depart from Central station in an easterly direction, immediately branching off the line to Barnetby and heading south along the former GN & GE Joint Railway double-track route, which opened in 1882. Most of the stations along this level route through sparsely populated Lincolnshire farmland have long closed, with the exception of Metheringham and Ruskington — both closed in 1961 but were reopened as basic unstaffed stations in 1975. Approaching the market town of Sleaford, trains loop westwards via North and West Junctions before arriving at the station — at the time of writing there were still 4 manually operated signalboxes guarding the 4 junctions. Passengers for Skegness change trains here.

From Sleaford, Skegness-bound trains head east along the initially single-track route to Heckington — here the 19th-century station building is now a museum, while a windmill and working signalbox complete this rural scene. The line reverts to double track through Swineshead station, followed by little-used Hubberts Bridge with its signal box and traditional level crossing gate. From here the track is single again to Boston. This once-busy station with its imposing GNR arched façade is now but a shadow of its former self, although a short branch to the docks is still retained for freight. From Boston trains head in a dead-straight line northeast across the Lincolnshire Fens to the site of Firsby South Junction — this route is single track as far as Sibsey and features no less than 14 level crossings. At Firsby the railway takes a sharp curve southeast through Thorpe Culvert, Wainfleet and Havenhouse stations (all unstaffed with the latter seeing little passenger usage) before arriving at Skegness's 4-platform terminus.

DESTINATION HIGHLIGHTS
extensive Blue Flag Central Beach; Butlins; Tower Esplanade and Compass Gardens; pier; carnival (August); Fairy Dell paddling pool; seal sanctuary; Church Farm Museum; Meccano exhibition; amusement park; stock car racing

FREQUENCY OF TRAINS
1 per hour (Mon-Sat)

62¼ MILES
1 HOUR 50 MINUTES

Viewed from the top of Boston Stump in 1979, a pair of BR Class 25s head a long holiday train across the River Witham on the approach to Boston station.

This day trip to the seaside resort of Cleethorpes begins at Lincoln Central station. Served by trains from Grimsby, Spalding/Peterborough, Newark/Nottingham and Gainsborough/Doncaster, this 5-platform station was opened in 1848 by the Great Northern Railway. Trains for Grimsby leave in an easterly direction before heading north across undulating Lincolnshire countryside to Market Rasen. This former Great Central Railway route to Barnetby features 15 level crossings and once served 10 intermediate stations – Market Rasen is now the only one open. From here trains continue northwards across sparsely populated farmland dotted with small villages to Wrawby Junction, where the lines from Gainsborough and Doncaster come in from the west. Barnetby station soon follows while the stretch of line eastwards from here, serving Immingham Dock with its oil refineries and coal/iron ore importing facilities, is one of the busiest railfreight routes in Britain. Next is Brocklesby Junction, where the freight-only line to Ulceby and Immingham Dock branches off to the north, followed by Habrough station where the line from Barton-on-Humber (see page 148) joins from the north. From here the railway route heads southeastwards across a flat landscape to Grimsby Town station, serving small stations at Stallingborough, Healing and Great Coates en route.

A change of trains is usually necessary at Grimsby Town, its mid-19th century station once the northern terminus of the East Lincolnshire line from Peterborough and Boston until its closure as a through route in 1970. The final part of this route is along the short single-track line serving Grimsby Docks (now a shadow of its once important self) and little-used New Clee stations before terminating close to the seafront at Cleethorpes. Once served by through trains to and from King's Cross, the station is seeing a slow resurgence in passenger traffic with trains to and from Manchester Airport and Sheffield, as well as the local Class 153 single-car service to and from Barton-on-Humber.

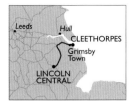

- **LINCOLN CENTRAL**
- MARKET RASEN
- BARNETBY
- HABROUGH
- STALLINGBOROUGH
- HEALING
- GREAT COATES
- **GRIMSBY TOWN**
- GRIMSBY DOCKS
- NEW CLEE
- **CLEETHORPES**

DESTINATION HIGHLIGHTS
Cleethorpes Coast Light Railway; Greenwich Meridian signpost; pier; boating lake; large leisure centre; Ross Castle; promenade; extensive sandy beach; Discovery Centre; Pleasure Island Family Theme Park

FREQUENCY OF TRAINS
1 every 2 hours (Mon-Sat) minimal service (Sun)

47¼ MILES
1 HOUR 25 MINUTES
(MON-SAT)
1 HOUR (SUN)

Far from the madding crowd and the sea on Cleethorpes' sandy beach.

CENTRAL ENGLAND

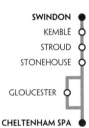

SWINDON ●
KEMBLE ○
STROUD ○
STONEHOUSE ○

GLOUCESTER ○

CHELTENHAM SPA ●

Our day trip to the Regency spa town of Cheltenham begins at Swindon's rather dreary modernized station, once a mecca for trainspotters in those good old days when ex-GWR 'Castles' and 'Kings' thundered through at the head of express trains to and from Paddington. Diesel trains for Cheltenham leave the station in a westerly direction and immediately branch off along the single-track route to Kemble, passing the remains of what were once the GWR's famous railway workshops before entering open country. Singled back in the late 1960s, this route was once used by the famous 'Cheltenham Flyer' and is now being rebuilt with double track. The attractive Cotswold stone station at Kemble, once the junction for Cirencester Town and Tetbury branches, is approached through a short tunnel. Beyond here the double-track route soon heads into Sapperton Short Tunnel, followed by the 1 mile 100 yds Sapperton Long Tunnel. Emerging from the tunnel, this scenic railway threads down the wooded Golden Valley in company with the Thames & Severn Canal to Stroud. After pausing at the station trains continue down the valley to Stonehouse, and at Standish Junction head north to join the former Midland Railway route from Bristol.

While some trains call at Gloucester Central station, where they have to then reverse direction, many trains along this route miss out the stop and bypass the city, which must be pretty galling for its 122,000 population. Cheltenham is soon reached, with trains calling at the former MR station of 'Lansdowne', located about a mile from the town. Sadly, the GWR's town-centre terminus station of St James was closed in 1966 so today's visitors will need to catch Stagecoach bus service D from here to complete their journey.

DESTINATION HIGHLIGHTS
Cheltenham Festival (March); The Times Literature Festival (October); Jazz Festival (late April/early May); Pittville Pump Room; Regency architecture and Montpellier shopping arcade; art gallery and museum; Holst Birthplace Museum; Gloucestershire-Warwickshire Railway (see page 91)

FREQUENCY OF TRAINS
1 per hour

43¼ MILES
1 HOUR 10 MINUTES

The famous 'Cheltenham Flyer' was the world's fastest train in the 1930s.

29P

CHELTENHAM FLYER

Opened by the GWR in 1908 as a north-south through route between Birmingham and the southwest, the line between Cheltenham and Stratford-upon-Avon finally closed to all traffic in 1976. Since then the section from Cheltenham Racecourse northwards to Toddington has been reopened by the Gloucestershire-Warwickshire Railway. Services now continue from Toddington to Laverton as part of the railway's extension to Broadway, and ultimately the national rail network at Honeybourne.

Fringed by Corsican pine trees, the attractive southern terminus at Cheltenham Racecourse was served by special trains for racegoers attending the Cheltenham Festival every March until the line closed in 1976. The station has a large free car park and is also served by buses from Cheltenham's Network Rail station. Passenger trains, normally steam hauled, first head north along the single-track line to the passing loop immediately south of Gotherington Halt, offering fine views to the east of Cleeve Hill and the Cotswold Escarpment en route. From Gotherington, where the privately owned station building, railway artefacts and a private siding are occasionally open to the public, the railway winds eastwards to enter the 693-yd-long Greet Tunnel before arriving at Winchcombe station where there is a passing loop. The original building here was demolished and was replaced by the former station at Monmouth Troy in 1986. A tea room and the nearby Winchcombe Railway Museum & Gardens (open most days April-Sept) with its fascinating collection of artefacts make this a pleasant place to break the journey.

From Winchcombe the railway once again heads north below the Cotswold Escarpment, passing the 13th-century Hailes Abbey (NT) en route before arriving at the railway's headquarters at Toddington station. From here, diesel railcars operate northwards on the Broadway extension as far as the Laverton loop (no public access).

CHELTENHAM RACECOURSE

GOTHERINGTON HALT

WINCHCOMBE

TODDINGTON

LAVERTON

DESTINATION HIGHLIGHTS
trip on steam-hauled heritage line; diesel railcar rides; Winchcombe Railway Museum; tea rooms; heritage trail; local walks; special events; narrow-gauge North Gloucestershire Railway

FREQUENCY OF TRAINS
5-6 per day (selected days, Feb-Oct)

10 MILES
40 MINUTES

Lovingly restored Winchcombe station, midway between Cheltenham and Toddington, on the Gloucestershire-Warwickshire Railway.

GLOUCESTER ●
CHELTENHAM SPA ○
ASHCHURCH FOR
TEWKESBURY ○
WORCESTER SHRUB HILL ●

Diesel trains for Worcester leave the former GWR Central station at Gloucester in an easterly direction, passing the site of Horton Road engine shed then crossing Horton Road at Tramway Crossing before taking the northern curve of the Gloucester triangle. After passing the site of the Midland railway engine shed, trains join the Bristol to Birmingham main line at Barnwood Junction. While Gloucester station has the second-longest platform in Britain, many north-south trains do not stop here as they have to reverse directions, instead taking the avoiding line. Once quadruple track, the main line to Cheltenham is now just double track, and at the halfway stage the site of the closed station at Churchdown is passed. The former MR station at Cheltenham Spa is soon reached – its restricted 2-platform layout is something of a bottleneck on this busy main line.

With views of the Cotswold escarpment to the east, trains head northwards away from Cheltenham to call at Ashchurch for Tewkesbury station. Once the junction for the lines to Great Malvern and Redditch, the original station was closed in 1971. The present rebuilt station was opened in 1997. Continuing northwards, trains pass the sites of long-closed stations at Bredon, Eckington, Defford and Wadborough while passengers are treated to views of the Malvern Hills to the west. At Abbotswood Junction, trains for Worcester branch off to the west, joining the single-track Cotswold Line from Oxford at Norton Junction. Worcester Shrub Hill station is soon reached – this Georgian-style building dates from 1865 and had an overall roof until it was removed in the 1930s. Train movements in Worcester are still controlled by GWR-style lower quadrant semaphore signals operated from three manual signal boxes. Shrub Hill station is about half a mile from the city centre although Foregate Street station, on the Hereford line, is much more conveniently located (see page 94).

DESTINATION HIGHLIGHTS
12th-century cathedral; Royal Worcester Porcelain Museum; canal walks along Worcester & Birmingham Canal; Tudor buildings; Art Gallery & Museum; Fort Royal Park; Three Choirs Festival (August, every three years)

FREQUENCY OF TRAINS
1 every 2 hours (Mon-Sat) minimal service (Sun pm)

25¾ MILES
40 MINUTES

Reflections in the River Severn at Worcester.

Our day trip to the pretty village of Parkend in the Forest of Dean starts at Gloucester station. Featuring the second-longest railway platform in the UK, the former GWR station here was once known as Central and was connected by a long footbridge to Eastgate station until the latter's closure in 1975. With views of the cathedral, diesel trains for Lydney head west out of the city to Over. Here, they cross the River Severn before heading southwest to follow the west bank of the widening river to Lydney, passing through the sites of closed stations at Oakle Street, Grange Court (once the junction for Hereford), Newnham (and Newnham Tunnel), Bullo Pill (once the junction for Cinderford) and Awre (once the junction for Coleford) en route. The line then hugs the river bank, passing the site of the Severn Bridge which collapsed following a collision by an oil tanker in 1960, before arriving at Lydney station where passengers for Parkend change trains.

Often steam hauled, Dean Forest Railway trains for Parkend depart from nearby Lydney Junction station and follow the route of a horse-drawn tramway which opened in 1813 to carry coal from forest collieries down to the Severn at Lydney. It was later rebuilt as a steam-operated line with northbound extensions to Lydbrook Junction, Coleford and Cinderford and eastbound across the Severn Bridge to Sharpness and Berkeley Road. Although passenger services northwards ended in 1929, the line remained open for freight until 1976. Trains climb north up the wooded valley, calling at St Mary's Halt and Lydney Town before arriving at the railway's headquarters at Norchard. Here, there is a low-level and high-level platform, museum and café. Trains for Parkend leave the high-level platform and continue to climb, calling at the recently reopened Whitecroft station, before reaching Parkend with village and walks close at hand.

● **GLOUCESTER**
● **LYDNEY**

▪ **LYDNEY JUNCTION**
○ ST MARY'S HALT
○ LYDNEY TOWN
○ NORCHARD
○ WHITECROFT
● **PARKEND**

DESTINATION HIGHLIGHTS
ride on Dean Forest Railway; Forest of Dean walks and railway path; village pubs; RSPB Nagshead Reserve

FREQUENCY OF TRAINS
Gloucester to Lydney:
1+ per hour (Mon-Sat)
1 every 2 hours (Sun)
Lydney to Parkend:
3 per day (Sun+BHs, Feb-Dec; Sat+Wed, Easter-Oct)

23¾ MILES
19 + 30 MINUTES

Restored GWR 0-6-0PT No. 9681 heads a train on the Dean Forest Railway in Gloucestershire.

WORCESTER
FOREGATE STREET ●

MALVERN LINK ○

GREAT MALVERN ○

COLWALL ○

LEDBURY ○

HEREFORD ●

Diesel trains for Hereford depart from Worcester Foregate Street station in a westerly direction. The station is located in the city centre and built on a viaduct, and is unusual as both tracks are bi-directional – one track is used by trains to and from Birmingham that avoid Shrub Hill station, while the other is used by trains to and from the latter. Both lines come together at Henwick, to the west, from where the line is normal double track as far as Malvern Wells. After leaving Foregate Street, trains soon cross the River Severn on a two-span girder bridge before heading off southwest across the Teme Valley on a series of bridges. Approaching the Malvern Hills, trains call at Malvern Link station followed by Great Malvern – built of local stone in 1862, the station with its decorated awning pillars has survived virtually unchanged.

A short distance south of Great Malvern the line becomes single track before it burrows under the Malvern Hills through the 1,589-yd-long single-bore Colwall New Tunnel – this was opened in 1926 to replace the original, parallel, tunnel which had a steep gradient, was difficult to operate and was in poor repair. Colwall's single-platform station is at the south end of the tunnel before the line heads west to enter the single-bore 1,323-yd-long Ledbury tunnel. On emerging, trains reach Ledbury station and passing loop, perched high above the attractive market town it serves and once the junction for the single-track line to Newent and Gloucester. Continuing on its westward route, the single-track railway soon crosses the Leadon Valley on a 30-arch, 330-yd-long viaduct, which was completed in 1860 using 5 million locally made bricks. After skirting Bunker's Hill and crossing the Frome and Lugg rivers, the railway joins the Welsh Marches main line at Shelwick Junction before making the final approach to Hereford station. Opened in 1853, the 4-platform station was named Hereford Barr's Court until 1893 and is located about a 15-minute walk from the attractions of the city centre.

DESTINATION HIGHLIGHTS
12th-century cathedral (inc the Mappa Mundi); Old House Jacobean Museum; Museum & Art Gallery; Cider Museum; Three Choirs Festival (August, every 3 years); International Cider Festival

FREQUENCY OF TRAINS
1+ per hour (Mon-Sat)
1 per hour (Sun)

28½ MILES
45 MINUTES

A Paddington to Hereford High Speed Train heads away from the Malvern Hills near Ledbury.

This day trip includes a journey along what is marketed as the Cotswold Line, which after decades of neglect is finally seeing a major upgrade with much its single-track rural route being replaced with double track. Diesel trains for Worcester depart northwards from Oxford station. At Oxford North Junction the line to Bicester branches off to the northeast and at Wolvercot Junction the Banbury main line branches off to follow a northwesterly route through attractive Cotswold countryside, villages and towns. The line from Wolvercot to Charlbury East is still single track with intermediate stations at Hanborough, Combe and Finstock. From Charlbury East the line is now double track to Evesham with intermediate stations at Charlbury, Ascott-under-Wychwood, Shipton, Kingham (once the junction for lines to Cheltenham and Chipping Norton), Moreton-in-Marsh and Honeybourne (once a railway crossroads serving the Stratford-upon-Avon to Cheltenham line). Between Moreton-in-Marsh and Honeybourne the line runs through Campden Tunnel where the railway's engineer, Isambard Kingdom Brunel, was forced to adopt heavy-handed tactics with a disgruntled contractor in 1852.

Closed in 1969, reopened in 1981 and the recent subject of a major upgrade, Honeybourne station is the ultimate goal for the Gloucestershire-Warwickshire Railway (see page 91) on its northern extension from Toddington. It is still the junction for the short line northwards to the former MOD depot at Long Marston. From Evesham station the line becomes single again, crossing the River Avon and serving Pershore before joining the Cheltenham to Worcester line at Norton Junction. A stop at Worcester Shrub Hill soon follows, after which trains for Foregate Street head west on the single-line section across the Worcester & Birmingham Canal. Foregate Street station is located in the very heart of the city, providing easy access to its rich heritage attractions.

- **OXFORD**
- HANBOROUGH
- COMBE
- FINSTOCK
- CHARLBURY
- ASCOTT-UNDER-WYCHWOOD
- SHIPTON
- KINGHAM
- MORETON-IN-MARSH
- HONEYBOURNE
- EVESHAM
- PERSHORE
- WORCESTER SHRUB HILL
- **WORCESTER FOREGATE STREET**

DESTINATION HIGHLIGHTS
12th-century cathedral; Royal Worcester Porcelain Museum; canal walks along Worcester & Birmingham Canal; Tudor buildings; Art Gallery & Museum; Fort Royal Park; Three Choirs Festival (August, every 3 years)

FREQUENCY OF TRAINS
1 per hour

57½ MILES
1 HOUR 25 MINUTES

A Class 165 diesel multiple unit departs from Moreton-in-Marsh station with a train for Oxford.

SHREWSBURY
• *Birmingham*

HEREFORD
• *Gloucester*

SHREWSBURY ●
CHURCH STRETTON ○
CRAVEN ARMS ○
LUDLOW ○
LEOMINSTER ○
HEREFORD ●

This day trip to Hereford takes in a journey along one of England's most scenic railway routes, the Welsh Marches Line. Diesel trains depart from Shrewsbury's grand Tudor-style station, located on the west bank of the River Severn. From here they head south along the former GWR&LNWR Joint Line through Severn Bridge Junction, site of the world's largest surviving manual signal box, English Bridge Junction and Sutton Bridge Junction, where the Cambrian Line heads off westwards into Wales. The railway continues south through a narrow gap in the Shropshire Hills, with the slopes of Long Mynd with its 1,693-ft summit soon coming into view to the west, to arrive at the former spa town of Church Stretton, overlooked from the east by the Iron-Age hill fort of Caer Caradoc. Further south the limestone escarpment of Wenlock Edge dominates the skyline as the railway winds its way through the hills to Craven Arms, junction for the Heart of Wales Line to Llanelli (see page 122).

From here, the line heads southeast, soon passing the 13th-century fortified manor house of Stokesay Castle, before arriving at Ludlow, one of the most attractive market towns in the country. After passing through the short Ludlow Tunnel the railway resumes its southerly route, calling at Leominster before following the valley of the River Lugg to the city of Hereford. The line takes a short cut away from the meandering river by burrowing through the hills in the twin Dinmore Tunnels en route. On the final approach to Hereford the single-track line from Worcester joins from the east at Shelwick Junction. Hereford station is located about a 15-minute walk from the city centre.

DESTINATION HIGHLIGHTS
12th-century cathedral (inc the Mappa Mundi); Old House Jacobean Museum; Museum & Art Gallery; Cider Museum; 3 Choirs Festival (August, every three years); International Cider Festival

FREQUENCY OF TRAINS
1+ per hour (Mon-Sat)
1 per hour (Sun: late am, pm)

51 MILES
55 MINUTES

RIGHT: *A Hereford to Shrewsbury train passes historic Stokesay Castle between Ludlow and Craven Arms.*

OPPOSITE: *The 17th-century timber-framed Old House in Hereford is now a museum.*

BIRMINGHAM SNOW HILL ●
JEWELLERY QUARTER ○
THE HAWTHORNS ○
SMETHWICK GALTON BRIDGE ○
LANGLEY GREEN ○
ROWLEY REGIS ○
OLD HILL ○
CRADLEY HEATH ○
LYE ○
STOURBRIDGE JUNCTION ○
HAGLEY ○
BLAKEDOWN ○
KIDDERMINSTER ●
KIDDERMINSTER TOWN ●
BEWDLEY ○
NORTHWOOD HALT ○
ARLEY ○
HIGHLEY ○
COUNTRY PARK HALT ○
HAMPTON LOADE ○
BRIDGNORTH ●

DESTINATION HIGHLIGHTS
Telford's 18th-century St Mary's
Church; Low Town and High
Town; The Cartway; funicular
railway; Castle Gardens;
Lavington Gardens Caves;
Northgate Museum

FREQUENCY OF TRAINS
B'ham to Kidderminster: 4 per hour
Kidderminster to Bridgnorth:
4-8 per day (Sat-Sun,
Feb-Nov; daily May-Sept)

35 MILES
40 + 70 MINUTES

*Restored GWR 'Manor' Class
'Erlestoke Manor' at
Kidderminster Town station with
a train for Bridgnorth.*

Originally opened in 1852 and greatly expanded in the early 20th century, Snow Hill was the GWR's main railway station in the centre of Birmingham. Amidst a public outcry the adjacent grand GWR hotel was demolished in 1969 and the station itself in 1977. The site was used as a car park until sense prevailed and it was rebuilt and reopened for services to Leamington and Stratford-upon-Avon in 1987 and to Worcester via Kidderminster in 1995. Our day trip to one of Britain's most scenic heritage railways follows this route westwards through the sprawling city suburbs, with diesel trains calling at Jewellery Quarter, The Hawthorns (home to West Bromwich Albion FC), Smethwick Galton Bridge, Langley Green and Rowley Regis, then through Old Hill Tunnel to Old Hill station, once the junction for the Bumble Hole Line to Dudley. Cradley Heath and Lye stations follow before trains arrive at Stourbridge Junction, where the diminutive Parry People Movers' Class 139 flywheel railcar shuttles to and fro along the short branch to Stourbridge Town.

From Stourbridge Junction trains head southwest, calling at Hagley and Blakedown before arriving at Kidderminster. Here, passengers need to change trains for the journey along the Severn Valley to Bridgnorth – the Severn Valley Railway's Victorian-style station, Kidderminster Town, is adjacent to the national rail network station. Trains, normally steam hauled, head west through Foley Park Tunnel before arriving at Bewdley's restored 3-platform GWR station. From here, the railway follows the picturesque Severn Valley northwards, crossing the river on the graceful Victoria Bridge to reach the village of Arley. All stations along this line have been superbly restored to their former GWR glory and Highley, the next station and location of the Engine House visitor centre, is no exception. Continuing northwards along the lush valley, trains serve Hampton Loade station before terminating at Bridgnorth, home to fine heritage architecture and the steepest inland funicular railway in Britain.

Our day trip to Stratford-upon-Avon, world-famous as the birthplace of William Shakespeare, begins at Birmingham's modern Snow Hill station (see page 98) with diesel trains heading through Snow Hill Tunnel to arrive at Moor Street station. The second-busiest station in Birmingham after New Street, Moor Street has recently been restored to its former GWR glory. Heading southwest through Bordesley and Small Heath, trains branch off the main line to Leamington Spa at Tyseley (home to the Birmingham Railway Museum) and head south through Birmingham's sprawling southern suburbs. Open countryside is eventually reached at Whitlock's End station, which is followed by Wythall, Earlwood and The Lakes. Serving nearby Earlswood Lakes, a popular destination for day trippers, The Lakes station has very short platforms and is a request stop. From here, trains continue southwards under the busy M42 to Wood End and Danzey stations, also both request stops.

Deep in the Warwickshire countryside, Henley-in-Arden follows – the station here was the end of the branch line from Tyseley until 1908 when the GWR extended it as part of the North Warwickshire Line to Stratford-upon-Avon, Honeybourne and Cheltenham. Rural Wootton Wawen station, another request stop, follows before trains join the single-track line from Hatton at Bearley Junction. The next station on our trip serves the village of Wilmcote, famous for Mary Arden's House, the home of Shakespeare's mother. From here it is but a short train ride to the newly opened Stratford Parkway station before trains terminate at Stratford-upon-Avon station. Once a through station served by trains on the GWR's main line between Birmingham and Cheltenham, the current terminus has seen passenger numbers almost double over the last 10 years – from here it is a 15-minute walk to the historic town centre. The former railway route continues southwards as a footpath and cycleway as far as Long Marston.

- **BIRMINGHAM SNOW HILL**
- BIRMINGHAM MOOR STREET
- BORDESLEY
- SMALL HEATH
- TYSELEY
- SPRING ROAD
- HALL GREEN
- YARDLEY WOOD
- SHIRLEY
- WHITLOCKS END
- WYTHALL
- EARLSWOOD
- THE LAKES
- WOOD END
- DANZEY
- HENLEY-IN-ARDEN
- WOOTTON WAWEN
- WILMCOTE
- STRATFORD-UPON-AVON PARKWAY
- **STRATFORD-UPON-AVON**

DESTINATION HIGHLIGHTS
Royal Shakespeare Theatre; Hall's Croft; Nash's House; New Place; Holy Trinity Church; historic town centre; boat hire on River Avon; Stratford-upon-Avon Canal; railway walk to Milcote and Long Marston

FREQUENCY OF TRAINS
1+ per hour

25 MILES
55 MINUTES

The River Avon and the Royal Shakespeare Theatre in Stratford-upon-Avon, the birthplace of William Shakespeare.

BIRMINGHAM
NEW STREET

GLOUCESTER
London
Swindon

BIRMINGHAM
NEW STREET ●
FIVE WAYS ○
UNIVERSITY ○
SELLY OAK ○
BOURNVILLE ○
KINGS NORTON ○
NORTHFIELD ○
LONGBRIDGE ○
BARNT GREEN ○
BROMSGROVE ○
ASHCHURCH
FOR TEWKESBURY ○
CHELTENHAM SPA ○
GLOUCESTER ●

Diesel trains for Gloucester depart in a southwesterly direction from Birmingham's gloomy subterranean New Street station, which at long last is at the centre of a major inner city redevelopment project. Trains first pass through a series of tunnels – Suffolk Street, Holiday Street, Canal Street, Granville Street and Bath Row – before emerging at Five Ways station alongside the Worcester & Birmingham Canal. Railway keeps company with canal through University, Selly Oak and Bourneville stations. At Kings Norton, the freight-only Camp Hill Line joins from the northeast and, following suburban stations at Northfield and Longbridge, at Barnt Green the single-track to Redditch strikes off in a southeasterly direction – this line extended southwards through Evesham to Ashchurch until closure in 1963.

After tunnelling under the M42, the railway climbs to the summit of the line at Blackwall before descending the 1-in-37 Lickey Incline – at 2 miles long, this is the steepest main-line railway incline in the UK and in steam days northbound trains required rear-end banking assistance from locomotives based at Bromsgrove. Bromsgrove station is reached at the bottom of the incline and just south of here, at Stoke Works Junction, the single line to Droitwich and Worcester strikes off in a southwesterly direction. The Worcester & Birmingham Canal rejoins the railway at Stoke Works, keeping company southwards for 6 miles before heading west to Worcester. After passing under the Cotswold Line and meeting the line from Worcester at Abbotswood Junction, trains head south offering passengers fine views of the Malvern Hills to the west before calling at Ashchurch (formerly junction for Tewkesbury and Redditch) and Cheltenham Spa. With the Cotswold escarpment to the east, the final part of our journey takes trains through the site of Churchdown station (one of the author's favourite trainspotting haunts in the early 1960s!) to Barnwood Junction, where the Gloucester avoiding line branches off, before terminating at Gloucester station.

DESTINATION HIGHLIGHTS
Gloucester Cathedral (Harry Potter film location); Historic Gloucester Docks; National Waterways Museum; Soldiers of Gloucestershire Museum; Gloucester City Museum & Art Gallery; Tailor of Gloucester House; 15th-century New Inn; Three Choirs Festival (every three years)

FREQUENCY OF TRAINS
1 per hour

**51¾ MILES
50 MINUTES**

Gloucester Cathedral is one of the locations used in filming the 'Harry Potter' films.

Our day trip to the European City of Culture 2008 and home of The Beatles starts at Birmingham's New Street station. From here, electric trains head west through New Street North tunnel before threading through the Black Country towns of Smethwick, Dudley and Tipton to reach Wolverhampton. The town once had 2 stations – High Level (which is now just Wolverhampton) and Low Level, which was served by trains on the former GWR line to Birmingham Snow Hill and Paddington until its closure in 1972. Fortunately, the Grade II-listed station building dating from 1855 has survived the demolition squad.

Trains for Liverpool depart northwards from Wolverhampton through Wolverhampton North and Bushbury junctions then out into the Staffordshire countryside through Penkridge. Listed for closure in 1962, the station here was saved by the local landowner, Baron Hatherton, who threatened to stop the railway crossing his land if it was closed. Soon, trains are gliding into Stafford where the West Coast Main Line joins from the east. From Stafford's Brutalist 1962-built station, trains head northeast running non-stop to Crewe, passing through the disused station at Norton Bridge (closed since 2004) where the electrified line to Stone and Stoke-on-Trent strikes off to the northeast.

After the obligatory stop at Crewe, trains head northwest across the Cheshire Plains through Winsford, Hartford and Acton Bridge before branching off the WCML at Weaver Junction to reach Runcorn. North of here, trains cross the Manchester Ship Canal and the River Mersey on the impressive Runcorn Railway Bridge (completed in 1868) before heading west to Speke Junction, then northwest through Mossley Hill to Edge Hill East Junction where the main line from Manchester joins from the east. The final 1½ miles down to Liverpool Lime Street station through deep rock cuttings and tunnels is along the route of the Liverpool & Manchester Railway which opened in 1830.

- **BIRMINGHAM NEW STREET**
- SMETHWICK ROLFE STREET
- SANDWELL & DUDLEY
- DUDLEY PORT
- TIPTON
- COSELEY
- WOLVERHAMPTON
- PENKRIDGE
- STAFFORD
- CREWE
- WINSFORD
- HARTFORD
- ACTON BRIDGE
- RUNCORN
- LIVERPOOL SOUTH PARKWAY
- WEST ALLERTON
- MOSSLEY HILL
- EDGE HILL
- **LIVERPOOL LIME STREET**

DESTINATION HIGHLIGHTS
Waterfront, Pier Head and Albert Docks; Museum of Liverpool; Merseyside Maritime Museum; International Slavery Museum; Tate Liverpool; The Beatles Story; Walker Art Gallery; World Museum; 20th-century Anglican Cathedral; 1960s Roman Catholic Cathedral; homes of John Lennon and Paul McCartney (NT)

FREQUENCY OF TRAINS
2 per hour (Mon-Sat)
1 per hour (Sun)

88¼ MILES
1 HOUR 45 MINUTES

A dockside view of restored warehouses and the Grade I-listed Royal Liver Building in Liverpool.

. Crewe

LEICESTER

BIRMINGHAM
NEW STREET

Milton .
Keynes

BIRMINGHAM
NEW STREET ●

WATER ORTON ○

COLESHILL PARKWAY ○

NUNEATON ○

HINCKLEY ○

NARBOROUGH ○

SOUTH WIGSTON ○

LEICESTER ●

Our day trip to the historic city of Leicester begins at Birmingham's New Street station – for years a dark and depressing place, it is now the subject of a major refurbishment. Diesel trains head northeast from the station and after burrowing through New Street Tunnels pass the boarded-up Curzon Street station. Designed by Philip Hardwick, this Grade I-listed building was opened by the London & Birmingham Railway in 1839 and will be the centrepiece of the new HS2 terminal in the city. After negotiating Proof House Junction and the flyunder at Grand Junction, trains reach the Midland main line at Landor Street Junction. Still heading northeast through Birmingham's suburbs the site of Saltley engine shed is passed, followed by Washwood Heath freight yard, Bromford Bridge oil terminal and the rail-connected Jaguar plant at Castle Bromwich. Castle Bromwich Junction and Water Orton West Junction both follow – here a triangular layout allows access to the freight-only line to Walsall, which heads off in a northwesterly direction. At Water Orton East Junction the Midland main line sweeps off northwards, while Leicester-bound trains head eastwards under the busy M42 then past Hams Hall Euroterminal and into open countryside.

After negotiating Arley Tunnel, trains cross over the West Coast Main Line to enter Nuneaton's 7-platform station. From here, Leicester-bound trains continue eastwards to Hinckley, Narborough and South Wigston before joining the Midland main line from St Pancras at Wigston North Junction. Now heading northwards, trains pass Knighton South Junction for the freight-only line to Coalville, and head through Knighton Tunnel before arriving at Leicester station. Here, the grand frontage of this late Victorian building has fortunately been preserved and the city centre is just a 10-minute walk away.

DESTINATION HIGHLIGHTS
Jewry Wall and Roman Museum; Abbey ruins and Abbey Park; 14th-century Guildhall; War Memorial; National Space Centre; cathedral; castle; outdoor market (largest in Europe); Watermead Country Park; Botanic Gardens; Great Central Railway (Leicester North by bus in summer); Grand Union Canal

FREQUENCY OF TRAINS
2 per hour

39½ MILES
55 MINUTES

Restored 'West Country' Class 4-6-2 No. 34007 'Wadebridge' speeds along the Great Central Railway in Leicestershire.

Our day trip to the historic city of Lichfield begins at Birmingham's New Street station – currently the subject of a major refurbishment. Electric trains head northeast from the station and after burrowing through New Street Tunnels pass the boarded-up Curzon Street station – designed by Philip Hardwick, this Grade I- listed building was opened by the London & Birmingham Railway in 1839 and will be the centrepiece of the city's new HS2 terminal. At Proof House Junction, Cross-City Line trains for Lichfield head north through Duddeston to Aston station, which is also served by trains on the Birmingham to Walsall line. On leaving Aston, trains for Lichfield call at Gravelly Hill, Erdington, Chester Road and Wylde Green before arriving at Sutton Coldfield.

North of Sutton Coldfield station, the Cross-City Line passes through a short tunnel and then under the freight-only line from Castle Bromwich to Walsall. Now into open countryside, trains continue northwards calling at Four Oaks, Butlers Lane, Blake Street and Shenstone before crossing the busy M6 and Watling Street. Our destination of Lichfield City station is soon reached and it is but a short walk from here to the city centre, with its beautifully preserved Tudor architecture. Trains continue to Lichfield Trent Valley station on the West Coast Main Line, beyond which the line through Alrewas to Wichnor Junction and Burton-upon-Trent was closed to passengers in 1965 but has been retained for freight and as a diversionary route.

- **BIRMINGHAM NEW STREET**
- DUDDESTON
- ASTON
- GRAVELLY HILL
- ERDINGTON
- CHESTER ROAD
- WYLDE GREEN
- SUTTON COLDFIELD
- FOUR OAKS
- BUTLERS LANE
- BLAKE STREET
- SHENSTONE
- **LICHFIELD CITY**

DESTINATION HIGHLIGHTS
unspoilt city centre with fine Tudor and Georgian architecture; 12th/13th-century cathedral and Close; ruined Franciscan Friary; Samuel Johnson Birthplace Museum; Erasmus Darwin House Museum; Heritage Centre in Market Square; Lichfield Festival; Beacon Park; restored Lichfield Canal; Staffordshire Regiment Museum (2½ miles); National Memorial Arboretum (4 miles)

FREQUENCY OF TRAINS
4 per hour (Mon-Sat)
2 per hour (Sun)

16¼ MILES
35 MINUTES

The 3-spired medieval cathedral in Lichfield is reflected in the tranquil waters of Minster Pool.

**BIRMINGHAM
NEW STREET** ●

SMETHWICK
ROLFE STREET ○

SANDWELL & DUDLEY ○

DUDLEY PORT ○

TIPTON ○

COSELEY ○

WOLVERHAMPTON ○

BILBROOK ○

CODSALL ○

ALBRIGHTON ○

COSFORD ○

SHIFNAL ○

TELFORD CENTRAL ○

OAKENGATES ○

WELLINGTON ○

SHREWSBURY ●

Diesel trains for Shrewsbury depart from the gloom of Birmingham's New Street station and head west through New Street North Tunnel before emerging in the city's sprawling suburbs. One of the powerhouses of the Industrial Revolution, this area is still known as the Black Country although much of the industry has long disappeared. Trains serve Smethwick, Dudley and Tipton (for the Black Country Museum) before arriving at Wolverhampton station. From here, trains travel north to Wolverhampton North Junction where they take the line past the sprawling Oxley Traincare Depot before reaching open countryside at Codshall. Now heading west again, the railway continues to Cosford (for the RAF Museum), Shifnal, Madeley Junction (for the freight-only line to Ironbridge Power Station), Telford Central, Oakengates Tunnel, Oakengates and Wellington. Now a suburb of the sprawling Telford New Town, Wellington was once a busy junction served by trains from Much Wenlock (closed 1962), Nantwich (closed 1963) and Stafford (closed 1964).

From Wellington, trains continue westwards into open country, paralleling the A5 dual carriageway for the last few miles to the outskirts of Shrewsbury. On the final approach to the station, trains take the northern curve of the triangular junction in which sits Severn Bridge Junction Signalbox – built in 1903 and housing a 180-lever frame, it is now the largest mechanical signal box in the world. A major railway crossroads, Shrewsbury station is itself worthy of an inspection. The Grade II-listed building was built in a Mock Tudor style and opened in 1848, with its platforms extended over the River Severn at the beginning of the 20th century. One unusual aspect is the screened Platform 8, which now sees no use but was once used for transporting prisoners to the adjacent prison. It is but a short walk from the station to the town centre, with its impressive Tudor and Georgian architecture and many historic attractions.

DESTINATION HIGHLIGHTS
600 Tudor and Georgian buildings; Shrewsbury Castle and Shropshire Regimental Museum; Lord Hill's Column; Shrewsbury Abbey; Flower Show; Parade Shopping Centre; The Quarry riverside park; Museum & Art Gallery; Coleham Pumping Station Museum; riverside walks; Folk Festival (late August)

FREQUENCY OF TRAINS
2 per hour (Mon-Sat)
1 per hour (Sun)

42 MILES
55-70 MINUTES

A train heads out of Shrewsbury station towards Severn Bridge Junction signalbox.

This day trip to Coventry starts at Oxford station from where diesel trains head north, keeping close company with the River Cherwell and the Oxford Canal through Tackley and Heyford. The canal opened in 1790 and was initially highly profitable but the coming of the railway in 1850 led to a decline in traffic, which was only arrested by the growing popularity of pleasure boating in the 1960s. At Aynho Junction the main line from Princes Risborough and Marylebone joins from the southeast and soon our train is slowing for the stop at King's Sutton, which now serves the town of Brackley, 6 miles to the east – the town lost its own rail link when the former Great Central route closed in 1966. King's Sutton was also once the junction for the GWR route to Kingham and Cheltenham until its complete closure in 1964.

From King's Sutton, trains continue northwards to Banbury station, which unusually features new GWR-style lower quadrant semaphore signals installed as recently as 2010. The station was once the junction for the former Great Central route to Woodford Halse, used by inter-regional passenger and freight trains until closure in 1966. Leaving Banbury in a northwesterly direction, trains speed through Fenny Compton, finally parting company with the Oxford Canal. This is also the junction for the freight-only branch to the MOD depot at Kineton, which uses part of the long-closed Stratford-upon-Avon & Midland Junction Railway route to reach its destination. The next stop is at Leamington Spa before Coventry-bound trains take the former LNWR route, now mainly single track, northwards through the closed station at Kenilworth where there is a passing loop. Our destination of Coventry is soon reached. The modern station, which has seen passenger numbers double over the last 10 years, features the crest and nameplate of LMS 'Coronation' Class 4-6-2 No. 46240 'City of Coventry' displayed on a wall. A good bus service links the station with the town centre.

- **OXFORD**
- TACKLEY
- HEYFORD
- KING'S SUTTON
- BANBURY
- LEAMINGTON SPA
- **COVENTRY**

DESTINATION HIGHLIGHTS
ruins of 14th-century St Michael's Cathedral; 1962 Coventry Cathedral; Herbert Art Gallery & Museum; Coventry Transport Museum; Midland Air Museum; walks along Coventry Canal; Time Zone Clock in Millennium Square

FREQUENCY OF TRAINS
1 per hour

52½ MILES
45 MINUTES

The spire of the war-damaged Coventry Cathedral towers over its 1960s replacement.

BEDFORD ST JOHNS ●
KEMPSTON HARDWICK ○
STEWARTBY ○
MILLBROOK ○
LIDLINGTON ○
RIDGMONT ○
ASPLEY GUISE ○
WOBURN SANDS ○
BOW BRICKHILL ○
FENNY STRATFORD ○
BLETCHLEY ●
MILTON KEYNES CENTRAL ●

Our short journey to discover the modern delights of Milton Keynes begins at Bedford's 1970s station, which is also served by trains on the Midland main line between St Pancras and Nottingham. Marston Vale Line trains for Bletchley first make the short journey southwards from here to Bedford St Johns station. This single-platform station with one rudimentary bus-type shelter replaced the original station that had been opened in 1846 by the Bedford Railway. It was once served by trains on the Varsity Line between Oxford and Cambridge but the closure of this as a cross-country route at the end of 1967 left just the Bedford to Bletchley section open for passenger traffic. The original station remained a terminus until 1984 when it was closed, replaced by the present basic structure and physically connected to Bedford Midland station using the trackbed of the closed MR line to Hitchin.

From Bedford, diesel trains head southwest along the double-track line passing Kempston Hardwick station (a request stop) to reach Stewartby, where the massive London Brick Company's works remained rail-served until closure in 1974. The empty clay pits are now used for waste landfill from London and 3 of the 4 tall chimneys have listed status. The next stop is Millbrook, once the site of another brickworks, where the half-timbered Gothic Revival station building is a private residence – this was the first of 4 stations built in this style as a sop to the Duke of Bedford when the line was built across his Woburn Estate. Millbrook is followed by Lidlington station (where the platforms are staggered either side of a level crossing), Ridgmont (for Woburn Safari Park), Aspley Guise, Woburn Sands (Gothic-Revival station building), Bow Brickhill (staggered platforms) and Fenny Stratford (Gothic-Revival station building). Bletchley station is next, where passengers change trains to travel north along the West Coast Main Line to the ultra-modern glass-fronted Milton Keynes Central station. A regular bus service links the station with the main shopping centre.

DESTINATION HIGHLIGHTS
modern 'covered high street' shopping centre; 125-mile network of footpaths and cycle tracks; art gallery; Bletchley Park Museum; Milton Keynes Museum; Milton Keynes Arts Centre; Westbury Arts Centre; National Bowl; public sculpture; walks along Grand Union Canal

FREQUENCY OF TRAINS
1 per hour (Mon-Sat)

**19 MILES
1 HOUR**

The old and new alongside the Grand Union Canal in the Wolverton district of Milton Keynes.

Our day trip to the Derbyshire Dales starts at Nottingham's Edwardian Baroque Revival station, which has recently been the subject of a major multi-million pound remodelling project. Trains for Matlock head southwest through Beeston and Attenborough before passing the junction for Toton Yard and taking the northbound curve of the triangular Trent Junction to Long Eaton and Spondon (for the rail-connected British Celanese works) to arrive at Derby. Although home to the Bombardier factory, Etches Park Maintenance Depot and the Railway Technical Centre, Derby as a railway town is now a shadow of its former self when it was one of Britain's most important railway works.

Trains for Matlock leave Derby in a northerly direction following the picturesque Derwent Valley to Duffield then plunging through the ½-mile Milford Tunnel to reach the town of Belper – north of here the railway crosses the Derwent 4 times before reaching Ambergate, the junction for Matlock. Once part of the Midland Railway route from London to Manchester, this scenic line through the Peak District was closed as a through route in 1968, leaving Matlock at the end of a single-track branch line. From Ambergate, the railway continues up the narrowing Derwent Valley keeping close company with the A6 and the Cromford Canal, calling at Whatstandwell (for Crich Tramway Museum), Cromford and Matlock Bath stations via a series of 4 tunnels and 4 river crossings. Once dubbed 'Little Switzerland' by the company, this line's stations still retain many original Midland Railway features such as latticework footbridges, ornate buildings and decorated cast-iron canopy supports. At Matlock station passengers for Rowsley change trains for the 5-mile trip along Peak Rail, calling en route at the restored Darley Dale station before arriving at Rowsley South. The village is 1 mile away to the north although the railway hopes to eventually extend its line beyond there as far as Bakewell.

- ● **NOTTINGHAM**
- ○ BEESTON
- ○ ATTENBOROUGH
- ○ LONG EATON
- ○ SPONDON
- ○ DERBY
- ○ DUFFIELD
- ○ BELPER
- ○ AMBERGATE
- ○ WHATSTANDWELL
- ○ CROMFORD
- ○ MATLOCK BATH
- ● **MATLOCK**
- ○ DARLEY DALE
- ● **ROWSLEY SOUTH**

DESTINATION HIGHLIGHTS
Matlock: Victorian town centre; Hall Leys Park and boating lake. *Rowsley South*: Peak Rail, Derbyshire Dales Narrow Gauge Railway

FREQUENCY OF TRAINS
Nottingham to Matlock:
1 per hour (Mon-Sat)
1 every 2 hours (Sun)
Matlock to Rowsley: 5 per day (Sat-Sun, Apr-Nov; selected weekdays June-Sept)

38 MILES
66 + 22 MINUTES

A Matlock to Derby train heads along the wooded Derwent Valley near Duffield.

CREWE ●
NANTWICH ○
WRENBURY ○
WHITCHURCH ○
PREES ○
WEM ○
YORTON ○
SHREWSBURY ●

One of the busiest railway junctions in Britain, Crewe station is still served by six railway routes radiating out to all points of the compass. Diesel trains for Shrewsbury initially head south from the station and soon branch off the West Coast Main Line at Crewe South Junction. At Gresty Lane Junction the freight-only line from the extensive Basford Hall Freight Yard swings in from the south and, now heading southwest, our train soon reaches open countryside before calling at Nantwich. The town is not only the junction for the Shropshire Union and Llangollen canals but was also the junction for the former GWR line to Market Drayton and Wellington until its closure in 1963. Our journey to Shrewsbury takes us along the former LNWR line through Wrenbury (request stop) before reaching the summit of the line on the Cheshire/Shropshire border just north of Whitchurch station.

Whitchurch was an important junction for the Cambrian Railways route to Oswestry and Welshpool until the line's closure in 1965. It was also served by trains on the former LNWR line from Tattenhall, which closed to passengers in 1957 and to freight in 1963. From Whitchurch, trains head southwards through open countryside to Prees (request stop), Wem and Yorton (request stop) stations before arriving at Shrewsbury's ornate mock-Tudor station. The historic town centre is but a short walk from here.

DESTINATION HIGHLIGHTS
medieval street plan with over 600 Tudor and Georgian buildings; Shrewsbury Castle and Shropshire Regimental Museum; Lord Hill's Column; Shrewsbury Abbey; Flower Show; Parade Shopping Centre; The Quarry riverside park; Museum & Art Gallery; Coleham Pumping Station Museum; riverside walks; Folk Festival (late August)

FREQUENCY OF TRAINS
1+ per hour (Mon-Sat)
1 per hour (Sun)

32½ MILES
35-45 MINUTES

A flashback to 1988, with Class 37/4 diesel No. 37428 leaving Shrewsbury with a Manchester to Cardiff express.

The ornate Victorian station of Stoke-on-Trent is the starting point for this day trip to the historic city of Chester. Built in the style of a Jacobean manor house, the station was opened in 1848 by the North Staffordshire Railway and was the company's headquarters until the Big Four Grouping of 1923. Electric trains for Crewe head north from here, first calling at Longport station, which has seen a remarkable 600% rise in passenger usage in the last 10 years. Still heading north, trains pass through Harecastle Tunnel to emerge at Kidsgrove station where the line to Manchester via Macclesfield branches off to the north. Close by, the Trent & Mersey Canal emerges from the 2,926-yd-long Harecastle Tunnel before reaching the junction with the Macclesfield Canal at Red Bull Junction.

Leaving Kidsgrove behind, trains for Crewe head off in a westerly direction across the Cheshire Plains, calling at Alsager then diving under the M6 before reaching Barthomley Junction, where the double-track line becomes single track for the last few miles into Crewe. Here, passengers for Chester need to change trains. Diesel trains head north out of Crewe and branch off the West Coast Main Line at Crewe North Junction before passing the Railway Age Museum and the Bombardier Depot and heading off in a northwesterly direction to continue their journey across the Cheshire Plains. Once the route of the famous 'Irish Mail', this 21¼-mile stretch of railway served 5 intermediate stations, although these are now long closed. Along much of this stretch the railway keeps close company with its erstwhile competitor, the Shropshire Union Canal, which following years of decline is now a popular route for pleasure boats. After passing through Christleton Tunnel trains arrive at Chester's important junction station. Built outside the city walls, the station is linked to the attractive city centre by a regular bus service.

Manchester
CHESTER
Crewe
STOKE-ON-TRENT
Shrewsbury

● STOKE-ON-TRENT
○ LONGPORT
○ KIDSGROVE
○ ALSAGER
● CREWE
● CHESTER

DESTINATION HIGHLIGHTS
Roman amphitheatre; city walls; Chester Castle; The Rows; 12th-century cathedral; 13th-century Old Dee Bridge; Chester Racecourse; Grosvenor Museum and Park; preserved lead shot tower; city-centre Victorian Jacobean-style architecture; walks along Shropshire Union Canal; boat cruises on River Dee and Shropshire Union Canal; Roman Gardens; Chester Zoo

FREQUENCY OF TRAINS
2 per hour (Mon-Sat)
1+ per hour (Sun)

36 MILES
1 HOUR 10 MINUTES

These black and white Tudor-style buildings in Bridge Street, Chester form part of the unique Chester Rows.

STOKE-ON-TRENT ●
LONGTON ○
BLYTHE BRIDGE ○
UTTOXETER ○
TUTBURY & HATTON ○
PEARTREE ○
DERBY ●

Our day trip to the industrial city of Derby takes us along the former North Staffordshire Railway route eastwards, skirting the Staffordshire Moorlands along the Blithe Valley before following the course of the River Dove for much of the remaining journey. Diesel trains for Derby leave Stoke-on-Trent's ornate station in a southerly direction before immediately branching off to the southeast at Derby Junction. Soon leaving the Potteries conurbation behind, trains first call at Longton station, located on an embankment overlooking the town. Immediately to the east, the railway crosses the town's busy King Street on a fine single-span cantilever bridge. After passing through Meir Tunnel, the next stop is Blythe Bridge station, jumping-off point for the nearby Foxfield Railway. A long stretch along the Blithe Valley then follows, with trains passing through the site of the closed station at Cresswell (once the junction for Cheadle) before Uttoxeter is reached. A favourite destination for racegoers to the adjacent racecourse, the station here was once an important junction serving lines northwards to Leek and North Rode via the Churnet Valley, and to Ashbourne and Buxton. It also serves as the nearest national rail network station for Alton Towers.

From Uttoxeter, the railway follows the course of the River Dove through dairy-farming country to Tutbury & Hatton station, home to a large, once rail-connected Nestlé factory. Continuing eastwards along the valley the railway soon joins the Birmingham to Derby main line at North Stafford Junction, passing through the closed joint station at Eggington, which was once the junction for the Great Northern Railway's route to Nottingham. From North Staffordshire Junction trains head northeast through Stenson Junction (for the freight-only line to Trent Junction), Melbourne Junction (for the freight-only branch to the Rolls-Royce factory at Sinfin) and Peartree station before terminating at Derby. A regular bus service links the station to the city centre (Monday-Friday) during university term time.

DESTINATION HIGHLIGHTS
14th-century cathedral; Derby Industrial Museum; Derby Gaol; Pickford's House Museum; Derby Museum & Art Gallery; 19th-century arboretum; Derby Tunnels via Tiger pub

FREQUENCY OF TRAINS
1 per hour (Mon-Sat; Sun pm)

36 MILES
51 MINUTES

An Art Deco clock on the wall of Compton House in Derby.

This day trip includes a journey along one of Britain's newest heritage railways, the Ecclesbourne Valley Railway. National rail network trains head northwards out of Derby station along the Midland Main Line, following the valley of the River Derwent to Duffield station. Passengers for Wirksworth and Ravenstor need to change trains at this unstaffed station, which has seen a remarkable rise in passenger usage since the heritage railway reopened completely in 2011.

Services on the Ecclesbourne Valley Railway are normally operated by heritage diesel trains, with steam also featuring on special events days. This scenic branch line follows the course of the River Ecclesbourne, itself a tributary of the Derwent, and was opened by the Midland Railway in 1867. Passenger services ceased in 1947 but the line remained open for limestone traffic until 1989. Diesel heritage trains head out of Platform 3 at Duffield station in a northwesterly direction, passing through the short Duffield Tunnel past the site of the closed Hazelwood station, which is now a timber yard. Now heading north, trains soon reach Shottle station where there is a passing loop. Although the station buildings here are privately owned, the platform was brought back into use in 2012. Continuing northwards up the valley the railway reaches Idridgehay station, where the station buildings and station master's house are now private residences. Wirksworth station is further 3½ miles to the north and it is here that passengers for Ravenstor need to change trains again. At weekends there are many visitor attractions at Wirksworth including a railway museum, model railways, a narrow-gauge line and a miniature railway. A separate diesel train carries passengers up the former mineral line to Ravenstor, which features gradients as steep as 1-in-27. From here visitors can access the Steeple Grange Light Railway, the National Stone Centre and the High Peak Trail via a disused incline.

- **DERBY**
- **DUFFIELD**
- SHOTTLE
- IDRIDGEHAY
- **WIRKSWORTH**
- **RAVENSTOR**

DESTINATION HIGHLIGHTS
journey along one of Britain's newest heritage railways; Steeple Grange Light Railway; National Stone Centre; railway walks along High Peak Trail

FREQUENCY OF TRAINS
Derby to Duffield:
1 per hour (Mon-Sat)
1 every 2 hours (Sun)
Duffield to Ravenstor:
3 per day (Sat-Sun+BHs, Mar-Oct; Tues, Apr-Sept; Thurs, July-Aug)

15¼ MILES
7 MINUTES + 1 HOUR

The diesel for the Ravenstor branch departs from Wirksworth station on the Ecclesbourne Valley Railway.

WORKSOP	●
WHITWELL	○
CRESWELL	○
LANGWITH-WHALEY THORNS	○
SHIREBROOK	○
MANSFIELD WOODHOUSE	○
MANSFIELD	○
SUTTON PARKWAY	○
KIRKBY-IN-ASHFIELD	○
NEWSTEAD	○
HUCKNALL	○
BULWELL	○
NOTTINGHAM	●

Our day trip to the historic city of Nottingham provides an opportunity to journey along a former Midland Railway line that became a victim of Dr Beeching's Axe when it lost its passenger service in 1964, causing Mansfield to become the largest town in the UK without a rail service. Fortunately the route remained open for coal traffic and, in more enlightened times, it was completely reopened to passengers in 1998 and marketed as the Robin Hood Line. Our starting point, Worksop station, is located on the former Great Central Railway's cross-country route between Sheffield and Lincoln via Retford. Nottingham-bound trains head west along this line before branching off southwards at Shireoaks East Junction. The first stop is at Whitwell, now a simple modern affair, where the original station building was dismantled and then reassembled at the Midland Railway Centre in Butterley in 1981. Continuing southwards through Whitwell Tunnel, the double-track line goes on to serve stations at Creswell, Langwith-Whaley Thorns and Shirebrook, the latter once an important centre of the Nottinghamshire coalfield. Just north of the station a freight-only line (once operated by the Great Central Railway) heads east to serve various coal plants and the Network Rail test track as far as Tuxford.

From Shirebrook, trains continue southwards calling at Mansfield Woodhouse, Mansfield, Sutton Parkway and Kirkby in Ashfield. Long gone are the coal mines that once kept this line busy, although the original MR station building at Mansfield has fortunately survived. South of Kirkby, and just north of Kirkby Tunnel, the Robin Hood Line becomes single track with intermediate stations at Newstead, Hucknall (the Nottingham Express Transit tram line parallels the railway from Hucknall to the outskirts of Nottingham) and Bulwell, before becoming double track once again. On reaching Mansfield Junction trains head east to terminate at Nottingham station. Built in an Edwardian Baroque Revival style, it was opened in 1904 and is currently the subject of a major redevelopment project.

DESTINATION HIGHLIGHTS
Nottingham Castle, museum and art gallery; Galleries of Justice; Old Market Square; City of Caves; 19th-century Gothic Revival cathedral designed by Pugin; fine Victorian architecture in Lace Market; Ye Old Trip to Jerusalem, The Bell Inn and Ye Olde Salutation Inn; Wollaton Hall for Industrial and Natural History museums

FREQUENCY OF TRAINS
1 per hour (Mon-Sat)
1 every 2 hours (Sun pm)

32 MILES
1 HOUR 6 MINUTES

The old and the new are reflected in the still waters of the Beeston & Nottingham Canal in Nottingham.

Our day trip to the beautiful city of Lincoln takes in a journey along a former Midland Railway route that was listed for closure in the 1963 'Beeching Report'. Opened in 1846 and engineered by George Stephenson, this 33-mile double-track route was fortunately reprieved. Diesel trains for Lincoln depart from Nottingham station in a northeasterly direction to follow the low-lying Trent Valley as far as Newark. At Netherfield Junction, a few miles outside Nottingham, the former Great Northern Railway route to Grantham, Sleaford and Skegness branches off to the east. From here, the Lincoln line heads out of the city's suburbs in a straight line down the valley, serving stations at Carlton (staggered platforms either side of a level crossing), Burton Joyce, Lowdham, Thurgarton (the last two still have their original MR station buildings), Bleasby, Fiskerton and Rolleston en route, before arriving at Newark Castle station. The attractive single-storey stone station building here is a remarkable survivor.

From Newark Castle, trains head over the flat crossing set at an angle to the East Coast Main Line – this is now the UK's last standard-gauge flat crossing where a railway crosses another railway on the level. Continuing northeastwards trains reach Collingham station, the second-busiest intermediate station on the line. Built in the style of a large Italian villa with heavy eaves and arched windows, this grand station building is now a private residence. The railway then crosses the Nottinghamshire/Lincolnshire border before arriving at Swinderby station with its small but attractive original brick building. The penultimate station is a Hykeham, where the basic modern platforms are staggered either side of a level crossing adjacent to a business park. The final part of our journey to Lincoln's conveniently situated Central station is via Boultham Junction and West Holmes Junction, where the line from Gainsborough joins from the northwest.

- **NOTTINGHAM**
- CARLTON
- BURTON JOYCE
- LOWDHAM
- THURGARTON
- BLEASBY
- FISKERTON
- ROLLESTON
- NEWARK CASTLE
- COLLINGHAM
- SWINDERBY
- HYKEHAM
- **LINCOLN**

DESTINATION HIGHLIGHTS
11th-century castle; 12th-century cathedral and Cathedral Close walls; medieval Old Quarter and Bishop's Palace; Steep Hill; 16th-century High Bridge; The Collection Museum; Museum of Lincolnshire Life; Sir Joseph Banks Conservatory at The Lawn; Christmas Market; 22-acre arboretum

FREQUENCY OF TRAINS
1 per hour (Mon-Sat; Sun late pm)

33 MILES
1 HOUR

Lincoln Cathedral was regarded by John Ruskin as 'the most precious piece of architecture in the British Isles'.

WALES

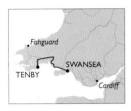

SWANSEA ●
GOWERTON ○
LLANELLI ○
PEMBREY & BURRY PORT ○
KIDWELLY ○
FERRYSIDE ○
CARMARTHEN ○
WHITLAND ○
NARBERTH ○
KILGETTY ○
SAUNDERSFOOT ○
TENBY ●

This day trip to the glorious seaside resort of Tenby starts in Wales's second-largest city, Swansea. Trains head northwards from the terminus and at Landore bear west to tackle the 1-in-52 gradient up to Cockett Tunnel. West of the tunnel the line becomes single track through Gowerton before crossing the River Loughor and reverting to double track just before Llandeilo Junction. Here, the Heart of Wales Line from Craven Arms and the Swansea Avoiding Line from Briton Ferry join from the northeast. After passing the rail-connected Tata tinplate works at Trostre, trains soon reach Llanelli station. Westwards from here the railway, engineered by Isambard Kingdom Brunel, follows a fairly level course, firstly along the north shore of the Loughor Estuary to Pembrey & Burry Port station then heading inland to avoid a vast area of sand dunes known as Pembrey Burrows. From Kidwelly the railway heads north, hugging the east bank of the tidal River Towy to Carmarthen.

Once an important junction serving lines from Aberystwyth and Llandeilo, Carmarthen station is now a terminus where trains bound for Tenby reverse direction before heading west through dairy-farming country to the town of Whitland (once the junction for Cardigan). Here, the single-track line to Tenby and Pembroke Dock branches off the main line to Milford Haven and Fishguard, heading first in a southwesterly direction up Lampeter Vale then through the hills to the Norman hilltop town of Narberth. Now heading directly south, trains call at Kilgetty and Saundersfoot – the latter, with its miles of golden sands overlooking Carmarthen Bay was an important exporter of coal and iron-ore in the 19th century. From here, the line descends through the hills to reach Tenby station. The attractive harbour, town centre and beaches are but a ten-minute walk from the station.

DESTINATION HIGHLIGHTS
2½ miles of sandy beaches;
13th-century town walls;
Tudor Merchant's House (NT);
Museum & Art Gallery;
Pembrokeshire Coast Path;
Palmerston Fort on St
Catherine's Island (at low tide);
boat trips from harbour to
monastic Caldey Island

FREQUENCY OF TRAINS
1 every 2 hours

58½ MILES
1 HOUR 35 MINUTES

Colourful houses overlook the sandy beach and harbour at Tenby.

The first part of our scenic railway journey from Swansea to the Victorian spa town of Llandrindod follows the same route as the day trip to Tenby (see page 116) as far as Llanelli. Here, trains for the Heart of Wales Line reverse direction and retrace their journey as far as Llandeilo Junction where they branch off northwards through Bynea and Llangennech stations to Morlais Junction. At this junction the double-track Swansea Avoiding Line heads west to Briton Ferry while the now single-track Heart of Wales Line follows the Loughor Valley to Pontarddulais and Pantyffynnon. Here, the freight-only line to the Gwaum-cae-Gurwen coal-loading terminal branches off to the east while the signalbox controls the whole length of the Heart of Wales Line as far as Craven Arms. Although threatened with closure in the 1963 'Beeching Report' and again in 1969, this highly scenic route, run as a Light Railway since 1972, is a remarkable survivor and well worth a visit.

Beyond Pantyffynnon the railway climbs northwards through Ammanford to Llandybie then descends into the Towy Valley to Llandeilo, former junction for Carmarthen and now a crossing place. From here the railways strikes off in a northeasterly direction up the narrowing valley, through Llangadog and Llanwrda to the town of Llandovery where there is a passing loop. Now following the ever-narrowing Bran Valley, the railway starts to climb to Cynghordy where it crosses the valley on a magnificent curving viaduct before making the final, gruelling climb up to Sugar Loaf Tunnel. After emerging from this 1,000-yd single-bore tunnel, the line passes Sugar Loaf Halt (the least-used station in Wales) before arriving at Llanwrtyd where trains cross and crews change over. From here, the railway continues northeast, winding through the hills to serve Llangammarch, Garth, Cilmeri and Builth Road (once junction for the Mid-Wales line) before finally reaching Llandrindod with its Victorian town centre. The station, which has a passing loop, is the busiest on the line and the only one with a ticket office.

- ● **SWANSEA**
- ○ GOWERTON
- ○ LLANELLI
- ○ BYNEA
- ○ LLANGENNECH
- ○ PONTARDDULAIS
- ○ PANTYFFYNNON
- ○ AMMANFORD
- ○ LLANDYBIE
- ○ FFAIRFACH
- ○ LLANDEILO
- ○ LLANGADOG
- ○ LLANWRDA
- ○ LLANDOVERY
- ○ CYNGHORDY
- ○ SUGAR LOAF
- ○ LLANWRTYD
- ○ LLANGAMMARCH
- ○ GARTH
- ○ CILMERI
- ○ BUILTH ROAD
- ● **LLANDRINDOD**

DESTINATION HIGHLIGHTS
Old Signal Box Museum at station; Victorian town centre; arts and crafts shops; Art Deco garages and National Cycle Collection; fishing in Rock Park; Victorian Festival (late August); Radnorshire Museum

FREQUENCY OF TRAINS
4 per day (Mon-Sat)
2 per day (Sun)

67¾ MILES
2 HOURS 20 MINUTES

BR Standard '5MT' No. 73036 approaches Cynghordy Viaduct on the climb to Sugar Loaf Tunnel in 1964.

SWANSEA ●
LLANSAMLET ○
SKEWEN ○
NEATH ○
BRITON FERRY ○
BAGLAN ○
PORT TALBOT PARKWAY ○
PYLE ○
BRIDGEND ○
PENCOED ○
LLANHARAN ○
PONTYCLUN ○
CARDIFF CENTRAL ●

This day trip to the capital city of Wales takes in a journey along Brunel's superbly engineered, level broad-gauge railway that was opened by the South Wales Railway in 1850. Taken over by the Great Western Railway in 1863, the line was converted to standard gauge in 1872. Today's modern diesel trains head north out of Swansea's terminus station to Swansea Loop East Junction, where the line to Carmarthen branches off westwards. Continuing past Landore diesel depot the railway then heads northwest from Landore Junction, crossing the River Tawe before passing through Llansamlet and Skewen stations to reach the historic town of Neath. On its curving approach to the town the railway crosses over the Neath Canal and the River Neath. From here, trains head south to Briton Ferry, where the Swansea Avoiding Line joins from the west, before paralleling the M5 motorway through Baglan to Port Talbot. The landscape beyond is dominated by the enormous Tata Margam Steelworks on the edge of Swansea Bay to the west and the forested slopes of the South Wales hills to the north and east.

After calling at Pyle station, once the junction for Porthcawl, trains head east across the Ogmore River to the large town of Bridgend. The station here is now the junction for the recently reopened passenger lines to Maesteg in the Llynfi Valley and the Vale of Glamorgan line to Cardiff via Barry (see page 120). Continuing eastwards, the railway meanders along the Ewenny Valley to Pencoed and Llanharan before winding down the picturesque, widening Ely Valley to Pontyclun and the western outskirts of Cardiff. On the final approach to the city's well-positioned Central station, trains pass Canton Depot before crossing the River Taff, from where passengers are treated to views of the Millennium Stadium and the city's skyline.

DESTINATION HIGHLIGHTS
Cardiff Castle; Cardiff Bay; Millennium Centre; Millennium Stadium; Llandaff Cathedral; National History Museum; National Museum & Gallery of Wales; Cathays Park; Bute Park; Roath Park; Victoria Park; Castell Coch; Cardiff Central Market; Spillers Records (worlds oldest record shop); Victorian shopping arcades

FREQUENCY OF TRAINS
2-3 per hour (Mon-Sat)
1-2 per hour (Sun)

45¾ MILES
55 MINUTES

Completed in 2009, the Wales Millennium Centre in Cardiff Bay is faced with copper oxide-coated sheet-steel cladding.

Our day trip from the Welsh capital city of Cardiff to the historic harbour city of Bristol takes in a journey through the 4-mile, 628-yd-long Severn Tunnel. The opening of the tunnel in 1886 shortened the rail journey from Paddington to South Wales by 25 miles – prior to that trains had to make the journey via Gloucester.

Trains for Bristol head northeast out of Cardiff Central station and take a straight and level course to the outskirts of Newport where, at Ebbw Junction, the recently reopened line to Ebbw Vale Parkway branches off to the west. To the east lie the rail-connected Newport Docks and, shortly after, the freight-only line from Machen joins from the southwest after emerging from Gaer Tunnel. The final approach to Newport station is through Hillfield Tunnel. After leaving Newport, trains head over the River Usk to the triangular Maindee Junction where the scenic Welsh Marches Line to Shrewsbury (see page 96) branches off to the north. After passing East Usk Junction freight yard, trains for Bristol head eastwards to Severn Tunnel Junction, passing the giant rail-connected Tata steelworks at Llanwern en route. A car-carrying service from Severn Tunnel Junction and through the tunnel to Pilning ended when the first Severn road bridge opened in 1966.

From Severn Tunnel Junction, Bristol-bound trains head down to enter the western portal of the tunnel – it is heartening to know that pumps work round the clock to keep the tunnel dry by pumping out 23-30 million gallons of water each day. After travelling under the River Severn, trains emerge near Pilning before heading through the 1-mile-long Patchway Tunnel to Patchway Junction. Here, the freight-only line to Avonmouth Docks heads west, the main line to Paddington heads east and Bristol-bound trains descend southwards through Filton Abbey Wood, Stapleton Road and Lawrence Hill before arriving at Bristol Temple Meads station. Regular bus services link the station to the historic city centre.

- **CARDIFF CENTRAL**
- NEWPORT
- SEVERN TUNNEL JUNCTION
- PILNING
- PATCHWAY
- FILTON ABBEY WOOD
- STAPLETON ROAD
- LAWRENCE HILL
- **BRISTOL TEMPLE MEADS**

DESTINATION HIGHLIGHTS
Bristol Zoo; Clifton Suspension Bridge; 'SS Great Britain'; Bristol Harbour Railway; Cabot Tower; Bristol Cathedral; St Nicholas Church Museum; Bristol Harbour Festival (end July/early August); International Balloon Festival (August); Industrial Museum; Museum & Art Gallery; Banksey street art; 17th-century Llandoger Trow pub

FREQUENCY OF TRAINS
2 per hour (Mon-Sat)
1 per hour (Sun)

37¼ MILES
50 MINUTES

Brunel's world-famous Clifton Suspension Bridge soars over the Avon Gorge in Bristol.

CARDIFF CENTRAL	●
GRANGETOWN	○
COGAN	○
EASTBROOK	○
DINAS POWYS	○
CADOXTON	○
BARRY DOCKS	○
BARRY	○
RHOOSE CARDIFF INTERNATIONAL AIRPORT	○
LLANTWIT MAJOR	○
BRIDGEND	●
WILDMILL	○
SARN	○
TONDU	○
GARTH (BRIDGEND)	○
MAESTEG (EWENNY ROAD)	○
MAESTEG	●

DESTINATION HIGHLIGHTS
Maesteg Market; Llynfi Valley walks around Garth Hill and Mynydd Bach

FREQUENCY OF TRAINS
1 per hour (Mon-Sat)

36 MILES
1 HOUR 30 MINUTES

A day trip to the town of Maesteg, at the head of the Llynfi Valley, may seem an odd choice but the surrounding hills and forests offer many walking opportunities. The ironworks and coal mines have long gone, but there are still reminders of the town's rich industrial heritage to be discovered today. Instead of taking the direct route along the main line westwards from Cardiff Central station, this trip starts with a ride along the coastal Vale of Glamorgan line via Barry. Trains for this route also leave the station in a westerly direction but branch off southwards to Grangetown, then through Cogan Junction where the single line to Penarth branches off southwards. Cogan station and tunnel soon follow as the line heads southwest to Cadoxton, Barry Docks and Barry. Barry station is also the junction for the short branch to Barry Island and the Barry Rail Centre.

Closed to passengers in 1964, the line between Barry and Bridgend remained open for freight and as a diversionary route, and passenger trains were reintroduced in 2005. After passing through Porthkerry Tunnel trains call at Rhoose (for Cardiff Airport) then past the rail-connected Aberthaw Power Station to Llantwit Major. Here, the line swings northwards to reach Bridgend where a change of trains is required.

The final part of our journey up the Llynfi Valley follows the course of early 19th-century horsedrawn tramways that were rebuilt by the broad-gauge Llynfi Valley Railway, opening in 1861 to serve ironworks and zinc smelters at Maesteg. A victim of the 'Beeching Axe', the line closed to passengers between Bridgend and Treherbert in 1970 but was reopened as far as Maesteg in 1992. The 8-mile single-track line serves stations at Wildmill, Sarn, Tondu, Garth, Maesteg Ewenny Road and Maesteg.

The Llynfi Valley Line in steam days – 0-6-0PT No. 4669 heads a short train through Tondu in June 1962.

Until the Second World War a day trip to the seaside resort of Barry Island was often the highlight of the year for the miners of the South Wales Valleys and their families. Steam-hauled excursion trains packed with day trippers would make the journey down the valleys on summer weekends and Bank Holidays – in the late 1920s up to 120,000 people would arrive by train at Barry Island on Bank Holiday weekends. Our day trip relives their experience although, sadly, the steam trains were replaced long ago by bland, modern diesel multiple units. Our trip starts at Merthyr Tydfil, once an important industrial centre with ironworks and coal mines. These have all long since disappeared and the town's basic station with its single platform is a rather dreary affair. Diesel trains depart southwards following the Taff Valley through Merthyr Vale and Quaker's Yard to Abercynon, where the single line down the Cynon Valley from Aberdare joins from northwest.

Following the Taff Valley, trains head southwards on the double-track line from Abercynon to Pontypridd. Still an important railway junction, the station here is also served by trains heading up the Rhondda Valley to Treherbert. From Pontypridd the railway continues on down the ever-widening Taff Valley to Radyr, where trains bound for Cardiff take the route through Llandaf and Cathays. The final approach takes the railway over the Newport main line before descending to Central station. Trains bound for Barry Island follow the Vale of Glamorgan route (see page 120) to Barry then branch off along a short single-track line to Barry Island station. With only very basic facilities this unstaffed station is a rather sad affair compared to the adjacent, original 1896 station building, which has been restored. Hopefully the weather will be good enough for a spot of sand-castle building on the beach!

- **MERTHYR TYDFIL**
- PENTRE-BACH
- TROED-Y-RHIW
- MERTHYR VALE
- QUAKERS YARD
- ABERCYNON
- PONTYPRIDD
- TREFFOREST
- TREFFOREST ESTATE
- TAFFS WELL
- RADYR
- LLANDAF
- CATHAYS
- CARDIFF QUEEN STREET
- CARDIFF CENTRAL
- GRANGETOWN
- COGAN
- EASTBROOK
- DINAS POWYS
- CADOXTON
- BARRY DOCKS
- BARRY
- **BARRY ISLAND**

DESTINATION HIGHLIGHTS
beach; Barry Island Pleasure Park; Barry Tourist Railway

FREQUENCY OF TRAINS
1 per hour (Mon-Sat)
1 every 2 hours (Sun)

33¼ MILES
1 HOUR 32 MINUTES

A 'Pacer' diesel unit approaches the important junction station of Pontypridd with a service to Barry Island.

SHREWSBURY	●
CHURCH STRETTON	○
CRAVEN ARMS	○
BROOME	○
HOPTON HEATH	○
BUCKNELL	○
KNIGHTON	○
KNUCKLAS	○
LLANGYNLLO	○
LLANBISTER ROAD	○
DOLAU	○
PEN-Y-BONT	○
LLANDRINDOD	●

DESTINATION HIGHLIGHTS
Old Signal Box Museum at
station; Victorian town centre;
arts and crafts shops; Art Deco
garages and National Cycle
Collection; fishing in Rock
Park; Victorian Festival (late
August); Radnorshire Museum

FREQUENCY OF TRAINS
4 per day (Mon-Sat)
2 per day (Sun)

51¾ MILES
1 HOUR 30 MINUTES

The first part of this day trip to the Victorian spa town of Llandrindod follows the same route as the Shrewsbury to Hereford day trip as far as Craven Arms (see page 96). At Craven Arms, diesel trains for the Heart of Wales Line branch off the Welsh Marches main line to head southwest to the first station at Broome. This highly scenic 90-mile single-track railway across central Wales to Llanelli is a remarkable survivor, having been threatened several times with closure in the 1960s. From Broome the railway bears south along the Clun Valley through Hopton Heath before joining the Teme Valley at Bucknall. Hugging the Wales/England border, the line then heads west up the narrowing valley to the historic market town of Knighton, whose station and passing loop are in England while the town itself is located across the river in Wales. Crossing into Wales, the railway reaches Knucklas where the fine castellated viaduct overlooks the ruined Norman castle and village below.

From Knucklas, the Heart of Wales Line climbs up through the curving Llangynllo Tunnel to Llangynllo station (the summit of the line, at 980 ft above sea level) before weaving around the contours to Llanbister Road and heading southwest down the Aran Valley to Dolau station. Set in hill-farming countryside, this remote station is famous for its award-winning garden. Leaving Dolau, the railway crosses the Ithon Valley for the first time before taking a short cut through Pen-y-Bont Tunnel and crossing the valley again at Crossgates. Following the meandering Ithon, the railway soon reaches Llandrindod station, by far the busiest on the entire line and the only one with a booking office.

BR Standard Class '4MT' 2-6-4T
No. 80069 heads a Swansea to
Shrewsbury train over Knucklas
Viaduct in 1960.

Our day trip to the delightful Banwy Valley starts at Shrewsbury's ornate mock-Tudor station, an important railway crossroads set alongside the River Severn. Diesel trains for the Cambrian Line head south from the station, passing the triangular Severn Bridge Junction and its enormous signalbox before branching off westwards at Sutton Bridge Junction. The 19¾-mile single-track route through rolling farmland to Welshpool once served intermediate stations at Hanwood, Yockleton, Westbury, Plas-y-Court, Breidden and Buttington but these were all closed in the 1960s. Crossing into Wales at Middletown, the railway heads down to cross Offa's Dyke before meeting the River Severn once again at Welshpool. Here, passengers for the Welshpool & Llanfair Railway should alight and make their way on foot westwards through the unspoilt market town to Raven Square station.

Still operated by the two original Beyer Peacock steam locomotives, train services along this delightful 8½-mile narrow-gauge line start their journey at Raven Square terminus, close to the grounds of Powis Castle. First climbing the 1-in-24 Golfa Bank to the 600-ft summit of the line, the railway traces contours round sharp curves, crossing country lanes on 4 level crossings and passing through little halts at Sylfaen and Castle Caereinion before reaching Cyfronydd. Here the line joins the fast-flowing River Banwy, crossing it near Heniarth and hugging the north bank to end at the delightful little terminus at Llanfair Caereinion.

- **SHREWSBURY**
- **WELSHPOOL**
- **WELSHPOOL RAVEN SQUARE**
- ○ SYLFAEN
- ○ CASTLE CAEREINION
- ○ CYFRONYDD
- ○ HENIARTH
- **LLANFAIR CAEREINION**

DESTINATION HIGHLIGHTS
Powis Castle (NT/Welshpool); ride on Welshpool & Llanfair narrow-gauge steam railway; riverside walks in Banwy Valley

FREQUENCY OF TRAINS
Shrewsbury to Welshpool:
1 every 2 hours
Welshpool Raven Square to Llanfair Caereinion:
3-5 per day (July-Aug; Sat-Sun+BHs, Apr-Oct)

27¾ MILES
22 + 50 MINUTES

The National Trust's medieval Powis Castle is located on the outskirts of Welshpool.

WELSHPOOL ●
NEWTOWN ○
CAERSWS ○
MACHYNLLETH ●

Our day trip along the Cambrian Line to the historic market town of Machynlleth starts at Welshpool station – the original Victorian Gothic station, now a café and shop, was replaced in the 1990s by a relocated and very basic platform and shelter. Leaving Welshpool the railway heads south, climbing gradually up the narrowing Severn Valley and closely following the river's winding course for the next 20 miles. The line also keeps company with the Shropshire Union Canal through Abermule, scene of a catastrophic head-on crash in 1921, as far as Newtown. With a population of nearly 13,000 it is the largest town in mid-Wales and was an important administration centre during the reign of Edward I of England.

The railway continues westwards to Caersws, where it leaves the Severn behind and begins its long climb up the steep-sided Carno Valley towards the Cambrian Mountains. With gradients as steep as 1-in-71, the line climbs for the next 8 miles to the 692-ft summit of the line at Talerddig. Here it passes through gritstone in a 120-ft-deep cutting which, when excavated, was the deepest railway cutting in the world. The line then descends down the Iaen Valley on gradients as steep as 1-in 52 to Cemmaes Road where it joins the broad valley of the River Dyfi. Following the valley westwards, the railway reaches the town of Machynlleth, an important railway centre where westbound trains divide before setting off for their respective destinations of Aberystwyth and Pwllheli.

DESTINATION HIGHLIGHTS
13th-century market (Wednesdays); Owain Glyndwr interpretive centre in Parliament House; Glyndwr Festival (early Sept); The Tabernacle Museum of Modern Art; Corris Railway Museum (by bus, hourly on weekdays); Centre for Alternative Technology (by bus, hourly on weekdays); riverside walks in Dyfi Valley

FREQUENCY OF TRAINS
1 every 2 hours

41¼ MILES
57 MINUTES

'Hinton Manor' calls at Machynlleth with the Cambrian Coast Express in September 1963.

Cambrian Line trains for Aberystwyth leave Machynlleth station in a southwesterly direction and head down the broad Dyfi Valley to reach the remote outpost of Dovey Junction, where the single line divides. Only accessible on foot, the single-island platform station is mainly used as an interchange point for the few passengers travelling between Aberystwyth and Pwllheli. Trains for Aberystwyth then skirt the southern shore of the Dyfi Estuary through the Dyfi National Nature Reserve before reaching the coast at Borth. Here, close to Borth Sands, the imposing station building is now a museum. Avoiding the difficult coastal terrain to the south, the railway heads inland on a switchback route through the hills before joining the broad Rheidol Valley and terminating on the coast at Aberystwyth.

Narrow-gauge steam trains for the 11¾-mile journey to Devil's Bridge depart from a separate platform at the national rail network station at Aberystwyth. First paralleling the standard-gauge line, the railway heads off up the southern wooded slopes of the Rheidol Valley, climbing continuously through Nantyronen, Aberffrwd and Rheidol Falls stations. The river now is far below and the final, dramatic approach up the 1-in-50 gradient to Devil's Bridge station is through a narrow rock cutting. From here, 639 ft above sea level, there are walks to the nearby beauty spots of Jacob's Ladder, Devil's Punchbowl and Mynach Falls.

- ● MACHYNLLETH
- ○ DOVEY JUNCTION
- ○ BORTH
- ● ABERYSTWYTH
- ○ LLANBADARN
- ○ GLANYRAFON
- ○ CAPEL BANGOR
- ○ NANTYRONEN
- ○ ABERFFRWD
- ○ RHEIDOL FALLS
- ○ RHIWFRON
- ● DEVIL'S BRIDGE

DESTINATION HIGHLIGHTS
ride on Vale of Rheidol narrow-gauge steam railway; walks to Jacob's Ladder, Devil's Punchbowl, Devil's Bridge and Mynach Falls in Rheidol Gorge

FREQUENCY OF TRAINS
Machynlleth to Aberystwyth:
1 every 2 hours
Aberystwyth to Devil's Bridge:
2-4 per day (May-Sept; selected days, Mar-Oct)

32¼ MILES
37 MINUTES + 1 HOUR

With panoramic views over Aberystwyth, the top of Constitution Hill is reached by a cliff railway.

PORTHMADOG ●
MINFFORDD ○
PENRHYNDEUDRAETH ○
LLANDECWYN ○
TALSARNAU ○
TYGWYN ○
HARLECH ○
LLANDANWG ○
PENSARN ○
LLANBEDR ○
DYFFRYN ARDUDWY ○
TALYBONT ○
LLANABER ○
BARMOUTH ○
MORFA MAWDDACH ○
FAIRBOURNE ○
LLWYNGWRIL ○
TONFANAU ○
TYWYN ●
┊
TYWYN WHARF ●
BRYNGLAS ○
DOLGOCH ○
ABERGYNOLWYN ○
NANT GWERNOL ●

DESTINATION HIGHLIGHTS
ride on Talyllyn narrow-gauge
steam railway; Dolgoch Falls;
forest walks from Nant Gwernol
to Bryn Eglws quarries; Narrow
Gauge Railway Museum (Tywyn)

FREQUENCY OF TRAINS
Porthmadog to Tywyn:
1 every 2 hours (Mon-Sat)
3 per day (Sun)
Tywyn to Nant Gwernol:
2-6 per day (Mar-Oct)

38¾ MILES
80 + 53 MINUTES

Our day trip to discover the delights of Britain's first preserved railway, the narrow-gauge Talyllyn Railway, starts at Porthmadog's national rail network station (now home to a pub). From here, Cambrian Line trains from Pwllheli head east across the reclaimed Traeth Mawr to Minffordd, the interchange station for the Ffestiniog Railway (see page 127). En route, the standard-gauge line crosses the narrow-gauge Welsh Highland Railway on the level, the only such place that this occurs in the UK. From Minffordd, the Cambrian Line heads up the Vale of Ffestiniog to Penrhyndeudraeth before crossing the Afon Dwyryd on a curving timber bridge shared with a toll road. Now heading south, the railway serves halts at Llandecwyn, Talsarnau and Tygwyn before reaching Harlech where Edward I's mighty 13th-century castle dominates the town. Continuing southwards, the railway reaches the coast at Llandanwg before heading inland to serve halts at Pensarn, Llanbedr, Dyffryn Ardudwy, and Talybont. Rejoining the coast at Llanaber, it soon reaches the seaside resort of Barmouth, once a popular destination for holidaymakers from the West Midlands.

After slowly crossing the 121-span Barmouth Bridge across the Mawddach Estuary, trains call at Morffa Mawddach (for the Mawddach Trail to Dolgellau) then hug the coastline from Fairbourne (for the miniature railway) to Llwyngwril and Tonfanau before arriving at Tywyn station. Here, passengers must alight and make their way on foot to nearby Wharf station. Saved from closure by the world's first group of preservationists in 1951, the Talyllyn Railway follows a 7½-mile scenic route up the Fathew Valley to the terminus at Nant Gwernol. Vintage steam trains call at Brynglas, Dolgoch (for nearby Dolgoch Falls) and Abergynolwyn en route. From Nant Gwernol, visitors can explore the tracks and footpaths that weave their way through the surrounding woodland and the old slate workings at Bryn Eglwys.

Closed in 1946 as a slate-carrying line, the narrow-gauge Ffestiniog Railway was gradually opened by preservationists between Porthmadog and Blaenau Ffestiniog between 1955 and 1982. Using unique Double-Fairlie steam locomotives to haul trains of vintage carriage, the railway has its headquarters at Portmadog Harbour station, which it now shares with the recently reopened Welsh Highland Railway (see page 128). On leaving the station, trains head across the mile-long Cob, an embankment built to reclaim land from the sea in 1811. Fine views of Snowdonia can be enjoyed from the train en route to Boston Lodge, the railway's historic 19th-century workshops at the far end of the Cob.

At Minffordd station the railway interchanges with the standard-gauge Cambrian Line (see page 126). From here, steam engines work hard to climb up the Vale of Ffestiniog to Penrhyn station before following the contours through the wooded slopes to Tan-y-Bwlch station. At 430 ft above sea level, this tranquil spot is a jumping-off point for woodland walks. Beyond Tan-y-Bwlch the railway clings to a ledge high above the valley floor, passing the private Campbell's Platform before diving under the spiral 360-degree loop to arrive at Dduallt station. After pausing at this remote spot, trains continue to climb around the loop before heading through Moelwyn Tunnel and emerging alongside Tanygrisiau Reservoir. Following the reservoir, the railway reaches Tanygrisiau station, 669 ft above sea level. The final stretch into Blaenau Ffestiniog takes the line past enormous man-made mountains of slate spoil and the remains of inclines that once served the slate quarries here. The station at Blaenau is shared with the standard-gauge Conwy Valley Line (see page 130) from Llandudno Junction.

- **PORTHMADOG HARBOUR**
- BOSTON LODGE HALT
- MINFFORDD
- PENRHYN
- TAN-Y-BWLCH
- CAMPBELL'S PLATFORM
- DDUALLT
- TANYGRISIAU
- **BLAENAU FFESTINIOG**

DESTINATION HIGHLIGHTS
ride on Ffestiniog narrow-gauge steam railway; Llechwedd Slate Caverns; walks to disused slate quarries

FREQUENCY OF TRAINS
2-7 per day (Mar-Oct; selected days, Feb-Dec)

13½ MILES
1 HOUR 10 MINUTES

LEFT: A train on the narrow-gauge Ffestiniog Railway crosses The Cob on the approach to Porthmadog.

OPPOSITE: A vintage train hauled by 'Talyllyn' pulls in to Rhydyronen station on the narrow-gauge Talyllyn Railway.

Llandudno Junction

CAERNARFON

PORTHMADOG HARBOUR

Aberystwyth

PORTHMADOG HARBOUR ●
PONT CROESOR ○
NANTMOR ○
BEDDGELERT ○
MEILLIONEN ○
RHYD DDU ○
SNOWDON RANGER ○
PLAS-Y-NANT ○
WAUNFAWR ○
TRYFAN JUNCTION ○
DINAS ○
BONTNEWYDD ○
CAERNARFON ●

DESTINATION HIGHLIGHTS
ride on Welsh Highland
narrow-gauge steam railway
through Snowdonia National
Park; 14th-century Caernarfon
Castle; harbour; Blue Flag
beach; haunted 16th-century
Black Boy Inn; market square;
Royal Welch Fusiliers Museum

FREQUENCY OF TRAINS
2-3 per day (July-Sept;
selected days, Mar-Oct)

25 MILES
2 HOURS 25 MINUTES

RIGHT: *Now a UNESCO World
Heritage Site, Caernarfon Castle
is reflected in the harbour
waters at Caernarfon.*

OPPOSITE: *An ex-South African
Garratt locomotive threads
Aberglaslyn Pass with a Welsh
Highland Railway train
for Porthmadog.*

This is definitely a day trip to remember. Britain's longest heritage railway, the recently reopened narrow-gauge Welsh Highland Railway, carries passengers through glorious scenery in the Snowdonia National Park before depositing them close to the walls of Caernarfon Castle. Reopened throughout in 2011, it follows the course of two long-closed narrow-gauge railways and a former standard-gauge line. Hauled by massive (by narrow-gauge standards) ex-South African Garratt articulated steam locomotives, trains depart from Porthmadog Harbour station, which is shared with the Ffestiniog Railway (see page 127). After threading behind the town and crossing the standard-gauge Cambrian Line on the level (see page 126), the railway heads northeast across flat pastureland reclaimed from the sea to reach Pont Croesor. Soon the railway heads northwards up the Glaslyn Valley and into the Snowdonia National Park to Nantmor, beyond which it enters the narrow and dramatic Pass of Aberglaslyn, passing through three rock-cut tunnels on the most spectacular part of this journey.

After crossing the Glaslyn on a bridge, the railway soon reaches the picturesque village of Beddgelert, once an important centre for copper mining but today heavily dependent on tourism. Leaving the station's curving platform and passing loop behind, the line climbs steadily through tortuous reverse curves up to the summit of the line at Pitts Head before paralleling the A4085 road to Rhyd Ddu. This remote station has a passing loop and is also a jumping-off point for a footpath to the summit of Snowdon, which looms to the east.

From Rhyd Ddu the line heads down along the shore of Llyn Cwellyn, where Snowdon Ranger station is the starting point of a steep path to the summit of Snowdon. Now heading northwest down the Gwyfrai Valley, trains call at Plas-y-Nant and the former slate-mining village of Waunfawr before heading west through Tryfan Junction to Dinas, where the WHR has its workshops, engine and carriage sheds. The rest of the journey northwards follows the route of the standard-gauge Afonwen to Caernarfon line that closed in 1964. The Lon Eifion cycleway parallels the WHR along this section. With an intermediate station at Bontnewydd, the railway ends at Caernarfon station, a short distance from the harbour, medieval city walls and the castle, which are encompassed as a UNESCO World Heritage Site.

LLANDUDNO ●
DEGANWY ○
LLANDUDNO JUNCTION ○
GLAN CONWY ○
TAL-Y-CAFN ○
DOLGARROG ○
NORTH LLANRWST ○
LLANRWST ○
BETWS-Y-COED ○
PONT-Y-PANT ○
DOLWYDDELAN ○
ROMAN BRIDGE ○
BLAENAU FFESTINIOG ●

The single-track railway along the scenic Conwy and Lledr valleys into the heart of the Snowdonia National Park is a fortunate survivor of the 'Beeching Axe'. Diesel trains for Blaenau Ffestiniog depart from Llandudno's terminus station, beginning their journey along the double-track line through Deganwy station to Llandudno Junction. From here, they branch off the North Wales Coast main line to follow the single-track route along the east bank of the tidal Conwy Estuary, calling at Glan Conwy – a request stop, as are most of the stations along this line – before reaching Tal-y-Cafn station, jumping-off point for the strenuous uphill walk to the famous Bodnant Gardens. The railway continues south along the narrowing wooded valley, keeping close company with the river to Dolgarrog before reaching North Llanrwst. Here, the original station buildings have survived and there is a passing loop and working signalbox. The well-patronized station of Llanwrst follows, then the line makes its only crossing of the river as it enters the Snowdonia National Park before hugging the forested west bank to Betws-y-Coed.

The busiest intermediate station on the line, the restored station at Betws-y-Coed is also the jumping-off point for the adjacent Conwy Valley Railway Museum. Trains for Blaenau continue southwards along the valley then head westwards to follow the narrow wooded Lledr Valley, crossing over Pont Gethin Viaduct before reaching Pont-y-Pant station. Continuing up the valley, the railway serves small halts at Dolwyddelan and Roman Bridge before heading south through the 2-mile 338-yd single-bore Ffestiniog Tunnel, the longest railway tunnel in Wales. After negotiating its murky depths, trains emerge into a man-made world of slate spoil tips and other reminders of this once-important industry before terminating at Blaenau Ffestiniog. The station here is shared with the narrow-gauge Ffestiniog Railway, which operates steam trains down to Porthmadog (see page 127).

DESTINATION HIGHLIGHTS
Conwy Valley Railway Museum
(Betws-y-Coed); Ffestiniog
narrow-gauge steam railway
to Porthmadog (see page 127);
Llechwedd Slate Caverns;
walks to disused slate quarries

FREQUENCY OF TRAINS
5 per day (Mon–Sat)
3 per day (Sun)

30¼ MILES
1 HOUR 20 MINUTES

*Old slate mine workings
litter the landscape around
Blaenau Ffestioniog.*

The first part of this day trip follows the same route as the Llandudno to Blaenau Ffestiniog day trip as far as Llandudno Junction where a change of train is required. Trains for Holyhead leave Llandudno Junction in a westerly direction and immediately cross the Conwy Estuary through George Stephenson's impressive wrought-iron tubular bridge that was completed in 1848. The railway then passes close to Conwy Castle and through an archway in the town's walls to arrive at Conwy station. The line soon reaches the coast, tracing it through Penmaenbach Tunnel to Penmaenmawr station. Here, the original impressive station building has survived while a nearby rail-connected quarry remains a source of heavy aggregate traffic. Still squeezed between hills and the sea, the railway continues west through Penclip Tunnel and Llanfairfechan before approaching the university town of Bangor through Llandegai and Bangor tunnels.

Bangor station is the busiest (and windiest) railway station in North Wales and its 4-track layout is approached through tunnels at both ends. On leaving the station, trains immediately enter Belmont Tunnel before heading across the Menai Strait to Anglesey – the original Britannia tubular bridge was destroyed in a fire in 1970 and replaced by the current road/rail 2-level structure which opened to rail traffic in 1972. On reaching Anglesey, trains call at Llanfairpwll station, whose full title of 58 characters is the longest station name in the UK. From here, the railway heads west across rolling Anglesey farmland, serving stations at Bodorgan, Ty Croes, Rhosneigr and Valley, which serves the nearby RAF base and is rail-linked to the nearby nuclear power station. The final approach to Holyhead is across Stanley Embankment to Holy Island and past a disused aluminium smelter. Located alongside the Irish ferry terminal, the impressive station at Holyhead was opened by the LNWR in 1866.

- **LLANDUDNO**
- DEGANWY
- **LLANDUDNO JUNCTION**
- CONWY
- PENMAENMAWR
- LLANFAIRFECHAN
- BANGOR
- LLANFAIRPWLL
- BODORGAN
- TY CROES
- RHOSNEIGR
- VALLEY
- **HOLYHEAD**

DESTINATION HIGHLIGHTS
Holyhead Breakwater and Country Park; beach; Maritime Museum; bird watching; St Cybi's Church; ancient ruins, burial chambers and standing stones; walks to Holyhead Mountain and North Stack RSPB observatory

FREQUENCY OF TRAINS
1 per hour

43¼ MILES
1 HOUR 11 MINUTES

The marina and long breakwater at Holyhead on Holy Island, Anglesey.

CHESTER ●
SHOTTON ○
FLINT ○
PRESTATYN ○
RHYL ○
ABERGELE & PENSARN ○
COLWYN BAY ○
LLANDUDNO JUNCTION ○
DEGANWY ○
LLANDUDNO ●

Our day trip along the north coast of Wales to the Victorian seaside resort of Llandudno starts at Chester's recently refurbished station. Opened in 1848 to serve the new main line to Holyhead, the impressive Grade II*-listed station building was designed in Italianate style with a train shed. It is now a major railway crossroads, with five routes radiating out to all points of the compass. Trains for Llandudno head southwest through Windmill Lane and Northgate Street tunnels to Saltney Junction, where the single-track line to Wrexham branches off to the south. Here, trains for the coastal route take a northwesterly course through Shotton before hugging the south shore of the Dee Estuary to call at Flint station. The railway then continues its journey alongside the Dee Estuary, passing the disused steel terminal at Mostyn Docks before reaching the Point of Ayr (the northernmost point of mainland Wales and, until 1996, also the site of a deep colliery), where the Dee enters the sea in Liverpool Bay. En route passengers can glimpse the strange sight of a land-locked ship near the coast – the 'TSS Duke of Lancaster', a former railway passenger steamer, was retired to Mostyn as a Fun Ship in 1979 and, after years of neglect, has recently reopened as an art gallery for graffiti artists. Heading inland for a short distance, the line avoids the shifting sand dunes which are now an RSPB reserve, before arriving at the seaside resort of Prestatyn.

The coming of the railway in 1848 soon led to the development of popular resorts along this stretch of coastline – after Prestatyn trains hug the coastline to call at Rhyl (for the famous miniature railway), Abergele & Pensarn and Colwyn Bay. Llandudno Junction soon follows and it is here that trains for the seaside resort branch off the coastal main line and head northwards through Deganwy before terminating at their destination.

DESTINATION HIGHLIGHTS
Great Orme Tramway, cable car and Bronze Age Copper Mine; promenade and beaches; Punch and Judy; amusement pier; Happy Valley Gardens; Victorian Extravaganza (May BH)

FREQUENCY OF TRAINS
1 per hour

47¼ MILES
1 HOUR 11 MINUTES

This Victorian electric tramway carries passengers from Llandudno to the top of the Great Orme.

Although now only a basic 1-platform terminus, Wrexham Central station was once a busy through station, with passenger services running southeast to Ellesmere and north to Bidston, at the top of the Wirral Peninsula. It was also a far-flung outpost of the Great Central Railway and, from 1923, the London & North Eastern Railway. Both routes were listed for closure in the 1963 'Beeching Report', but while the line to Ellesmere closed in 1962 the railway to Bidston was reprieved and operates today as the Borderlands Line. It is double track throughout apart from the short section between Wrexham General and Wrexham Central. All the stations are unstaffed and passenger facilities are minimal and modernistic!

Diesel trains for Bidston leave Wrexham Central and, after calling at Wrexham General (once named Exchange), head in a northerly direction into open countryside, serving stations at Gwersyllt, Cefn-y-Bedd, Caergwrle, Hope, Penyffordd, Buckley, Hawarden (with a fine latticework footbridge) and Shotton en route. Here, the Borderlands Line serves a high-level station while the low-level line is served by trains on the North Wales Coast Line from Chester. Continuing northwards from Shotton, trains cross the River Dee to call at Hawarden Bridge station before crossing from Wales into England. To the west of the line is the rail-linked Corus steelworks and UPM paper mill, which provide much freight traffic for the line. Now heading up the flat Wirral Peninsula, the railway serves stations at Neston, Heswall and Upton before arriving at remote Bidston where passengers for Liverpool need to change trains.

At the top of the Wirral Peninsula, the lines from West Kirby and New Brighton were electrified using third rail by the LMS in 1938. Merseyrail electric trains depart from Bidston in a southeasterly direction and, after calling at Birkenhead North (the main traction depot for Merseyrail) and Birkenhead Park, head underground to call at Conway Park and Birkenhead Hamilton Square. From here the railway dives under the river through the Mersey Tunnel before reaching the conveniently located Liverpool James Street station – opened in 1886 it is the oldest deep-level underground station in the world.

- **WREXHAM CENTRAL**
- WREXHAM GENERAL
- GWERSYLLT
- CEFN-Y-BEDD
- CAERGWRLE
- HOPE
- PENYFFORDD
- BUCKLEY
- HAWARDEN
- SHOTTON
- HAWARDEN BRIDGE
- NESTON
- HESWALL
- UPTON
- **BIDSTON**
- BIRKENHEAD NORTH
- BIRKENHEAD PARK
- CONWAY PARK
- BIRKENHEAD HAMILTON SQUARE
- **LIVERPOOL JAMES STREET**

DESTINATION HIGHLIGHTS
Waterfront, Pier Head and Albert Docks; Museum of Liverpool; Merseyside Maritime Museum; International Slavery Museum; Tate Liverpool; The Beatles Story; Walker Art Gallery, World Museum; 2 modern cathedrals; Mathew Street Music Festival (August); former homes of John Lennon and Sir Paul McCartney (NT)

FREQUENCY OF TRAINS
1 per hour (Mon-Sat)
1 every 2 hours (Sun)

32½ MILES
1 HOUR 25 MINUTES (M-SA)
1 HOUR 54 MINUTES (SUN)

A dramatic bird's-eye view of Liverpool's waterfront on the banks of the Mersey Estuary.

MANCHESTER PICCADILLY ●
LEVENSHULME ○
HEATON CHAPEL ○
STOCKPORT ○
DAVENPORT ○
WOODSMOOR ○
HAZEL GROVE ○
MIDDLEWOOD ○
DISLEY ○
NEW MILLS NEWTOWN ○
FURNESS VALE ○
WHALEY BRIDGE ○
CHAPEL-EN-LE-FRITH ○
DOVE HOLES ○
BUXTON ●

Our day trip to the Victorian spa town of Buxton starts at Manchester Piccadilly station. One of the busiest stations in the UK, modern Piccadilly has been rebuilt several times but still retains its 1860 Grade II-listed train shed. Diesel trains for Buxton depart in a southeasterly direction, threading through Manchester's sprawling suburbs past Ardwick Junction and Slade Lane Junction before calling at Levenshulme station. This is one of many stations on this line that have seen an enormous increase in passenger usage over the last ten years. Heaton Chapel station is next, followed by Stockport – this ugly modern station is set high above the Mersey Valley and is best known for its confusing signs for pedestrians. South of Stockport, Buxton-line trains branch off at Edgeley Junction to call at Davenport, Woodsmoor and Hazel Grove.

Hazel Grove is the limit of the 25 kV AC overhead electric working from Manchester. It is also the junction for the Hope Valley line to Sheffield via the new Chord Line, which opened in 1986, and the 2-mile 346-yd Disley Tunnel. Buxton-bound trains branch off at Hazel Grove to start the climb up into the hills, first calling at Middlewood – this is one of only a handful of stations in the country which has no road access and is used mainly by walkers on the Middlewood Trail. Still climbing, the scenic railway heads eastwards along the Goyt Valley to Disley before joining company with the Peak Forest Canal to reach New Mills Newtown. Here in the valley below, the Hope Valley line heads eastwards to Chinley and Sheffield. Continuing its climb, the railway winds round through Furness Vale and Whaley Bridge then passes alongside Combs Reservoir to Chapel-en-le-Frith. The final, curving climb up through Eaves and Barmoor Clough tunnels takes trains to Dove Holes station (183 ft below is the long Dove Holes tunnel on the freight-only line from Chinley to Peak Forest) and the summit at Bibbington before terminating at Buxton station.

DESTINATION HIGHLIGHTS
Poole's Cavern; St Anne's Well; Devonshire Dome; Pavilion Gardens; Pump Room and Crescent; Grinlow Tower (Solomon's Temple); Museum & Art Gallery; Buxton Festival and Fringe (July); Real Ale Trail

FREQUENCY OF TRAINS
1 per hour

25¾ MILES
1 HOUR

A Manchester to Buxton train climbs into the hills near Chapel-en-le-Frith.

Our day trip across (and through) the Pennines to Bradford – the world's first UNESCO City of Film – begins at Manchester Victoria Station. Caldervale Line trains for Bradford first head east up to Miles Platting Junction before branching off through Manchester's northern suburbs to reach Rochdale Castleton station. Closely following the course of the Rochdale Canal, the railway enters the narrowing Roch Valley through Littleborough before plunging beneath the Pennine Moors in the 1-mile 1,125-yds Summit Tunnel. Dug entirely by navvies using basic tools, it was the longest railway tunnel in the world at the time of its completion in 1841. It was closed for eight months in 1984 following a serious fire caused by a derailed train of loaded petrol tankers.

After emerging from the tunnel into West Yorkshire, the railway resumes its company with the Rochdale Canal, passing through Winterbutlee Tunnel to reach Walsden and then Todmorden. East of the station, at Hall Royd Junction, the Copy Pit line from Burnley joins from the west. From here, the scenic Caldervale Line heads east, burrowing through 4 tunnels along the narrow Calder Valley, keeping close company with road, river and canal through Hebden Bridge's restored station and Mytholmroyd before arriving at Sowerby Bridge. Here, the Rochdale Canal links up with the Calder & Hebble Navigation while the line to Bradford branches off to the north at Milner Royd Junction, passing through Bank House Tunnel and Dryclough Junction to reach Halifax's island platform station.

The heavily engineered line through the hills from Halifax to Bradford opened in 1850. On leaving the station trains burrow through Beacon Hill Tunnel, Hipperholme Tunnel, Wyke Tunnel and Bowling Tunnel before reaching Bradford Interchange station. This combined railway, bus and coach station is conveniently located close to the city centre.

- **MANCHESTER VICTORIA**
- MOSTON
- MILLS HILL
- CASTLETON
- ROCHDALE
- SMITHY BRIDGE
- LITTLEBOROUGH
- WALSDEN
- TODMORDEN
- HEBDEN BRIDGE
- MYTHOLMROYD
- SOWERBY BRIDGE
- HALIFAX
- **BRADFORD INTERCHANGE**

DESTINATION HIGHLIGHTS
14th-century Bolling Hall Museum (by bus); 15th/16th-century cathedral; National Media Museum; Bradford Industrial Museum (inc railway exhibits); Italianate Lister Mills; fine Victorian architecture (City Hall, Wool Exchange; Little Germany); City Park and Mirror Pool; Peel Park

FREQUENCY OF TRAINS
2 per hour (Mon-Sat)
1 per hour (Sun)

40 MILES
1 HOUR 5 MINUTES

The imposing Victorian Gothic Town Hall in Bradford, West Yorkshire.

MANCHESTER VICTORIA
ASHTON-UNDER-LYNE
STALYBRIDGE
MOSSLEY
GREENFIELD
MARSDEN
SLAITHWAITE
HUDDERSFIELD
DEIGHTON
MIRFIELD
RAVENSTHORPE
DEWSBURY
BATLEY
MORLEY
COTTINGLEY
LEEDS

DESTINATION HIGHLIGHTS
Trinity shopping complex;
Fairburn Ings RSPB reserve;
Roundhay Park; Leeds City
Museum; Abbey House
Museum; Armley Mills
Museum (Industrial Museum
with railway exhibits); Thwaite
Mills Watermill Museum;
Thackray Museum; Royal
Armouries Museum; Leeds Art
Gallery; Clarence Docks;
Millennium Square; Mandela
Gardens; Leeds Minster;
Middleton Railway

FREQUENCY OF TRAINS
3 per hour (Mon-Sat)
1 per hour (Sun)

42¾ MILES
1 HOUR 35 MINUTES

OPPOSITE: *Full moon over
Clarence Dock and the Royal
Armouries Museum in Leeds.*

Our day trip across (and under) the Pennines to the city of Leeds begins at Manchester Victoria station. Opened by the Manchester & Leeds Railway in 1844, the station was considerably enlarged in 1909 and, until 1969 when the adjacent Exchange station closed, was home to the longest platform in Europe. Diesel trains for Leeds follow the original route of the Manchester & Leeds Railway, heading east up to Miles Platting Junction where the Caldervale Line (see page 137) to Sowerby Bridge branches off to the north. Continuing eastwards, Ashton-under-Lyne's island platform station is the first stop, followed by Stalybridge station with its award-winning buffet bar. From here, trains head north up the narrowing Tame Valley, paralleling the Huddersfield Narrow Canal through Mossley and Greenfield before burrowing under the Pennines at Diggle through the 3-mile 60-yds Standedge Tunnel. This double-track tunnel was opened in 1894 to replace 2 earlier single-bore tunnels, which opened in 1848 and 1871 respectively. It is the fifth-longest railway tunnel in the UK and parallels the Huddersfield Narrow Canal's tunnel that opened in 1811.

Emerging from the tunnel into West Yorkshire, trains reach Marsden, the jumping-off point for a local exhibition in the former goods shed and the Huddersfield Narrow Canal's exhibition near the tunnel mouth. From Marsden the railway heads down the Colne Valley, keeping close company with the canal, through Slaithwaite, Gledholt Tunnel, Springwood Junction (for the single-track Penistone Line – see page 142) and Huddersfield Tunnel to reach Huddersfield station. Built in neo-classical style in the mid-19th century, this magnificent Grade I-listed building features two pubs. From here, trains for Leeds continue to follow the Colne Valley through Deighton before joining the Calder Valley near Mirfield. The station here is also served by the Caldervale Line, which joins from the west at Heaton Lodge Junction.

Eastwards from Mirfield, Leeds-bound trains branch off northwards at Thornhill LNW Junction and climb away from the Calder Valley through Ravensthorpe, Dewsbury and Batley before burrowing through the 1-mile 1,609-yds Morley Tunnel. Trains emerge from the tunnel into Morley station, which has seen a remarkable 600% rise in patronage over the last ten years. Still heading north, we follow a long S-shaped route through Cottingley before approaching Leeds through a maze of junctions. The 17-platform station is built over the River Aire and is the busiest in the North of England. With its bus interchange, it is conveniently located for visits to the thriving city centre.

MANCHESTER VICTORIA	●
WOODLANDS ROAD	○
ABRAHAM MOSS	○
CRUMPSALL	○
BOWKER VALE	○
HEATON PARK	○
PRESTWICH	○
BESSES O' TH' BARN	○
WHITEFIELD	○
RADCLIFFE	○
BURY INTERCHANGE	●
BURY BOLTON STREET	●
SUMMERSEAT	○
RAMSBOTTOM	○
IRWELL VALE	○
RAWTENSTALL	●

DESTINATION HIGHLIGHTS
Bury: market; Burrs Country
Park; art museum;
ruined 13th century castle;
Lancashire Fusiliers Museum;
Transport Museum;
East Lancashire Railway.
Rawtenstall: Fitzpatrick's
Herbal Health Bar; Whitaker
Park for Rossendale Museum
& Art Gallery

FREQUENCY
Manchester to Bury:
5 trams per hour
Bury to Rawtenstall:
4-6 trains per day (Wed-Sun,
Mar-Sept; Sat-Sun Jan-Nov)

17¾ MILES
30 + 30 MINUTES

*'Duke of Gloucester' speeds
along the Irwell Valley on the
East Lancashire Railway.*

Our day trip to the Irwell Valley in Lancashire involves journeys on two railway routes that were both closed and then reopened – one as part of the Manchester Metrolink light rail system and the other as a heritage railway.

The first 9¾ miles from Manchester to Bury is along the former Lancashire & Yorkshire Railway's route that was electrified using high-voltage DC collected through a side-contact third rail in 1916. The line was closed in 1991 when it was converted to form part of the Manchester Metrolink, reopening a year later. Trams for Bury depart from Manchester Victoria in an easterly direction through Collyhurst Tunnel then head north through Queens Road, junction for Oldham and Rochdale and the Metrolink Depot. After calling at Woodlands Road, Abraham Moss, Crumpsall and Bowker Vale trams head through Heaton Park Tunnel to arrive at Heaton Park station. Nearby Heaton Park is one of the largest municipal parks in Europe – its 600 acres are the grounds of 18th-century Grade I-listed neoclassical country house. Features include a golf course, tennis courts, boating lake, woodlands, ornamental gardens, an observatory and a restored tramway. From Heaton Park station, trams head northwest, calling at Prestwich, Besses o' th' Barn, Whitefield and Radcliffe before terminating at Bury Interchange.

Mainly steam hauled, heritage trains for Rawtenstall depart northwards from nearby Bury Bolton Street station. The railway also extends eastwards to Heywood. Closely following the River Irwell, the line heads through Bury Tunnel and then crosses a loop of the river before arriving at Summerseat station. Continuing northwards up the valley, it crosses the river on Brooksbottom Viaduct then burrows through Brooksbottom and Nuttall tunnels to arrive at Ramsbottom station where there is a passing loop. Continuing north, the railway crosses from Greater Manchester into Lancashire and continues up the narrowing valley to call at Irwell Vale before terminating at Rawtenstall.

Ribble Valley Line trains for Clitheroe depart from Manchester Victoria station in a southwesterly direction and, after calling at Salford Central and Salford Crescent, branch off the Wigan line at Windsor Bridge Junction to head through Manchester's northeastern suburbs, passing through little-used Clifton station (one train a day in each direction) to Kearsley then through the 295-yd twin-bore Farnworth Tunnel to Farnworth station. Still heading northeast, trains call at Moses Gate before arriving at Bolton Interchange (formerly Trinity Street station). From here Clitheroe-bound trains branch off the Horwich and Preston line to climb due north along a single-track section to Hal I' Th' Wood station (for a local museum). The line becomes double track again until the next station, Bromley Cross where it reverts to single as far as Blackburn,

From Bromley Cross the railway, still climbing into the hills, eventually reaches open countryside, skirting Jumbles Reservoir before reaching Entwistle station (request stop). Just north of here we reach the summit of the line at Sough before descending through the 1-mile 255-yd Sough Tunnel through the East Lancashire hills to reach Darwen, where there is a passing loop. From here, the railway continues northwards, snaking beneath the M65 and meeting the Preston to Burnley line at Bolton Junction before arriving at Blackburn. The station here features a restored late 19th-century building and a long piece of stainless steel artwork by Stephen Charnock.

From Blackburn, trains head west through Blackburn Tunnel then branch northwards at Daisyfield Junction before calling at Ramsgreave & Wilpshire, Langho (staggered platforms) and Whalley, where the line crosses the River Calder on a 48-arch viaduct. The final stretch of this journey carries us up the Ribble Valley to the award-winning interchange station at Clitheroe. This last section from Blackburn lost its passenger service in 1962 but was reopened in 1990.

- **MANCHESTER VICTORIA**
- SALFORD CENTRAL
- SALFORD CRESCENT
- CLIFTON
- KEARSLEY
- FARNWORTH
- MOSES GATE
- BOLTON
- HALL I' TH' WOOD
- BROMLEY CROSS
- ENTWISTLE
- DARWEN
- BLACKBURN
- RAMSGREAVE & WILPSHIRE
- LANGHO
- WHALLEY
- **CLITHEROE**

DESTINATION HIGHLIGHTS
Norman castle; Sausage Day (5 January); Clitheroe Food Festival (early August); original 1894 station building now the Platform Gallery; rail trips along Ribble Valley to Hellifield (summer Sundays)

FREQUENCY OF TRAINS
1 per hour

35¼ MILES
1 HOUR 17 MINUTES

The meandering River Ribble near Clitheroe, Lancashire

HUDDERSFIELD
LOCKWOOD
BERRY BROW
HONLEY
BROCKHOLES
STOCKSMOOR
SHEPLEY
DENBY DALE
PENISTONE
SILKSTONE COMMON
DODWORTH
BARNSLEY INTERCHANGE
WOMBWELL
ELSECAR
CHAPELTOWN
MEADOWHALL
INTERCHANGE
SHEFFIELD

This day trip to the city of Master Cutlers starts at Huddersfield's superbly restored 1850 station, described as one of the finest early railway stations in Britain. Our journey is along the highly scenic route via Penistone, which abounds with viaducts and tunnels and has survived several closure threats. Supported by the Penistone Line Partnership, the single-track railway across the Pennines has become famous for its jazz and real-ale trains. Diesel trains head west out of Huddersfield station and, after passing through Huddersfield Tunnel, branch off southwards at Springwood Junction, crossing the Colne Valley on a large viaduct and passing through Lockwood Tunnel to Lockwood station. Still heading south, trains then cross the River Holme on another large viaduct to reach Berry Brow station before passing through Robin Hood Tunnel to arrive at Honley.

Beyond Honley, the railway turns east to serve Brockholes then through Thurstonland Tunnel to Stocksmoor, where the line becomes double-track as far as Clayton West Junction. Trains call at Shepley station en route, the jumping-off point for the narrow-gauge Kirklees Light Railway to Clayton West. Reverting to single track again, the railway heads south at Clayton West Junction, through Cumberworth Tunnel to Denby Dale. South of here the line is carried high above the village on an impressive viaduct before passing through Wellhouse Tunnel to reach Penistone. Once the junction for the electrified line to Manchester via Woodhead, the station here is now a passing loop.

From Penistone the railway heads due east along a stretch of line that was reopened in 1983, passing through Oxspring Tunnel en route then serving Silkstone Common and Dodworth before arriving at Barnsley's modern interchange station. The rest of the journey south to Sheffield is along the former Midland Railway route, now known as the Hallam Line. Intermediate stations are at Wombwell, Elsecar, Chapeltown and Meadowhall Interchange.

DESTINATION HIGHLIGHTS
restored Sheffield Midland
station; 200 parks, woodlands
and public gardens; Peace
Gardens; Millennium
Galleries; Winter Gardens;
Sheffield Supertram system;
The Wheel; Kelham Island
Museum; Castle Market;
Weston Park Museum and
Mappin Art Gallery; Botanical
Gardens; cathedral; Abbeydale
Industrial Hamlet

FREQUENCY OF TRAINS
1 per hour

37 MILES
1 HOUR 15 MINUTES

*The imposing 29-arch,
98-ft-high Penistone Viaduct
was built in 1850.*

Our day trip to Manchester starts at Sheffield's only station. Although opened by the Midland Railway in 1870, its wonderful stone façade was added in 1905 and has been fully restored in recent years, along with the station approach in Sheaf Square. A new real ale pub was opened in the building in 2009 and has since won several awards. Trans-Pennine diesel trains for Manchester leave the station in a southwesterly direction following the Midland main line to Dore Station Junction, where the scenic Hope Valley Line is taken westwards through Dore & Totley station before burrowing through Totley Tunnel. Over 3½ miles long, the tunnel was completed in 1893 and is the third longest in the UK.

Emerging from the tunnel, the railway enters the Peak District National Park and follows the Hope Valley in a northwesterly direction through Grindleford, Bamford and Hope stations. This highly scenic route is also heavily used by freight trains, some of which originate from the large cement works at Earles Sidings near Hope. From here, the line heads northwards up the Noe Valley before turning west along the beautiful Vale of Edale – here, overlooked by the Pennine peaks of Kinder Scout to the north and Mam Tor to the south, the little station of Edale is the jumping-off point for the start of the Pennine Way Long Distance Path. West of Edale, the railway burrows through the 2-mile 182-yd Cowburn Tunnel to emerge at Chinley Junction (for the freight-only line to Peak Forest) before calling at Chinley station's island platform.

Beyond Chinley, fast trains take the direct route to Stockport and Manchester via the 2-mile 346-yd Disley Tunnel. Slower trains follow the Goyt Valley, calling at New Mills Central, Strines (on Sundays), Marple and Romiley, continuing via Reddish North. Both routes join at Ardwick Junction for the final approach into Manchester's centrally located Piccadilly station.

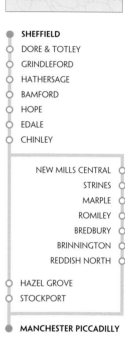

- SHEFFIELD
- DORE & TOTLEY
- GRINDLEFORD
- HATHERSAGE
- BAMFORD
- HOPE
- EDALE
- CHINLEY

- NEW MILLS CENTRAL
- STRINES
- MARPLE
- ROMILEY
- BREDBURY
- BRINNINGTON
- REDDISH NORTH

- HAZEL GROVE
- STOCKPORT

- MANCHESTER PICCADILLY

DESTINATION HIGHLIGHTS
Museum of Science & Industry; Museum of Transport; Salford Quays; Town Hall; Imperial War Museum North; Manchester Museum; Manchester Art Gallery; Whitworth Art Gallery; Manchester Jewish Museum; Lowry Art Centre (Salford Quays); Canal Street; National Football Museum; Manchester United Museum

FREQUENCY OF TRAINS
2+ per hour

46 MILES
51-78 MINUTES

The Sheffield to Manchester railway passes through the Peak District National Park at Edale.

LIVERPOOL CENTRAL	●
MOORFIELDS	○
SANDHILLS	○
BANK HALL	○
BOOTLE ORIEL ROAD	○
BOOTLE NEW STRAND	○
SEAFORTH & LITHERLAND	○
WATERLOO	○
BLUNDELLSANDS & CROSBY	○
HALL ROAD	○
HIGHTOWN	○
FORMBY	○
FRESHFIELD	○
AINSDALE	○
HILLSIDE	○
BIRKDALE	○
SOUTHPORT	●

This day trip to Southport takes in a journey along Merseyrail's Northern Line, which was electrified by the Lancashire & Yorkshire Railway using 750V DC third rail as long ago as 1904. Although listed for closure in the 1963 'Beeching Report', the line was subsequently reprieved and now sees passenger usage in the millions every year.

Electric trains depart from Liverpool Central underground station and head north, calling at Moorfields before emerging into the city's suburbs and calling at Sandhills's island platform station, which overlooks the River Mersey and Liverpool Docks. At Sandhills Junction, north of the station, the Kirkby/Ormskirk line branches off to the northeast while Southport-bound trains head off in a northwesterly direction, calling at Bank Hall, Bootle Oriel Road, Bootle New Strand and Seaforth & Litherland, which was also served by the Liverpool Overhead Railway (or 'Dockers' Umbrella') from 1905 until its untimely closure in 1956. Continuing northwestwards towards the coast, the line serves stations at Waterloo, Blundellsands & Crosby and Hall Road (scene of major railway accidents in 1905, 1961 and 1977), not far from the coastline and the vast sand dune systems that are a feature of this coastline up to Southport.

From Hall Road the railway heads north into open countryside, though never far from the coast, through Hightown to the commuter town of Formby. Here, the beaches, sand dunes and nature reserves, managed by the National Trust, are a popular destination for day trippers in the summer months. After Formby, trains call at Freshfields before heading northeast, paralleling the sand dunes and their nature reserves in a dead-straight line to Southport, calling at the seaside resort village of Ainsdale, Hillside (for the Royal Birkdale golf course) and Birkdale, where the station still retains its attractive Victorian glass platform canopies. Southport station was opened as Chapel Street station in 1851 and is conveniently located in the town centre and a short distance from the broad, sandy beach and seafront attractions.

DESTINATION HIGHLIGHTS
Lord Street; Southport Pier and Pier Tramway; extensive beach and sand dunes; Marine Lake; Southport Air Show (September); Southport Flower Show (late August); New Pleasureland; Model Railway Village; Lawnmower Museum

FREQUENCY OF TRAINS
4 per hour

19 MILES
45 MINUTES

A tramway carries visitors along Southport Pier – at 1,216 yds, the second-longest pier in Britain.

Our day trip to Blackpool starts at Liverpool Lime Street station and follows the original route of the Liverpool & Manchester Railway, opened in 1830, eastwards from Crown Street as far as Huyton. Lime Street station is a rather grand affair, completed in 1849 with an overall single curved glass roof and fronted by the former North Western Hotel, built in the style of a French chateau. Diesel trains for Blackpool head east out of the station and begin their climb through a dramatic series of deep cuttings and 3 tunnels to reach Edge Hill. Here the electrified line to Runcorn and Crewe heads off southwards while Blackpool-bound trains continue eastwards along this historic route through Wavertree, Olive Mount Junction, Broad Green and Roby to arrive at Huyton. East of the station, trains branch off in a northeasterly direction at Huyton Junction on a route that was listed for closure in the 'Beeching Report', through Prescot, Eccleston Park and Thatto Heath to St Helens Central – the ultra-modern glass station building here makes reference to the town's world-famous company, Pilkington Glass.

Heading northeast from St Helens, the railway enters open countryside, serving Garswood and Bryn (with its quaint original station building) before joining the West Coast Main Line at Springs Branch Junction. After a stop at Wigan North Western station, trains head north along the main line, serving stations at Euxton Balshaw Lane and Leyland en route before crossing the River Ribble to reach Preston. This busy and spacious station features a grand double-span glass overall roof supported on decorated cast-iron columns dating from 1880.

Trains for Blackpool head north out of Preston and soon branch off westwards from the WCML at Fylde Junction. From here the railway cuts across through Salwick and Kirkham & Wesham (for the Blackpool South branch) then heads northwest to reach the flat coastal plain known as the Fylde. After serving Poulton-le-Fylde (once the junction for Fleetwood), the railway loops southwards through Layton before arriving at Blackpool's modern, 8-platform, North station, conveniently located for the town's many famous attractions.

- **LIVERPOOL LIME STREET**
- EDGE HILL
- WAVERTREE TECHNOLOGY PARK
- BROAD GREEN
- ROBY
- HUYTON
- PRESCOT
- ECCLESTON PARK
- THATTO HEATH
- ST HELENS CENTRAL
- GARSWOOD
- BRYN
- WIGAN NORTH WESTERN
- EUXTON BALSHAW LANE
- LEYLAND
- PRESTON
- SALWICK
- KIRKHAM & WESHAM
- POULTON-LE-FYLDE
- LAYTON
- **BLACKPOOL NORTH**

DESTINATION HIGHLIGHTS
beach and promenade; 3 piers; Sandcastle Water Park; Stanley Park; Blackpool Tower; Illuminations (late Aug-early Nov); Pleasure Beach; Madame Tussauds Waxworks; Sea Life Centre; Zoo; Winter Gardens; Model Village & Gardens; street tramway to Fleetwood

FREQUENCY OF TRAINS
1 per hour

50½ MILES
1 HOUR 30 MINUTES

Blackpool's long seafront with the North Pier, sea wall and iconic Blackpool Tower.

LEEDS ●
SHIPLEY ○
SALTAIRE ○
BINGLEY ○
CROSSFLATTS ○
KEIGHLEY ●
INGROW WEST ○
DAMEMS ○
OAKWORTH ○
HAWORTH ○
OXENHOPE ●

This day trip from Leeds begins at the city's busy 17-platform junction station, much of which is supported on Victorian brick-vaulted arches over the River Aire. Although it has been rebuilt and enlarged many times in the past, predicted growth in passenger traffic will mean further expansion in the future.

Electric trains for Keighley head out of the station in a northwesterly direction, negotiating Leeds West Junction, Whitehall Junction, Armley Junction and Apperley Junction en route before arriving at Shipley. The junction for Bradford Forster Square, the station here is one of only two with triangular platform layouts in the UK. Trains for Keighley continue westwards up the Aire Valley, closely following the Leeds & Liverpool Canal, to Saltaire, jumping off point for Sir Titus Salt's mid 19th-century model village and mills that are now a UNESCO World Heritage Site. Following closure in 1965 the station was reopened in 1984 and still has traditional wooden platforms. Next stop is Bingley, approached through Bingley Tunnel, followed by Crossflats (opened in 1982) and then Keighley where passengers for the Keighley & Worth Valley Railway change trains.

One of the earliest preserved railways in the UK, the branch line to Oxenhope closed in 1962 but was reopened by a group of preservationists in 1967. The line became famous as the location for the filming of 'The Railway Children' starring Jenny Agutter and Bernard Cribbins, released in 1970.

Trains, mostly steam hauled, leave Keighley station's branch platforms to begin their 5-mile climb up the scenic Worth Valley. First stop is at Ingrow West, for the Vintage Carriages Trust Museum and the Bahamas Locomotive Society Museum. Continuing up the valley, trains plunge through Ingrow Tunnel to arrive at tiny Damems station, the smallest standard-gauge station in the UK. The next stop is Oakworth where the gas-lit station has been restored to its early 20th-century appearance. The penultimate stop is at Haworth station (jumping-off point for the Brontë Museum), which has been restored as it would have appeared in BR days. Trains terminate at Oxenhope, home to the Heritage Lottery-funded Exhibition Shed.

DESTINATION HIGHLIGHTS
ride on Keighley & Worth Valley railway; Vintage Carriage Trust Museum (Ingrow); 'Railway Children' film locations; Brontë Museum (Haworth); Oxenhope Straw Race (July); Railway Museum (Oxenhope); Beer & Music Festival (Oxenhope, late October)

FREQUENCY OF TRAINS
Leeds to Keighley:
3-4 per hour (Mon-Sat)
2 per hour (Sun)
Keighley to Oxenhope:
5-7 per day (June-Sept; Sat-Sun+BHs, Feb to Dec)

22 MILES
25 + 25 MINUTES

A vintage steam train climbs out of Keighley towards Oxenhope on the Keighley & Worth Valley Railway.

With an early departure from Leeds, a good day's walking on Ilkley Moor can be enjoyed on this day trip. Wharfedale Line electric trains head west out of the city's busy station and, after negotiating Leeds West Junction and Whitehall Junction, head up the Aire Valley in close company with the Leeds & Liverpool Canal to Apperley Junction. Here, Ilkley-bound trains branch off northwards from the main line – the first few miles are single track as far as Springs Junction, where it reverts to double track. Continuing northwards, trains pass through Esholt Junction, where the electrified single line from Bradford via Shipley joins from the southwest, then through Greenbottom Tunnel before arriving at Guiseley station.

Heading northwest from Guiseley, trains serve Menston, where the derelict station building has been restored and brought back into use, before entering the Wharfe Valley at Burley-in-Wharfedale. The station here was once the junction for the line to Leeds via Otley and Arhington until its closure in 1965. Continuing up the valley, trains call at Ben Rhydding station, which until the First World War was used mainly by clients visiting the nearby hydropathic establishment. From here, trains continue westwards before terminating at Ilkley's 2-platform station – Ilkley Moor and the famous Cow and Calf Rocks are but a short walk from here. The railway once continued up the valley to Bolton Abbey and Skipton but became a victim of the 'Beeching Axe' when it was closed in 1965. Today, the section from Bolton Abbey to Embsay operates as the Embsay & Bolton Abbey Steam Railway.

- **LEEDS**
- GUISELEY
- MENSTON
- BURLEY-IN-WHARFEDALE
- BEN RHYDDING
- **ILKLEY**

DESTINATION HIGHLIGHTS
walks to Ilkley Moor and Cow and Calf Rocks; start of Dales Way Long Distance Path; 18th-century White Wells spa bath; Ilkley Pool & Lido; 18th-century Flying Duck pub and microbrewery

FREQUENCY OF TRAINS
2 per hour (Mon-Sat)
1 per hour (Sun)

18¾ MILES
28 MINUTES

The Cow and Calf Rocks on Ilkley Moor and, below, the town of Ilkley in Wharfedale.

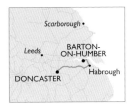

DONCASTER
KIRK SANDALL
HATFIELD & STAINFORTH
THORNE SOUTH
CROWLE
ALTHORPE
SCUNTHORPE
BARNETBY
HABROUGH
ULCEBY
THORNTON ABBEY
GOXHILL
NEW HOLLAND
BARROW HAVEN
BARTON-ON-HUMBER

Our day trip to discover the hidden delights of Barton-on-Humber begins at Doncaster station, from where diesel trains head northeast away from the East Coast Main Line at Marshgate Junction. Our route takes us along a busy stretch of quadruple-track line that sees heavy freight traffic from Immingham Dock and the Corus Steelworks at Scunthorpe. Heading in a dead-straight line through Kirk Sandall Junction, where the freight-only line from Shireoaks joins from the south, trains serve Kirk Sandall and Hatfield & Stainforth – here, the freight-only line from Adwick Junction joins from the west. Just to the east, a major landslip from Hatfield Colliery's spoil tip disrupted rail services between Doncaster and Scunthorpe/Goole throughout 2013. With the line now reopened, trains head east through Thorne Junction (for the Goole line), paralleling the Sheffield & South Yorkshire Navigation across flat peatland to Thorne South, Crowle and Althorpe.

Continuing eastwards from Althorpe, trains soon cross the River Trent on the King George V Bridge before arriving at Scunthorpe – the present station here was opened by the LNER in 1928 to replace an earlier one located to the east. The giant Tata Steelworks complex to the south, which generates much freight traffic along this route, dominates the next stretch of our journey. At Barnetby, the line from Gainsborough joins from the southwest while the Lincoln line joins from the south. The next stop is Habrough, where passengers for Barton-on-Humber change trains.

Diesel trains depart in a westerly direction from Habrough and take the single-line spur northwards to Ulceby, where the freight-only line to Immingham Docks branches off to the east. Continuing northwards in a straight line across flat Lincolnshire farmland, the railway serves little-used Thornton Abbey station, Goxhill (original station building and traditional level crossing gates) and tiny New Holland station. From here the now single-track line heads west through Barrow Haven before arriving at Barton-on-Humber's basic one-platform terminus.

DESTINATION HIGHLIGHTS
Saxon Church of St Peter's;
Water's Edge Country Park,
Visitor Centre and Nature
Reserves; Humber Bridge
viewing point; Wilderspin
National School Museum;
Baysgarth House Museum;
start of Viking Way Long
Distance Path

FREQUENCY OF TRAINS
1 every 2 hours (Mon-Sat)

52½ MILES
2 HOURS 10 MINUTES
NB includes 50-70 minutes'
wait at Harbrough

A single-car diesel unit stands at Ulceby station.

This day trip to the former cotton-milling town of Colne is ideal for walkers out to enjoy the beautiful countryside of the surrounding hills. For much of its route the railway follows the Leeds & Liverpool Canal, which first brought prosperity to the area when it opened in 1816 – it also follows the route of the more modern M65 which ends at Colne.

Diesel trains for Colne depart southwards from Preston's grand overall-roofed station, first heading down the West Coast Main Line to Lostock Hall Junction. Here, trains for Colne branch off to the southwest before climbing eastwards to cross over the main line and arriving at Lostock Hall station – a large steam engine shed here was one of the last to close, on 4 August 1968. Next stop is Bamber Bridge where several level crossings are controlled from a signal box – the original 1846 station building here is a remarkable survivor albeit with a different use. Still heading east the railway burrows under the M6 and M65 link road to enter open countryside and, after passing through Pleasington (request stop), Cherry Tree and Mill Hill (island platform) stations, arrives at Blackburn's late 19th-century station.

Trains for Colne head northeast from Blackburn, through Blackburn Tunnel and Daisyfeld Junction (where the Clitheroe branch (see page 141) heads northwards), and calling at Rishton, Church & Oswaldtwistle and Accrington, where the station was rebuilt in 2011 as a prototype for sustainable energy use. Huncoat and Hapton request stops are next and from here the railway keeps close company with canal and motorway up the valley to Colne. At Rose Grove, where the line up to Copy Pit Summit and the Calder Valley heads off southeastwards, trains for Colne branch off northwards along the single-track route up the narrowing Pendle Valley to call at Burnley Barracks, Burnley Central, Brierfield and Nelson before terminating at Colne.

- **PRESTON**
- LOSTOCK HALL
- BAMBER BRIDGE
- PLEASINGTON
- CHERRY TREE
- MILL HILL
- BLACKBURN
- RISHTON
- CHURCH & OSWALDTWISTLE
- ACCRINGTON
- HUNCOAT
- HAPTON
- ROSE GROVE
- BURNLEY BARRACKS
- BURNLEY CENTRAL
- BRIERFIELD
- NELSON
- **COLNE**

DESTINATION HIGHLIGHTS
walks to Castercliffe Iron Age Fort, Boulsworth Hill, Noyna Hill and Weets Hill; Rhythm & Blues Festival (August Bank Holiday weekend); Colne Museum; grave of Wallace Hartley (bandmaster on the 'Titanic'); market; British in India Museum; Leeds & Liverpool Canal towpath

FREQUENCY OF TRAINS
1 per hour (Mon-Sat)
1 every 2 hours (Sun)

28 MILES
1 HOUR 10 MINUTES

Pendle Hill and its mantle of snow overlooks the town of Nelson, Lancashire.

Middlesbrough

YORK

LEEDS

Manchester

LEEDS ●
BURLEY PARK ○
HEADINGLEY ○
HORSFORTH ○
WEETON ○
PANNAL ○
HORNBEAM PARK ○
HARROGATE ○
STARBECK ○
KNARESBOROUGH ○
CATTAL ○
HAMMERTON ○
POPPLETON ○
YORK ●

There are two rail routes between Leeds and York but this one, via Harrogate and Knaresborough, is by far the most scenic – travel times are longer but it is well worth the detour. Diesel trains for Harrogate and York depart westwards from Leeds station, heading northwestwards at Armley Junction through Burley Park, Headingly (for Headingley Stadium and cricket ground) and Horsforth before passing through the 2-mile 241-yd Bramhope Tunnel. Opened in 1849, the tunnel was dug out by thousands of navvies and is noted for its Grade II-listed castellated north portal. After emerging from the tunnel, trains soon cross from West Yorkshire to North Yorkshire before burrowing through Wescoehill Tunnel to arrive at Weeton, jumping-off point for walks to Almscliffe Crags. Heading northeast through open countryside, the railway reaches Pannal where the former station building is now a pub.

After leaving Pannal, trains take a looping route to cross the Crimple Valley on a 31-arch viaduct before reaching Harrogate's southern suburbs at Hornbeam Park station and arriving at Harrogate shortly afterwards – the modern station here replaced the original Victorian structure demolished in the 'enlightened' 1960s. The 'main line' once extended northwards from here to Northallerton via Ripon but this became a victim of the 'Beeching Axe' in 1967. Today's route eastward to York was also threatened with closure but was fortunately reprieved.

From Harrogate the railway loops eastward to Starbeck and Knaresborough, whose 1851 station is approached by a fine viaduct across the River Nidd. The line becomes single track through Knareborough Tunnel to Cattal, where double track resumes as far as Hammerton, crossing the meandering River Nidd once more en route. Now heading in a straight line across a fairly flat rural landscape, trains reach Poppleton, where double track resumes for the final approach to the historic city of York via Skelton Junction on the East Coast Main Line.

DESTINATION HIGHLIGHTS
York Minster; York Castle Museum; city walls; narrow medieval streets (The Shambles); Yorkshire Museum; Museum Gardens; JORVIK Viking Centre; York Art Gallery; Richard III Museum; Treasurer's House (NT); National Railway Museum; boat trips on River Ouse; railway path to Selby

FREQUENCY OF TRAINS
1 per hour

38¾ MILES
1 HOUR 20 MINUTES

The railway viaduct over the River Nidd at Knaresborough.

Diesel trains for Morecambe depart from Skipton station in a northwesterly direction up the Aire Valley and follow the same route as the day trip to Carlisle (see page 152) as far as Settle Junction. From Settle Junction, trains climb away westwards from Ribblesdale to Giggleswick station before descending to the valley of the River Wenning – to the north are the wild Pennine fells of the Yorkshire Dales National Park while to the south looms the fell country of the Forest of Bowland. Threading through this dramatic scenery, trains continue down the valley to Clapham station, opened in 1849 by the 'little' North Western Railway as part of their ill-fated Anglo-Scottish route northwards via Ingleton. The next stop is Bentham, followed by Wennington – the station here was also the junction for the direct line to Lancaster (Green Ayre) and Morecambe until 1966. Passengers for Morecambe now have to take the longer route from Wennington along the former Furness & Midland Joint Railway via Carnforth.

Trains for Morecambe leave Wennington and head north out of the valley, burrowing through the hills in Melling Tunnel and crossing the Lune Valley to take a northerly loop into the Keer Valley. Now heading southwest, trains soon reach Carnforth station. After years of neglect, the station, famous as the outdoor location for the film 'Brief Encounter', has been refurbished and now houses a refreshment room and visitor centre. From here, trains head south along the West Coast Main Line to Lancaster, offering passengers a fleeting glimpse of Morecambe Bay at Hest Bank en route. At Lancaster, trains reverse direction to head north before branching off the WCML at Morecambe South Junction. After calling at Bare Lane, trains soon reach Morecambe's basic modern station – the restored Midland Railway Promenade station and seafront is a short walk from here.

- **SKIPTON**
- GARGRAVE
- HELLIFIELD
- LONG PRESTON
- GIGGLESWICK
- CLAPHAM
- BENTHAM
- WENNINGTON
- CARNFORTH
- LANCASTER
- BARE LANE
- **MORECAMBE**

DESTINATION HIGHLIGHTS
restored Morecambe Promenade station; taking tea in Art Deco Midland Hotel; promenade and extensive beaches; local potted shrimps; bird watching in Morecambe Bay

FREQUENCY OF TRAINS
4 per day

41½ MILES
1 HOUR 35 MINUTES

The long, sandy beach and promenade at Morecambe overlook the vast expanse of Morecambe Bay.

DESTINATION HIGHLIGHTS
11th-century Carlisle Castle;
King's Own Royal Border
Regiment Museum;
13th/17th-century cathedral;
Carlisle Citadel tours (July
and August); Tullie House
Museum & Art Gallery;
14th-century Guildhall
Museum

FREQUENCY OF TRAINS
1 per hour (Mon-Sat)
4 per day (Sun)

86¾ MILES
2 HOURS

OPPOSITE: *Haymaking time
near Dent Head Viaduct on the
Settle-Carlisle Line.*

This day trip to the border city of Carlisle is along what is arguably Britain's most scenic railway route, the Settle & Carlisle Line. Involving the construction of 22 viaducts and 14 tunnels across and through the remote Pennine Hills, the railway was a pinnacle of Victorian engineering achievement when it was opened by the Midland Railway in 1876. Costly to maintain and operate and with negligible intermediate traffic, the line was listed for closure in the 1963 'Beeching Report' – it not only survived this threat but also another in the 1980s. Today, it is a major freight and diversionary route, taking pressure off the congested West Coast Main Line, and local passenger traffic has increased, with 8 stations that closed in 1970 having been reopened. Manually operated signal boxes and semaphore signalling are still a feature along this superb route.

Diesel trains for Carlisle leave Skipton station in a northwesterly direction, following the Aire Valley through Gargrave before heading over the hills to join the Ribble Valley at Hellifield. Here, the restored station building is now privately owned – a feature of many of the stations along this line – while the freight-only line from Hellifield joins from the south. From here, trains head up the Ribble Valley into the Pennine Hills, calling at Long Preston before heading north at Settle Junction where the line to Carnforth heads off to the northwest. The next stop is at Settle, with its restored 'Derby Gothic'-style building, where the signal box has been restored as a visitor attraction by the Friends of the Settle-Carlisle Line.

From Settle, the railway climbs for 16 miles at a gradient of 1-in-100 to Blea Moor – during steam days this stretch of line was known to engine crews as 'the long drag' – passing through Stainforth Tunnel and calling at Horton-in-Ribblesdale and Ribblehead stations en route. From here, the railway crosses the iconic 24-arch Ribblehead Viaduct, burrows through the 1-mile 869-yd Blea Moor Tunnel and crosses Dent Head and Artengill viaducts to reach remote Dent station (the highest main-line station in England). Continuing to climb northwards through a series of tunnels, trains call at Garsdale to reach the summit of the line at Ais Gill (1,169 ft above sea level).

From Ais Gill the railway begins its descent down the Eden Valley, through Birkett Tunnel to Kirkby Stephen, crossing Smardale Viaduct and then cutting across the hills through Crosby Garrett and Helm tunnels to rejoin the valley south of Appleby. The station here still retains a booking office and is the busiest intermediate station on the line. From Appleby, the railway descends along the Eden Valley all the way to Carlisle. En route, trains pass through 6 more tunnels, calling at Langwathby (Brief Encounter Tea Room), Lazonby & Kirkoswald and Armathwaite, before joining the main line from Newcastle at Petterill Bridge Junction for the final mile into Carlisle's centrally located station.

Our day trip to the seaside resort of Scarborough begins at Hull's magnificent Paragon station terminus. As with many of the stations along this route, it was designed by the notable architect George Townsend Andrews for George Hudson's York & North Midland Railway and opened in 1848. It was considerably enlarged by the North Eastern Railway in 1904 and in recent times its 5–bay train shed with barrel-vaulted glass and iron roofs has been converted into an interchange station for trains, buses and coaches.

Yorkshire Coast Line trains for Scarborough head west out of the station before turning north through the city's suburbs to Cottingham station – G T Andrews's station, stationmaster's house and goods shed here are all Grade II-listed buildings. Heading northwards into open countryside, trains then call at Beverley, where the G T Andrews station with its elegant train shed has been superbly restored. The station was once the junction for the line to Market Weighton and York until closure in 1965. Continuing northwards on a fairly straight and level route, trains call at Arram, Hutton Cranswick and Driffield (the junction for trains to Malton until 1950 and to Selby until 1965).

From Driffield the railway turns to the northeast, avoiding the Yorkshire Wolds to the north, and heads towards the coast, calling at Nafferton (Grade II-listed Italianate station) before arriving at Bridlington. The original G T Andrews station here was replaced by a much larger structure in 1912 to cope with the huge increase in excursion trains that were then descending on the growing resort. The railway, now single track, then loops inland to Bempton and Hunmanby where it reverts to double track as far as Filey (the junction for the Butlins Holiday Camp branch, 1947-1977). Once more single track, it then heads west to Seamer Junction and joins the line from York for the final few miles to Scarborough's recently downsized Victorian terminus.

DESTINATION HIGHLIGHTS
ruined 11th-century castle;
Rotunda Museum; South Cliff
Promenade; South Bay Beach
and entertainment; North Bay
Beach; Peasholm Park;
Northstead Manor Gardens,
North Bay miniature railway
and boating lake; Central
Tramway and South Cliff Lift
(funicular railways);
Scarborough Mere;
Seafest (July); street art

FREQUENCY OF TRAINS
1-2 per hour (Mon-Sat)
4 per day (Sun)

53¾ MILES
1 HOUR 30 MINUTES

*Sunrise on Scarborough's
North Beach.*

Our day trip to the seaside at Scarborough starts at York's imposing curving glass-roofed station. Strategically located on the East Coast Main Line between London and Edinburgh, it was opened in 1877 and at the time was the largest railway station in the world.

Opened in 1845, the York to Scarborough railway was built by George Hudson's York & North Midland Railway and once served 14 intermediate stations. Apart from Malton and Seamer (near Scarborough), these were all closed in 1930 because increased traffic from holiday and excursion trains meant that the line was full to capacity and could not accommodate local stopping trains. Diesel trains for Scarborough leave York to the north, crossing the River Ouse and heading out into the city's northern suburbs through Haxby and Strensall (both these closed stations may reopen in the near future) before heading northeast across country to the first stop at Malton (21¼ miles from York). Trains pass through the long-closed stations of Flaxton and Barton Hill en route before following a scenic, meandering trail up the Derwent Valley, through the closed stations of Kirkham Abbey, Castle Howard and Huttons Ambo.

Malton station, once a busy junction served by lines from Ampleforth, Whitby and Driffield, lost its G T Andrews-designed overall roof in 1989 and is now reduced to just one platform, with a canopy that once stood on Whitby station. Trains for Scarborough head east from Malton, following the Derwent Valley through the long-closed stations of Rillington, Knapton, Heslerton, Weaverthorpe and Ganton before meeting the Yorkshire Coast Line (see page 154) at Seamer Junction. After calling at Seamer station, trains head north to Scarborough. Although retaining its grand façade, clock tower and part of its decorative overall roof, the terminus station here is much reduced in size compared to the heady days of the 1930s when trainloads of day trippers and holidaymakers would descend on the town in the summer months.

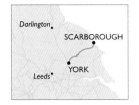

- ● **YORK**
- ○ MALTON
- ○ SEAMER
- ● **SCARBOROUGH**

DESTINATION HIGHLIGHTS
ruined 11th-century castle; Rotunda Museum; South Cliff Promenade; South Bay Beach and entertainment; North Bay Beach; Peasholm Park; Northstead Manor Gardens, North Bay miniature railway and boating lake; Central Tramway and South Cliff Lift (funicular railways); Scarborough Mere; Seafest (July); street art

FREQUENCY OF TRAINS
1 per hour

53¾ MILES
50 MINUTES

South Bay and castle, Scarborough, North Yorkshire.

MIDDLESBROUGH ●
MARTON ○
GYPSY LANE ○
NUNTHORPE ○
GREAT AYTON ○
BATTERSBY ○
KILDALE ○
COMMONDALE ○
CASTLETON MOOR ○
DANBY ○
LEALHOLM ○
GLAISDALE ○
EGTON ○
GROSMONT ○
SLEIGHTS ○
RUSWARP ○
WHITBY ●

Although listed for closure in the 1963 'Beeching Report', the highly scenic, 35-mile single-track Esk Valley Line between Middlesbrough and Whitby is a fortunate survivor. Diesel trains for Whitby depart from Middlesbrough station, which still retains its ornate Gothic-style frontage and original North Eastern Railway tiled map, but misses its overall roof which was destroyed by the Luftwaffe in 1942. Esk Valley Line trains head east to Guisborough Junction before branching southwards off the Saltburn line, through the town's suburbs to the first stop at Marton. The explorer and navigator Captain Cook was born in the village in 1728, subsequently moving to Great Ayton further down the line. Next stop is Gypsy Lane, followed by Nunthorpe – once the junction for the line to Guisborough – and Whitby via Staithes, which has a passing loop and a signal box that supervises all train movements on the branch.

From Nunthorpe the railway heads southeast into open countryside towards the Cleveland Hills, calling at Great Ayton before arriving at Battersby. Once the junction for the mineral line southwards to Rosedale and westwards to Picton, Battersby is a now a lonely railway outpost (complete with water towers) where trains for Whitby reverse direction. Heading east, the railway then enters the North Yorkshire Moors National Park and on this scenic stretch down the Esk Valley serves the pretty villages of Kildale (for the Cleveland Way), Commondale, Castleton Moor, Danby, Lealholm, Glaisdale, Egton, Grosmont (for North Yorkshire Moors Railway), Sleights and Ruswarp, before passing under Larpool Viaduct to arrive at Whitby. George Townsend Andrews designed the impressive station building here which, although reduced to just one platform, still retains its original North Eastern Railway tiled map.

DESTINATION HIGHLIGHTS
Whitby Abbey ruins; harbour; beaches; Old Town Hall; Church Stairs; Whitby Museum; whalebone arch and statue of Captain Cook; replica of Cook's 'Endeavour'; Whitby Lighthouse (Ling Hill); Whitby Regatta (August); Gothic Weekend; Bram Stoker Film Festival (October); Cleveland Way National Trail; North Yorkshire Moors Railway (see page 157)

North Yorkshire Moors Railway (see page 157)

FREQUENCY OF TRAINS
4 per day

35 MILES
1 HOUR 27 MINUTES

The ruins of Whitby Abbey overlook the North Sea from the East Cliff above this popular tourist destination.

This day trip along the North Yorkshire Moors Railway, through the wild grandeur of the North Yorkshire Moors National Park to the historic market town of Pickering, starts at Whitby station. The route is along one of the country's earliest railways, the Whitby & Pickering, which was engineered by George Stephenson and opened, initially using horse haulage, in 1836. Since closure between Grosmont and Pickering in 1965 it has been reopened as a heritage railway and has, deservedly, become one of the most popular in the UK. During the summer months three trains a day visit Whitby using the national rail network track from Grosmont.

From Whitby station, steam trains follow the north bank of the River Esk under the imposing brick-built Larpool Viaduct (until 1965 used by trains from Scarborough) along the Esk Valley Line through Ruswarp (where the Esk is crossed) and Sleights before arriving at Grosmont station. Here, NYMR trains for Pickering branch off southwards through Grosmont Tunnel and past the engine shed to begin the 1-in-49 climb up to Goathland – the station here is famous for its appearances in the 'Heartbeat' TV series and the Harry Potter films (as Hogsmeade station). Continuing to climb up through moorland, the railway reaches Lockton High Moor before starting the descent to Newton Dale Halt – from here there are way-marked walks across the moors and to the adjacent North Riding Forest Park. Continuing through the superb scenery of Newton Dale, trains reach Levisham station, whose peaceful location features a camping coach for hire and the studio of the NYMR's 'Artist in Residence'. Continuing its descent through Newton Dale, the railway finally arrives alongside Pickering Beck at Pickering – designed for George Hudson's York & North Midland Railway by G T Andrews in 1845, the restored station has recently had its overall timber roof reinstated. The town's other tourist attractions are close to hand.

- **WHITBY**
- RUSWARP
- SLEIGHTS
- GROSMONT
- GOATHLAND
- NEWTON DALE HALT
- LEVISHAM
- **PICKERING**

DESTINATION HIGHLIGHTS
ride on steam-operated North Yorkshire Moors Railway; visit film and TV locations at Goathland; moorland walks from Newtondale Halt; Artist in Residence studio at Levisham; *Pickering*: Pickering Castle, Beck Isle Museum, Jazz Festival (July)

FREQUENCY OF TRAINS
3 trains per day (Mar-Nov)

24½ MILES
1 HOUR 35 MINUTES

A steam train runs through the North Yorkshire Moors National Park near Levisham.

BISHOP AUCKLAND ●
SHILDON ○
NEWTON AYCLIFFE ○
HEIGHINGTON ○
NORTH ROAD ○
DARLINGTON ○
DINSDALE ○
TEES-SIDE AIRPORT ○
ALLENS WEST ○
EAGLESCLIFFE ○
THORNABY ○
MIDDLESBROUGH ○
SOUTH BANK ○
BRITISH STEEL REDCAR ○
REDCAR CENTRAL ○
REDCAR EAST ○
LONGBECK ○
MARSKE ○
SALTBURN ●

Much of this journey to the seaside follows the route of the Stockton & Darlington Railway, which opened in 1825. Listed for closure in the 1963 'Beeching Report', the branch line from Bishop Auckland was subsequently reprieved, but the other routes serving the town were not so lucky. Bishop Auckland is also the eastern terminus of the Weardale Railway to Stanhope and Eastgate, although no heritage trains currently use this line. Tees Valley Line trains for Saltburn depart in a southeasterly direction along the single-line section through Shildon Tunnel before arriving at Shildon, jumping-off point for the adjacent Locomotion Museum (a branch of the National Railway Museum at York). From here, the line becomes double track through Newton Aycliffe as far as Heighington, where it reverts to single track to Darlington, calling en route at historic North Road station, located next to the Darlington Railway Centre & Museum.

After calling at Darlington's impressive main-line Victorian station, trains for Saltburn head east to Dinsdale, Teesside Airport (served by two trains per week, only on Sundays, it is the least-used station in the UK), Allens West, Eaglescliffe, Thornaby and Middlesbrough.

Trains continue eastwards from the industrial town of Middlesbrough (also junction for the Esk Valley Line to Whitby) to Redcar Central, passing through the little-used British Steel Redcar station, set amidst an industrial landscape dominated by the giant Tata steelworks. The original train shed at Redcar Central is now home to a business park. From here the line follows the coast through Redcar East, Longbeck and Marske before arriving at the seaside resort of Saltburn. The restored ornate station building here is now a tourist information centre while the adjacent Zetland Hotel (once rail-connected with its own platform) is now home to luxury flats. Beyond Saltburn, the meandering coastal route to Skinningrove and Boulby is still used by freight trains.

DESTINATION HIGHLIGHTS
beach; promenade; surfing; restored station building; Saltburn Cliff Lift; Saltburn Pier; Saltburn Miniature Railway; Valley Gardens; Italian Gardens; coastal walks; Cleveland Way Long Distance Path

FREQUENCY OF TRAINS
1 per hour (Mon-Sat)
5 per day (Sun)

40¼ MILES
1 HOUR 25 MINUTES

RIGHT: *The superb long, sandy beach at Saltburn-by-the-Sea.*

OPPOSITE: *Saltburn-by-the-Sea's Victorian amusement pier and cliff railway.*

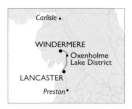

LANCASTER ●
OXENHOLME ●
LAKE DISTRICT
KENDAL ○
BURNESIDE ○
STAVELEY ○
WINDERMERE ●

Our journey to the Lake District for a boat trip on beautiful Lake Windermere begins at Lancaster station. From here, fast electric trains head north on the West Coast Main Line, offering brief views of Morecombe Bay at Hest Bank, before passing through Carnforth. Trains on this route no longer stop here but passengers can glimpse the station made famous in the 1945 film 'Brief Encounter' (still served by Furness Line trains – see page 161) and the engine shed and workshops of the West Coast Railway Company. Continuing northwards, the railway starts its climb into the Cumbrian Hills before arriving at Oxenholme station, where passengers change trains for the single-track Windermere branch.

Lakes Line diesel trains for Windermere leave Oxenholme in a northwesterly direction, calling at Kendal, Burneside, and Staveley stations en route. Most of this short scenic line lies in the Lake District National Park. Until 1973 it was double track and was once served by through trains from London Euston and Manchester as well as being a popular destination for excursion trains. Today, the branch ends at the basic single-platform modern terminus at Windermere, where the original station building and train shed have been incorporated into a supermarket. Located about a mile from Lake Windermere, the station is a hub for bus services to the lakeside attractions and steamer pier at Bowness-on-Windermere and other destinations in the Lake District.

DESTINATION HIGHLIGHTS
Windermere Steamboat Museum; Holehird Gardens; Mountain Goat bus day tours; cruises on Lake Windermere to Lakeside (for Lakeside & Haverthwaite Railway) and Ambleside; boat hire; The World of Beatrix Potter

FREQUENCY OF TRAINS
1+ per hour

50 MILES
45 MINUTES

Reflections in Lake Windermere – England's largest natural freshwater lake.

A day trip to Barrow-in-Furness might not be everyone's idea of fun, but the town and neighbouring Walney Island (reached by bus) have a surprising amount to offer. Furness Line diesel trains for Barrow head north from Lancaster station, following the West Coast Main Line briefly alongside Morecambe Bay at Hest Bank before branching off to call at Carnforth. The original station here was opened in 1846 and became famous as the outdoor location for the film 'Brief Encounter' in 1945. Following years of neglect the station buildings have been restored, with a visitor centre and Brief Encounter refreshment room. To the west of the station are the headquarters, engine shed and works of the West Coast Railway Company. Barrow trains head northwest from here, first calling at Silverdale (for Leighton Moss RSPB Reserve) before reaching Arnside station. Set alongside the tidal Kent Estuary, the station is a jumping-off point for birdwatchers visiting the Gait Barrow National Nature Reserve. From here trains head west, crossing the Kent Estuary on an impressive 1,558-ft-long, 50-span viaduct then hugging the shoreline of Morecambe Bay through Grange-over-Sands (restored 1864-station building) and Kents Bank. Here, the railway turns west across a small peninsula to Cark & Cartmel station – once used by the Dukes of Devonshire and their guests visiting nearby Holker Hall – then across the 49-span Leven Viaduct to arrive at Ulverston. Dating from 1873, the grand Furness Railway station here features an Italianate restored clock tower, graceful glass awnings and an unusual layout with an island platform that once served trains for the Lakeside branch.

From Ulverston, trains head southwest across the peninsula through Lindall Tunnel, Dalton and Dalton Tunnel to Dalton Junction, where the freight-only line used by nuclear flask trains for Sellafield heads north. Barrow-bound trains continue southwards through Roose then loop round to the northeast at Salthouse Junction (for nuclear flask trains from Ramsden Dock) before arriving at Barrow-in-Furness station.

- **LANCASTER**
- CARNFORTH
- SILVERDALE
- ARNSIDE
- GRANGE-OVER SANDS
- KENTS BANK
- CARK & CARTMEL
- ULVERSTON
- DALTON
- ROOSE
- **BARROW-IN-FURNESS**

DESTINATION HIGHLIGHTS
large indoor market; Dock Museum; Furness Abbey; Walney Island (by bus via Jubilee Bridge); Walney Island Nature Reserves; Earnse Bay beach (Walney Island); South Lakes Wild Animal Farm; Piel Island and Castle (by bus - not Sundays or Bank Holidays)

FREQUENCY OF TRAINS
1 per hour (Mon-Sat)
1 every 2 hours (Sun)

34¾ MILES
1 HOUR 5 MINUTES

A morning view of the shoreline at Arnside, Cumbria, with the Lake District Fells beyond.

Our journey to Eskdale starts at Barrow-in-Furness station, which was completely rebuilt following destruction by the Luftwaffe in 1941. From here, Cumbrian Coast Line diesel trains head north along the single-track line to Park South Junction, where the freight-only spur from Dalton Junction joins from the south and the line becomes double-track. The whole of the Cumbrian Coast Line south of Workington was listed for closure in the 'Beeching Report' but was reprieved, no doubt due to its strategic value in serving the Sellafield nuclear reprocessing plant. Trains carrying nuclear waste contained in secure flasks continue to arrive at Sellafield from many parts of the UK. The line still features signal boxes and semaphore signalling, and most of the stations are request stops.

Skirting the shore of the Duddon Estuary, trains first call at Askam before continuing northwards along the coast to windswept Kirkby-in-Furness and Foxfield. Dominated by the superb working signal box, the station here was once the junction for the Coniston branch. From Foxfield the railway loops round southwards, first crossing the River Duddon to serve stations at Green Road (award-winning gardens) and Millom (museum and visitor centre) then heading north, close to the coast, to Silecroft and Bootle before arriving at Ravenglass. Here, passengers for Eskdale change trains and make their way to the Ravenglass & Eskdale Railway's nearby station.

Originally opened in 1875 as a 3-ft-gauge line serving iron-ore mines in Eskdale, the 7-mile R&ER was converted to 15-in gauge in 1915. Today its miniature, mainly steam-hauled trains carry passengers up the valley from its well-kept terminus at Ravenglass, calling at Muncaster Mill, Irton Road, The Green, Fisherground and Beckfoot en route before terminating amidst stunning scenery at Dalegarth. From here, visitors can enjoy the peace, tranquillity and scenery of the valley, visit nearby Boot village (two pubs), explore Stanley Force waterfall or go hillwalking on the Fells.

DESTINATION HIGHLIGHTS
Ravenglass & Eskdale
miniature railway; railway
museum; Ratty Arms pub;
Muncaster Castle and World
Owl Trust; Roman Bath House
(Walls Castle); fell walking
from Dalegarth

FREQUENCY OF TRAINS
Barrow to Ravenglass:
1 per hour (Mon-Sat)
Ravenglass to Dalegarth:
2-14 per day (Mar-Nov)

36½ MILES
45 + 45 MINUTES

*'River Mite' hauls a train on the
15-in-gauge Ravenglass &
Eskdale Railway near
Irton Road station.*

This day trip to explore the scenic delights of Eskdale begins at Carlisle's busy junction station. Originally opened in 1847 and considerably expanded in 1875, the station is served by lines radiating out to Dumfries, Glasgow, Newcastle, Leeds, Preston and the Cumbrian Coast. Trains on the latter line depart southwards from Carlisle and soon branch off the West Coast Main Line to strike off in a southwesterly direction across fertile Cumbrian farmland, through Dalston (request stop), Wigton and Aspatria (request stop). The intermediate stations along this route to the coast still feature their original and distinctive station buildings, built for the opening of the Maryport & Carlisle Railway in 1841, and to the south, the peaks of the Cumbrian Mountains are ever-present. From Aspatria, the railway follows the Ellen Valley before reaching the coast at Maryport – sadly, the grand M&CR station buildings here have been replaced by boring shelters.

From Maryport, trains head south, hugging the coast to Flimby and crossing the River Derwent to Workington. Here, the original station has survived although its days as an important hub for iron-ore and steel trains and through coaches to and from Euston are now a distant memory. Continuing southwards along the coast, the railway heads through Harrington (request stop) and Parton to Whitehaven, where it becomes single track to Sellafield. After passing through Whitehaven Tunnel to Corkickle station, the railway heads inland briefly before reaching the coast again at St Bees (original 1860 station building). The most scenic part of this journey now follows, with the railway literally at the water's edge through Nethertown, Braystones and Sellafield (you can't miss the giant rail-connected nuclear reprocessing plant here!). From here, the line becomes double track, first serving Seascale then heading inland to Drigg, before crossing the Mite Estuary to arrive at Ravenglass where passengers for Eskdale should alight .

For details of the scenic journey up Eskdale see page 162.

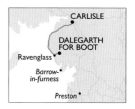

- **CARLISLE**
- DALSTON
- WIGTON
- ASPATRIA
- MARYPORT
- FLIMBY
- WORKINGTON
- HARRINGTON
- PARTON
- WHITEHAVEN
- CORKICKLE
- ST BEES
- NETHERTOWN
- BRAYSTONES
- SELLAFIELD
- SEASCALE
- DRIGG
- **RAVENGLASS**
- MUNCASTER MILL
- MITESIDE HALT
- MURTHWAITE HALT
- IRTON ROAD
- THE GREEN
- FISHERGROUND HALT
- BECKFOOT
- **DALEGARTH FOR BOOT**

DESTINATION HIGHLIGHTS
see page 162

FREQUENCY OF TRAINS
Carlisle to Ravenglass:
1 per hour (Mon-Sat)
Ravenglass to Dalegarth:
2-14 per day (Mar-Nov)

64½ MILES
1 HOUR 40 MINUTES
+ 45 MINUTES

A train for Barrow-in-Furness heads along the scenic Cumbrian Coast Line near Siddick.

NEWCASTLE
CENTRAL
CARLISLE
Darlington
Lancaster

CARLISLE
WETHERAL
BRAMPTON
HALTWHISTLE
BARDON MILL
HAYDON BRIDGE
HEXHAM
CORBRIDGE
RIDING MILL
STOCKSFIELD
PRUDHOE
WYLAM
BLAYDON
METRO CENTRE
DUNSTON
NEWCASTLE CENTRAL

Following the course of Hadrian's Wall and, for much of its length, the River Tyne, England's northernmost cross-country line from Carlisle to Newcastle was opened in 1838. In addition to the regular passenger service, the double-track line is also used as a diversionary route and for freight traffic. Along with its highly scenic qualities, the line features many original station buildings, iron latticework footbridges and graceful signal boxes from a bygone age.

Diesel trains for Newcastle head southeast from Carlisle's busy station before striking east through Petteril Bridge Junction, where the Settle-Carlisle Line joins from the south. The first stop is at Wetheral station, after which trains cross the River Eden on a fine stone viaduct before heading up into the hills to Brampton, which until 1923 was the junction for a short branch line to Brampton Town. From here, the railway continues to climb northeastwards, crossing Hadrian's Wall twice before looping southwards to join the South Tyne Valley at Haltwhistle. Featuring a graceful and lofty signal box, the station here was also the junction for the Alston branch until 1976.

Now heading eastwards along the valley, trains call at Bardon Mill and Haydon Bridge before crossing the South Tyne to reach Hexham. Built in 1835 and still with some original features, Hexham is the busiest intermediate station on the line and also one of the oldest in the world. From Hexham, trains continue eastwards, closely following the course of the Tyne through Corbridge, Riding Mill, Stocksfield, Prudhoe, Wylam (superb elevated signal box) and Blaydon. Just east of here, trains for Newcastle crossed the Tyne via Scotswood Bridge until it was closed in 1982 – today's trains follow a new route via Metro Centre and Dunston before heading north to cross King Edward VII Bridge, high over the Tyne, to Newcastle station.

DESTINATION HIGHLIGHTS
BALTIC Centre for Contemporary Art; Centre for Life; Discovery Museum; Great North Museum; Laing Art Gallery; Victorian Grainger Market; Quayside architecture and Tyne bridges; 11th-century Newcastle Castle; Grey Street and Grey's Monument; Chinatown; Segedunum Roman Fort, Baths and Museum (Wallsend); North Tyneside Steam Railway and Museum (Percy Main)

FREQUENCY OF TRAINS
1 per hour

60 MILES
1 HOUR 30 MINUTES

The dramatic Gateshead Millennium Bridge across the River Tyne in Newcastle.

Our day trip along the East Coast Main Line to York starts at Newcastle's 12-platform station, which was opened by Queen Victoria in 1850. With a neo-classical Grade I-listed station building and three curved, arched roofs it was first linked across the Tyne by Robert Stephenson's High Level Bridge. However, this involved Anglo-Scottish trains having to reverse direction at the station until the King Edward VII Bridge was opened in 1906, thus allowing through running.

Although the ECML is electrified, cross-country services using the route are operated by diesel multiple units. Trains for York depart southwards to cross the Tyne on the King Edward VII Bridge, offering great views of the city to east and west. Heading south, trains soon pass the busy Tyne Yard, which lies to the west and handles all heavy freight movements in the area – to the east, Antony Gormley's iconic Angel of the North sculpture can be seen on high ground. At Chester-le-Street, the railway joins the valley of the meandering River Wear, following its course to Durham before soaring high above this historic city on a curving viaduct. South of the city, the railway loops westward to meet the river for the last time before resuming its southerly course through Ferryhill and Newton Aycliffe to Darlington (junction for Bishop Auckland and Stockton-on-Tees).

South of Darlington the ECML follows a more-or-less dead-straight and level route all the way to York – for good reason this stretch was called the 'Race Track' in steam days. Trains speed through Northallerton (for the Wensleydale Railway) and Thirsk before making the final approach past the National Railway Museum into York's magnificent curving, overall-roofed station. The city's many historic attractions are within easy reach of the station.

- **NEWCASTLE CENTRAL**
- CHESTER-LE-STREET
- DURHAM
- DARLINGTON
- NORTHALLERTON
- THIRSK
- **YORK**

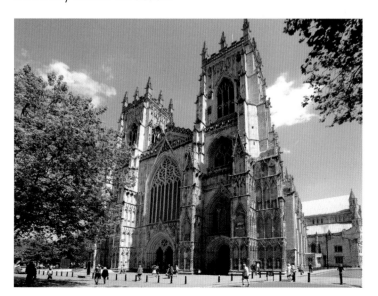

DESTINATION HIGHLIGHTS
York Minster; York Castle Museum; city walls; narrow medieval streets (The Shambles); Yorkshire Museum; Museum Gardens; JORVIK Viking Centre; York Art Gallery; Richard III Museum; Treasurer's House (NT); National Railway Museum; boat trips on River Ouse; railway path to Selby

FREQUENCY OF TRAINS
5 per hour (Mon-Sat)
4 per hour (Sun)

80½ MILES
1 HOUR

The magnificent York Minster is one of many tourist attractions in this historic city.

NEWCASTLE CENTRAL ◉	
ST JAMES ○	MONUMENT ○
MONUMENT ○	HAYMARKET ○
MANORS ○	JESMOND ○
BYKER ○	WEST JESMOND ○
CHILLING-HAM ROAD ○	ILFORD ROAD ○
WALKER-GATE ○	SOUTH GOSFORTH ○
WALLSEND ○	LONG-BENTON ○
HADRIAN ROAD ○	FOUR LANE ENDS ○
HOWDON ○	BENTON ○
PERCY MAIN ○	PALMERS-VILLE ○
MEADOW WELL ○	NORTHUM-BERLAND PARK ○
NORTH SHIELDS ○	SHIREMOOR ○
TYNE-MOUTH ○	WEST MONKSEATON ○
CULLER-COATS ○	MONKSEATON ○
	WHITLEY BAY ◉

Geordies have been making this trip to the seaside resort of Whitley Bay for well over a century. With its long golden sandy beach, the destination is well worth a visit on a fine day. The route is along the North Tyneside Loop, which developed following the opening of the Newcastle & North Shields Railway and the Blyth & Tyne Railway in the 19th century. Primarily coal-carrying lines, both companies were taken over by the North Eastern Railway which introduced electric trains in 1904 – this move was in response to increasing competition from electric street trams. The 30-mile network was electrified using the third-rail system and remained in use until British Railways de-electrified it in 1967, when diesel multiple units were introduced. This remained the *status quo* until it was converted into an overhead electric light rail system, which reopened in 1980. Known as the Tyne & Wear Metro, the network has been expanded south of the Tyne to South Shields, Sunderland and South Hylton and also to Newcastle Airport.

Heading in a clockwise direction, Yellow Route trains for Whitley Bay begin their journey underground from Newcastle Central Metro station before emerging into daylight at Jesmond Junction to head north to South Gosforth (original NER footbridge). Here the Airport line strikes off to the west while the North Tyneside Loop branches off eastwards through Benton, Northumberland Park and Monkseaton (1933 Art Deco station building) before arriving at Whitley Bay. Dating from 1910, the station here is Grade II listed and has retained its glass overall roof. Continuing clockwise from here, Metro trains head south, never far from the coast, to Cullercoats (original station building and footbridge) and Tynemouth where the grand 1882 NER station is well worth a visit. The journey westwards to Newcastle features the 1890 NER station at North Shields, while at Percy Main passengers can detour to ride on the North Tyneside Steam Railway to the George Stephenson Museum at Middle Engine Lane.

DESTINATION HIGHLIGHTS
promenade and long Blue Flag golden sandy beach; Spanish City Dome; coastal walk to St Mary's Lighthouse Museum (low tide); sea kayaking; surfing

FREQUENCY OF TRAINS
5 per hour (Mon–Sat)
4 per hour (Sun)

10–10½ MILES
28 MINUTES

The historic town of Tynemouth, south of Whitley Bay.

This day trip to the historic border town of Berwick-upon-Tweed takes in a journey northwards along the electrified East Coast Main Line. Trains leave Newcastle's bustling station in an easterly direction, taking a lofty course high above the Tyne and the city centre before following a northerly route through the sprawling suburbs and heading into open country. After crossing the River Blyth, trains slow down for the 50-mph speed limit through Morpeth – the curve here is the most severe of any main line in Britain. The imposing 1847-built station at Morpeth still features an original North Eastern Railway tile map which can be see on the up platform. From here, the railway crosses the River Wansbeck to Pegswood before heading north into rolling farmland through Widdrington and Acklington, passing two rail-connected open-cast coal mines to the east en route.

With our first view of the North Sea, trains approach Alnmouth station, once the junction for the short Alnwick branch, which closed in 1968 but is now being reopened as a heritage railway. Heading north from Alnmouth, the railway crosses the River Alne to head northwest, paralleling the coastline a mile-or-so inland. Beyond Chathill station, once the junction for the eccentric North Sunderland Railway to Seahouses, there are views of Bamburgh Castle to the east and the Cheviot Hills to the west before the railway finally approaches the Northumberland coast. From the train, there are fine views to the east of Lindisfarne (or Holy Island) – the famous priory and castle here can only be reached at low tide across a causeway. After the coastal approach to Berwick, the railway loops inland before crossing the River Tweed on the iconic Royal Border Bridge – designed by Robert Stephenson and opened by Queen Victoria in 1850, this graceful stone viaduct is 2,162 ft long, 120 ft high and has 28 arches. After crossing the Tweed, trains soon reach Berwick's island platform station, which is linked by a footbridge to the original station building. Modern conservationists will be shocked to learn that the Great Hall of Berwick Castle was demolished in 1847 to make way for the station!

- NEWCASTLE CENTRAL
- MANORS
- CRAMLINGTON
- MORPETH
- PEGSWOOD
- WIDDRINGTON
- ACKLINGTON
- ALNMOUTH
- CHATHILL
- BERWICK-UPON-TWEED

DESTINATION HIGHLIGHTS
12th-century castle and Elizabethan fortified town walls; Berwick Barracks and Gymnasium Art Gallery; tours of old courtroom and jail (Town Hall); Royal Border Bridge; Riding of the Bounds (1 May); Lowry Trail; Food and Beer Festival (September)

FREQUENCY OF TRAINS
1-2 per hour

67 MILES
46 MINUTES

The iconic Royal Border Bridge carries the East Cast Main Line across the River Tweed at Berwick.

SCOTLAND

AYR ●
MAYBOLE ○
GIRVAN ○
BARRHILL ○
STRANRAER ●

Opened in stages between 1856 and 1877, the highly scenic, steeply graded line from Ayr to Stranraer fortunately escaped threatened closure in the 1960s but now faces an uncertain future having recently lost its *raison d'être* – the Northern Ireland ferry link at Stranraer Harbour. Diesel trains for Stranraer head south from Ayr station, famous for the adjacent Station Hotel that was originally opened by the Glasgow & South Western Railway in 1866.

The double track becomes single track at Dalrymple Junction (for the freight-only line to Chalmerston) and is soon climbing steeply into open countryside along the Doon Valley to Maybole. From here, the railway follows a switchback route in a southwesterly direction, tracing the Water of Girvan to reach the coast at Girvan – out to sea is the distinctive shape of Ailsa Craig, source of blue hone granite used to make curling stones. From Girvan, the railway immediately starts its steep climb up to Pinmore Tunnel and the first summit of the line, crossing 4 viaducts in just 5 miles. From Pinmore, it descends to Pinwherry before steadily climbing once more to remote Barrhill station, where there is a passing loop and signal box. Continuing its ascent through the hills, the railway reaches Chirmorie Summit then descends through Glenwhilly (passing loop only) and New Luce to the site of Challoch Junction. A stone's throw from the glorious Sands of Luce, the 'Port Road' from Dumfries once joined here from the east until its closure in 1965.

From Challoch Junction, the railway turns west along a fairly level route through Dunragit and Castle Kennedy to Stranraer, where it bypasses the town to follow a long causeway alongside Loch Ryan before terminating at the old harbour station.

DESTINATION HIGHLIGHTS
medieval Castle of St John;
Stranraer Museum in Old
Town Hall; Agnew Park
miniature railway and boating
lake; Southern Upland Way;
boat trips to Ailsa Craig
(from Girvan)

FREQUENCY OF TRAINS
5 per day (Mon-Sat)
3 per day (Sun)

59¼ MILES
1 HOUR 25 MINUTES

The uninhabited island of Ailsa Craig can be reached by boat from the harbour at Girvan.

Our day trip 'doon the watter' to the Isle of Bute begins at Glasgow Central station. An architectural gem, it features the recently refurbished Central Hotel, an oval booking office and the famous glass-walled bridge across Argyle Street known as 'Heilanman's Umbrella'. By far the busiest in Scotland, the station has been enlarged several times since it opened in 1879. Inverclyde Line electric trains for Wemyss Bay depart southwards from here to cross the Clyde before heading west at Bridge Street Junction. After passing through Shields Junction (for the Paisley Canal line), trains serve suburban stations at Cardonald, Hillington East and Hillington West before arriving at Paisley Gilmour Street station. Featuring an ornate castellated station building, Gilmour Street is also the junction for the line to the Ayrshire Coast via Lochwinnoch, which heads off in a westerly direction.

Inverclyde Line trains take a northwesterly route from Paisley, paralleling the M8 and calling at Paisley St James and Bishopton before burrowing through 2 tunnels to reach the south bank of the Clyde at Langbank, where the original red sandstone station building features stepped gable ends. Now following the ever-widening river westwards, trains call at Woodhall and Port Glasgow, from where the service to Wemyss Bay branches off the Gourock line to follow a single-track route skirting the high moorlands of Clyde Muirshiel Regional Park. Trains call at Whinhill then head out into open country through Drumfrochar, Branchton, IBM Halt, Dunrod passing loop, Inverkip and Inverkip Tunnel before reaching the Clyde Coast at Wemyss Bay. The station here is built on a pier and was opened by the Caledonian Railway in 1903. With its sinuous, graceful curves and elegant glass canopies, mock-Tudor exterior and clock tower, it is truly an inspiring building and well deserves its Grade A architectural listing. Ferries for Rothesay on the Isle of Bute leave from the same pier.

- **GLASGOW CENTRAL**
- CARDONALD
- HILLINGTON EAST
- HILLINGTON WEST
- PAISLEY GILMOUR STREET
- BISHOPTON
- WOODHALL
- PORT GLASGOW
- WHINHILL
- DRUMFROCHAR
- BRANCHTON
- I.B.M.
- INVERKIP
- **WEMYSS BAY**
- **ROTHESAY (ISLE OF BUTE)**

DESTINATION HIGHLIGHTS
boat trip across Firth of Clyde; ruined 13th-century Rothesay Castle; Winter Gardens; Ascog Hall fernery; Ardencraig House walled garden

FREQUENCY OF TRAINS
1 per hour

37¼ MILES
48 + 35 MINUTES

Opened in 1903, the station building at Wemyss Bay is one of Scotland's finest railway buildings.

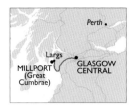

Perth

Largs
MILLPORT   GLASGOW
(Great   CENTRAL
Cumbrae)

GLASGOW CENTRAL
CARDONALD
HILLINGTON EAST
HILLINGTON WEST
PAISLEY GILMOUR STREET
JOHNSTONE
MILLIKEN PARK
HOWWOOD
LOCHWINNOCH
GLENGARNOCK
DALRY
KILWINNING
STEVENSTON
SALTCOATS
ARDROSSAN SOUTH BEACH
WEST KILBRIDE
FAIRLIE
LARGS

MILLPORT
(GREAT CUMBRAE)

Electric trains for the Ayrshire Coast Line follow the same route out of Glasgow Central as the day trip to Wemyss Bay (see page 171) as far as Paisley Gilmour Street station. From here the double-track line strikes off in a southwesterly direction along the route opened by the Glasgow, Paisley, Kilmarnock & Ayr Railway in 1840. After calling at Johnstone, Milliken Park and Howwood stations, trains follow the Black Cart Water Valley along the east shore of Castle Semple Loch to Lochwinnoch station, jumping-off point for the RSPB Nature Reserve and Castle Semple Country Park. Continuing southwest down the valley, the railway skirts the east shores of Barr Loch and Kilbirnie Loch to enter the Garnock Valley at Glengarnock. It then follows the Garnock River on its southward course to the sea, serving stations at Dalry and Kilwinning.

The 4-platform station at Kilwinning is the junction for the scenic Ardrossan and Largs branch lines. Trains bound for these seaside destinations head off in a southwestly direction to reach the coast at Stevenston. They then loop northwards along the coast to serve Saltcoats, where the line becomes single track, and Ardrossan South Beach, where the short branch line to Ardrossan Town and Ardrossan Harbour (for ferries to the Isle of Arran) extends to the west. Although the line northwards is single track, it is paralleled by a freight-only single-track line serving the vast coal import terminal and nuclear power station at Hunterston. Trains for Largs briefly head inland to call at West Kilbride before approaching the coast again at Hunterston, where our view from the train is dominated by the coal-handling terminal and our final destination, the island of Great Cumbrae, just visible beyond. After calling at Fairlie station, trains burrow through Fairlie Tunnel to follow the coast-hugging route before terminating at Largs. The small ferry terminal for the brief crossing to Great Cumbrae is a short distance from the station.

DESTINATION HIGHLIGHTS
bike hire; Millport Cathedral; Robertson Museum and Aquarium; sandy beaches; bird watching

FREQUENCY OF TRAINS
1 per hour

44½ MILES
1 HOUR + 10 MINUTES

Millport is the 'capital' of the island of Great Cumbrae, reached by ferry from Largs.

Glaswegians have been able to enjoy a day trip by train to Loch Lomond since 1850 when the Caledonian & Dumbartonshire Junction Railway opened its branch line from Bowling, on the north bank of the Clyde, and up the valley of the River Leven from Dumbarton to Balloch Pier. Initially, day trippers from Glasgow had to travel by Clyde steamer to Bowling, but in 1858 the line was linked to Glasgow by the opening of the Glasgow, Dumbarton & Helensburgh Railway. The North Clyde suburban lines were electrified in 1960 and, after steamer services ceased on Loch Lomond, the Balloch Pier branch was cut back to the present Balloch station in 1986.

North Clyde Line trains for Balloch depart westwards from Glasgow Queen Street Low Level station along the oldest stretch of underground railway in the city, calling at Charing Cross before emerging into daylight on the north bank of the Clyde. Note that on Sundays trains depart from Central station and join this route just before Partick station. With fine views of the river and the new Riverside Museum, trains then call at Partick's modern rail and underground interchange station (a short walk from the museum). After calling at Hyndland station, Balloch-bound trains take an inland route away from the river via Westerton and Singer before rejoining the riverside line via Yoker at Dalmuir. Kilpatrick is the next stop, before the railway follows a riverside course to Bowling (where the Forth & Clyde Canal from Falkirk meets the Clyde) and then crosses the River Leven to enter Dunbarton Central station – the original buildings here are Category A listed. At Dalreoch, trains branch off northwards along the single-track line up the Leven Valley, calling at Renton and Alexandria en route before terminating at Balloch's modern and conveniently located station.

GLASGOW QUEEN STREET	GLASGOW CENTRAL
	ANDERSTON
CHARING CROSS	EXHIBITION CENTRE
PARTICK	
HYNDLAND	
ANNIESLAND	
WESTERTON	
DRUMCHAPEL	
DRUMRY	
SINGER	
DALMUIR	
KILPATRICK	
BOWLING	
DUMBARTON EAST	
DUMBARTON CENTRAL	
DALREOCH	
RENTON	
ALEXANDRIA	
BALLOCH	

DESTINATION HIGHLIGHTS
boat cruises on Loch Lomond; canoe and kayak hire; restored 'Maid of the Loch' paddle steamer; Balloch Castle Country Park; Loch Lomond Sea Life Centre; National Park Visitor Centre; Loch Lomond Shores retail park

FREQUENCY OF TRAINS
2 per hour

19¼ MILES
48 MINUTES

The last paddle steamer to be built in Britain, the 'Maid of the Loch' is berthed at Balloch Pier.

This day trip to the seaside at up-market North Berwick begins at Glasgow's Queen Street High Level station. Set in a confined position between George Square and Cowlairs Tunnel, the station was opened by the Edinburgh & Glasgow Railway in 1842. The opening of the railway in the 19th century soon put paid to the aspirations of canal owners as the route closely follows the Forth & Clyde Canal between Glasgow and Falkirk (opened in 1790) and the Union Canal between Falkirk and Edinburgh (opened in 1822).

Diesel trains for Edinburgh depart northwards from the overall-roofed station and, after negotiating the tunnel, continue the steep climb up to Cowlairs where West Highland Line trains branch off westwards. To the east lies the modern Eastfield Depot, once the site of a large steam-engine shed popular with trainspotters in the 1950s and '60s. Edinburgh-bound trains head out to the suburbs in a northeasterly direction through Bishopbriggs and Lenzie before calling at Croy and Falkirk High. Now heading due east, trains call at Polmont before passing Bo'ness Junction at Manuel, where the Bo'ness & Kinneil Railway strikes off northwards to the Forth shoreline. After the stop at Linlithgow, trains closely follow the Union Canal as far as Winchburgh Junction then continue into Edinburgh's Waverley station, calling at Haymarket en route. Passengers for North Berwick change trains at Waverley.

From Waverley station, electric trains for North Berwick head east along the East Coast Main Line through Calton Tunnel and, after negotiating the junctions at Portobello, call at Musselburgh, Wallyford, Prestonpans, Longniddry and Drem. Leaving the ECML at Drem Junction, trains head north along the single-track branch line to reach the coast at North Berwick – to the east, the volcanic plug of North Berwick Law rises incongruously to a height of 613 ft.

DESTINATION HIGHLIGHTS
two sandy beaches; Seacliff private beach (entry fee); harbour; boat trips to Bass Rock and Fidra; Scottish Seabird Centre; walk up to North Berwick Law; John Muir Way; Fringe by the Sea Festival (August)

FREQUENCY OF TRAINS
1 per hour

69¾ MILES
1 HOUR 35 MINUTES

Reached by boat from North Berwick, 351-ft-high Bass Rock is now home to more than 150,000 gannets.

Our day trip from Scotland's largest city to its capital is along the Shotts Line, the most southerly of the 3 railway routes that link the two cities. This former Caledonian Railway route across the Central Lowlands was listed for closure in the 1963 'Beeching Report' but, apart from its Edinburgh terminus at Princes Street which closed in 1965, it was fortunately reprieved and in recent years has seen an upsurge in passenger usage.

Shotts Line diesel trains head south out of Glasgow Central station to cross the River Clyde and follow the electrified West Coast Main Line through Cambuslang as far as Newton East Junction. Here the WCML heads off in a southeasterly direction while trains for Edinburgh strike off eastwards to call at Uddingston and Bellshill before negotiating the complicated junction layout at Mossend (for the Mossend freight terminal). The next stop is Holytown and, east of here, Argyle Line electric trains branch off southwards to Wishaw at Holytown Junction.

Soon the Shotts Line reaches open country to serve Carfin, Cleland, Hartwood (the station here was originally built in the grounds of a psychiatric hospital!), Shotts, Fauldhouse, Breich (one of the least-used stations in Scotland), Addiewell, West Calder and Livingstone South (for the new town) before meeting the electrified line from Carstairs at Midcalder Junction. From here, trains call at Kirknewton, Curriehill (for Heriot-Watt University) and then Edinburgh suburban stations at Wester Hailes, Kingsknowe, Slateford and Haymarket before burrowing through Haymarket and The Mound tunnels to arrive at Edinburgh's centrally located Waverley station. The second-busiest station in Scotland, Waverley is set in a steep, narrow valley between the medieval Old Town and the 18th-century New Town. The valley was originally filled by Nor Loch, which was drained to make way for the railway and station in the 19th century. Covering 25 acres, Waverley is the second-largest station in Britain.

- **GLASGOW CENTRAL**
- CAMBUSLANG
- NEWTON
- UDDINGSTON
- BELLSHILL
- HOLYTOWN
- CARFIN
- CLELAND
- HARTWOOD
- SHOTTS
- FAULDHOUSE
- BREICH
- ADDIEWELL
- WEST CALDER
- LIVINGSTON SOUTH
- KIRKNEWTON
- CURRIEHILL
- WESTER HAILES
- KINGSKNOWE
- SLATEFORD
- HAYMARKET
- **EDINBURGH WAVERLEY**

DESTINATION HIGHLIGHTS
Edinburgh Castle; Arthur's Seat; Old Town and Royal Mile; Greyfriars Kirkyard; Grassmarket; Holyrood Palace and Queen's Gallery; Holyrood Park; Innocent Railway Path; Botanical Gardens; National Gallery of Scotland; Edinburgh Festivals (August); Military Tattoo (August)

FREQUENCY OF TRAINS
1 per hour (Mon-Sat)
1 every 2 hours (Sun)

46½ MILES
1 HOUR 27 MINUTES

Edinburgh by night – Waverley station, North Bridge, the Bank of Scotland building and Edinburgh Castle.

GLASGOW CENTRAL
MOTHERWELL
LOCKERBIE
CARLISLE

Our journey up the electrified West Coast Main Line to the border city of Carlisle takes the route of the Caledonian Railway's main line that opened throughout in 1848. The heavily engineered railway features 23 viaducts, which take it up the Clyde Valley and over the Southern Uplands to Beattock Summit before sweeping down Annandale for the approach to Carlisle.

Electric trains for Carlisle glide effortlessly out of Glasgow Central and, after crossing the Clyde, pick up speed through the city's sprawling suburbs to begin the journey up the Clyde Valley. Motherwell is the first stop, after which trains accelerate along Clydesdale through Carstairs Junction, where the electrified line from Edinburgh joins from the north. Continuing its gradual climb up the valley, the railway passes through many stations that were closed by the 'Beeching Axe' in 1965 – Thankerton, Symington, Lamington, Abington, Crawford, Elvanfoot and Beattock all bit the dust. South of Abington the line continues to follow the narrowing and winding valley, hemmed in by wild and remote hill country on both sides and keeping close company with the M74. Trains speed through Elvanfoot, until 1938 the junction for the light railway to Wanlockhead, and breast Beattock Summit (1,015 ft above sea level) before descending into the wilds of Annandale. After calling at Lockerbie – the only intermediate station now served on the 89½ miles between Motherwell and Carlisle – the railway heads southeast along the ever-broadening valley to pass the site of Britain's worst rail disaster at Quintinshill. A multiple train collision here in 1915 claimed the lives of 217 people, the vast majority of whom were officers and men of the Royal Scots Regiment. Just a mile beyond, the former Glasgow & Southwestern Railway route from Dumfries joins from the west at Gretna Junction before trains head across the flat flood plain of the Esk and Eden rivers to reach Carlisle station.

DESTINATION HIGHLIGHTS
Carlisle Castle; King's Own
Royal Border Regiment
Museum; cathedral; Carlisle
Citadel tours (summer); Tullie
House Museum & Art Gallery;
14th-century Guildhall
Museum

FREQUENCY OF TRAINS
2 per hour (Mon-Sat)
1 per hour (Sun)

102¼ MILES
1 HOUR 10 MINUTES

RIGHT: *Managed by English Heritage, Carlisle Castle is over 900 years old.*

OPPOSITE: *Preserved LNER 'A4' Paciific No. 60009 'Union of South Africa' waits to depart from Carlisle station.*

GLASGOW CENTRAL
Edinburgh

DUMFRIES
Carlisle

GLASGOW CENTRAL ●
CROSSMYLOOF ○
POLLOKSHAWS WEST ○
KENNISHEAD ○
PRIESTHILL & DARNLEY ○
NITSHILL ○
BARRHEAD ○
DUNLOP ○
STEWARTON ○
KILMAURS ○
KILMARNOCK ○
AUCHINLECK ○
NEW CUMNOCK ○
KIRKCONNEL ○
SANQUHAR ○
DUMFRIES ●

This day trip follows the route of the former Glasgow & South Western Railway's main line deep into Ayrshire and then down picturesque Nithsdale to the historic market town of Dumfries. The 1963 'Beeching Report' listed the line between Glasgow and Kilmarnock for closure and although it was reprieved, much of the route between Barrhead and Kilmarnock was singled and many intermediate stations closed. In more recent years, the relaying of double track has allowed a more frequent train service with a subsequent increase in patronage.

Glasgow South Western Line diesel trains leave Glasgow Central and head off in a southwesterly direction through the suburbs to Crossmyloof and Pollockshaws West. Kennishead station, dwarfed by tall tower blocks, is next, followed by Priesthall & Darnley, Nitshill and Barrhead. From here the line, single track as far as Lugton, heads out into open country to serve Dunlop and Stewarton before becoming single track again to Kilmaurs and Kilmarnock. Today the home of the Brush-Barclay Locomotive Works, Kilmarnock was served by one of earliest stations in Scotland when the horse-drawn Kilmarnock & Troon Railway opened in 1812. Featuring an elegant Italianate tower, the present station was opened by the Glasgow, Paisley, Kilmarnock Railway in 1846.

Trains for Dumfries head out of Kilmarnock across a 23-arch viaduct, and are soon heading southeast up into the Ayrshire Hills through Mossgeil Tunnel to Auchinleck and New Cumnock. Here, the railway joins the Nith Valley for the rest of the journey to Dumfries. Passing through sparsely populated hill-farming country, trains serve stations at Kirkconnel and Sanquhar – these, along with others on the line, were closed in 1965 but subsequently reopened. Without a doubt, the final 26 miles down the Nith Valley via Drumlanrig Tunnel is one of the most scenic railway journeys in southern Scotland while our destination of Dumfries, once the junction for the 'Port Road' to Stranraer, intriguingly beckons followers of Scotland's favourite son, the poet and lyricist Robert Burns.

DESTINATION HIGHLIGHTS
Old Bridge House Museum; Dumfries Museum and Camera Obscura; Robert Burns Centre; Robert Burns House; Robert Burns Mausoleum (St Michael's churchyard); Globe Inn (used by Robert Burns); Dumfries & Galloway Aviation Museum; ruined Lincluden Abbey

FREQUENCY OF TRAINS
1-2 per hour (Mon-Sat)

82½ MILES
1 HOUR 45 MINUTES

The Devorgilla Bridge and weir across the River Nith at Dumfries.

Until 1965 this day trip to Oban, the Gateway to the Isles, would have taken railway passengers on a route via Stirling, Dunblane and Callander. However, the closure of this highly scenic route up Glen Ogle now sees Oban-bound trains travelling via the equally scenic West Highland Line as far as Crianlarich, where the original line is rejoined.

Diesel trains for Oban depart from Glasgow Queen Street station in a northerly direction and, after climbing up through up through Queen Street Tunnel to Cowlairs, branch off westwards to follow the suburban route through Westerton to Dalmuir. From here, trains follow the north bank of the River Clyde through Bowling and Dumbarton to Craigendoran Junction where the line becomes single-track. Now heading north alongside Gare Loch, trains reach Garelochhead station before climbing up to the summit of the line alongside Loch Long at Glen Douglas.

From the summit, the line heads down to Arrochar & Tarbet station before heading north on a ledge alongside Loch Lomond to Ardlui and then up Glen Falloch to Crianlarich. Here the train is divided, with one half continuing to Fort William along the West Highland Line (see page 180) and the other half to Oban. From Crianlarich, trains for Oban head west along Strath Fillan to Tyndrum Lower and then down Glen Lochy to Dalmally. West of here, this scenic line skirts around the northern leg of Loch Awe, serving stations at Loch Awe (camping coach) and Falls of Cruachan (seasonal request stop), before weaving through the Pass of Brander to reach Taynuilt on the shore of Loch Etive. Following the south shore of the loch westwards, trains call at Connel Ferry station before heading inland and looping down through a rock cutting into Oban, where the modern station is conveniently located next to the ferry terminal and close to the town centre.

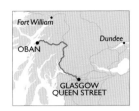

GLASGOW QUEEN STREET
DALMUIR
DUMBARTON CENTRAL
HELENSBURGH UPPER
GARELOCHHEAD
ARROCHAR & TARBET
ARDLUI
CRIANLARICH
TYNDRUM LOWER
DALMALLY
LOCH AWE
FALLS OF CRUACHAN
TAYNUILT
CONNEL FERRY
OBAN

DESTINATION HIGHLIGHTS
busy harbour; ferries to Kerrera and Lismore; seafood restaurants; Oban Distillery; McCaig's Tower; War and Peace Museum; St Columba's Cathedral

FREQUENCY OF TRAINS
3 per day

101¼ MILES
3 HOURS 8 MINUTES

A bridge carrying the Glasgow to Oban railway is reflected in the still, deep waters of Loch Awe.

GLASGOW QUEEN STREET	●
DALMUIR	○
DUMBARTON CENTRAL	○
HELENSBURGH UPPER	○
GARELOCHHEAD	○
ARROCHAR & TARBET	○
ARDLUI	○
CRIANLARICH	○
UPPER TYNDRUM	○
BRIDGE OF ORCHY	○
RANNOCH	○
CORROUR	●

The first part of this day trip to remote Corrour follows the same route as the Oban trip as far as Crianlarich (see page 179). Opened in 1894 between Glasgow and Fort William, the West Highland Line is deservedly one of the most scenic railways in the world. In common with all the stations on the line, Crianlarich station has an island platform with an attractive Swiss chalet-style waiting room which also features a tea room. Diesel trains for Fort William head northwards from the station, crossing a viaduct before beginning their climb up Strath Fillan to Upper Tyndrum station. From here, the line continues its ascent to County March Summit (1,024 ft above sea level) before following the contours of Beinn Dorain around the famous Horseshoe Curve and viaduct to Bridge of Orchy, where the station building is now a bunk house for walkers on the West Highland Way.

Heading northwards up Glen Orchy, the line continues its contour-hugging route high above Loch Tulla then heads away from all human habitation up Glen Tulla to reach wild and remote Rannoch Moor. The Victorian railway builders took five years to cross the moor, laying the line across the bogs on a raft of brushwood and heather. Human habitation is briefly touched at lonely Rannoch station, where a tea room and visitor centre is located in the station building, before the line plunges into Cruach cutting and Britain's only railway snow shed. Trains then head northwest across remote terrain to Corrour station. At 1,339 ft above sea level, Corrour is the highest standard-gauge station in Britain and one of the very few with no road access – although it is served by the Highland Caledonian Sleeper train from London, it is one of the loneliest spots on Britain's rail network. Beautiful and remote Loch Ossian is a short walk away while stunning hill-walking countryside is at your feet!

DESTINATION HIGHLIGHTS
Station House Restaurant; hill walking and Munro-bagging; walks around Loch Ossian and to Loch Treig; Ossian Hostel; 'Trainspotting' film location

FREQUENCY OF TRAINS
4 per day (Mon-Sat)
2 per day (Sun)

123 MILES
3 HOURS 45 MINUTES

Remote Loch Ossian can be reached on foot along a track from Corrour station.

Our day trip to Mallaig takes in a memorable railway journey through stunning scenery along a route recently made famous in the Harry Potter films. As well as the regular diesel trains that operate year round, 'The Jacobite' steam train also runs along the line in the summer months. Overlooked by Ben Nevis, trains for Mallaig depart northwards from Fort Willam's 1970s-style terminus and strike off westwards at Mallaig Junction to Banavie station. Beyond Banavie, the railway crosses the Caledonian Canal on a swing bridge before following the north shore of Loch Eil to the little-used stations at Loch Eil Outward Bound and Locheilside. Continuing westwards, the line then makes a loop high over Glen Finnan on the iconic 21-arch curving viaduct that was built by 'Concrete Bob' McAlpine for the line's opening in 1901 – the views southwards from here over the Glenfinnan Monument and along the length of Loch Shiel are truly awesome on a clear day. With gradients as steep as 1-in-40, numerous rock cuttings, viaducts and 11 tunnels, this heavily engineered route still demands the highest driving skills from the crew of the steam-operated summer service.

After slowly crossing the viaduct, trains reach Glenfinnan where the restored station building and signalbox are now a railway museum. From here, the railway heads west alongside idyllic Loch Eilt to Lochailort station before cutting across the Ardnish Peninsula through a series of tunnels and over Loch nan Uamh Viaduct to reach Beasdale. Beyond here, the railway continues westwards to reach the coast at Arisaig – the westernmost station in Britain – before turning northwards through Morar to terminate at Mallaig. The final coast-hugging part of this journey offers glorious views of the Sound of Sleat, the islands of Eigg and Rum and the White Sands of Morar (as featured in the film 'Local Hero').

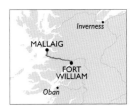

- **FORT WILLIAM**
- BANAVIE
- CORPACH
- LOCH EIL OUTWARD BOUND
- LOCHEILSIDE
- GLENFINNAN
- LOCHAILORT
- BEASDALE
- ARISAIG
- MORAR
- **MALLAIG**

DESTINATION HIGHLIGHTS
'Harry Potter' and 'Local Hero' film locations (route of Hogwarts Express); trip on steam-operated 'The Jacobite'; monument to Bonnie Prince Charlie (Glenfinnan); Glenfinnan Station Museum; White Sands of Morar

FREQUENCY OF TRAINS
4 per day (Mon-Sat)
3 per day (Sun)

41¾ MILES
1 HOUR 3 MINUTES

Train passengers have fine views of the Jacobite Monument and Loch Shiel from Glenfinnan's curving viaduct.

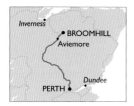

Inverness
BROOMHILL
Aviemore
Dundee
PERTH

PERTH
DUNKELD & BIRNAM
PITLOCHRY
BLAIR ATHOLL
DALWHINNIE
NEWTONMORE
KINGUSSIE
AVIEMORE
BOAT OF GARTEN
BROOMHILL

DESTINATION HIGHLIGHTS
trip on Strathspey Railway;
walks from Broomhill; railway
museum (Boat of Garten);
summit of Cairngorm (via bus
from Aviemore and
Cairngorm Mountain Railway)

FREQUENCY OF TRAINS
Perth to Aviemore: 1 every
90 mins (Mon-Sat),
7 per day (Sun)
Aviemore to Broomhill: 3 per
day (June-Aug; selected days,
Feb-June & Sept-Oct)

92½ MILES
1 HOUR 30 MINUTES +
45 MINUTES

OPPOSITE: *A restored industrial
tank engine hard at work on the
Strathspey Railway.*

This day trip along the scenic Highland Line to Aviemore and the Strathspey Railway begins at Perth's grand station, which was designed by Sir William Tite and opened in 1848. Following river valleys to the summit of the line at Druimuachdar, Highland Line diesel trains head northwards from Perth, following the Tay Valley to the site of Stanley Junction where steam-hauled Glasgow-Aberdeen expresses once branched of eastwards until their demise in 1966. From here, the line becomes single track, briefly cutting across country before rejoining the river valley to the east of Dunkeld. The scenery has changed from fertile farmland to the heavily wooded gorges of the Strath Tay by the time trains reach the first stop, Dunkeld & Birnam. Continuing northwards, the railway crosses the river on an impressive castellated iron girder bridge before sweeping through the site of Ballinluig station, until 1965 the junction for the Aberfeldy branch.

At Ballinluig the railway enters the wooded valley of the River Tummel, which it follows to Pitlochry – the original Highland Railway stations and their gardens here are a welcoming sight for visitors to this popular destination. North of Pitlochry the railway threads through the Pass of Killiecrankie, crossing the river on a 10-span viaduct to start the long climb northwestwards through Glen Garry. After calling at Blair Atholl, where the Duke of Atholl's Blair Castle is a notable landmark, the line becomes double track once more and trains continue their climb up the narrowing valley, keeping close company with the A9 before breasting the summit at Druimuachdar, 1,484 ft above sea level.

From the summit, the line heads northwards down Glen Truim to Dalwhinnie where it reverts to single track – the view down Loch Ericht as the train approaches Dalwhinnie station is one of the highlights of this scenic route. Continuing down Glen Truim, the railway enters the Spey Valley, following the river through Newtonmore and Kingussie stations to Aviemore, where passengers change trains. The attractive and spacious station here was opened in 1898 when the direct line to Inverness via Slochd Summit was opened. It is also the southern terminus of the Strathspey Railway to Broomhill.

A victim of the 'Beeching Axe' in 1965, this delightful 8¼-mile single-track heritage line follows a northeasterly course along the scenic Spey Valley, en route serving the intermediate station at Boat of Garten where there is a railway museum. While trains (steam or diesel) currently terminate at Broomhill station, the line is being extended along the valley to Grantown-on-Spey. Broomhill station has also featured as 'Glenbogle' station in the TV series 'Monarch of the Glen'.

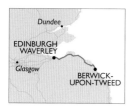

EDINBURGH WAVERLEY
DUNBAR
BERWICK-UPON-TWEED

Our day trip to the historic border town of Berwick-upon-Tweed starts at Edinburgh's Waverley station, which has recently been the subject of a major refurbishment. Diesel and electric trains provide the service along the East Coast Main Line to Berwick. Trains depart in an easterly direction through Calton Tunnel and, after passing through the city's suburbs, head out into the rich farming country of fertile East Lothian. As they speed through Prestonpans and Longniddry, passengers are treated to views northwards of the Firth of Forth and the Fife hills beyond. Between Drem and Longniddry the 613-ft volcanic plug of North Berwick Law comes into view, while at Dunbar, where the railway meets the coast, the steep-sided Bass Rock can be seen to the north. From Dunbar, the railway heads southeast along the coast, passing the rail-connected Oxwellmains cement works, waste disposal terminal and Torness nuclear power station en route before heading inland again at Cockburnspath.

From Cockburnspath, the railway takes a meandering route along the Eye Water Valley, slowing down at Penmanshiel to follow the diversion that was opened following the collapse of Penmanshiel Tunnel in 1979. Continuing to trace the valley, trains speed through Reston, once the junction for Duns and St Boswells, and past Ayton Castle to reach the coast again at Burnmouth. Once the junction for the short branch line to Eyemouth, the station here closed in 1962. For the final, dramatic, part of the journey to Berwick the railway heads south along the cliff tops, passing the historic lineside indicators marking the Scotland-England boundary along the way. On arrival at Berwick-upon-Tweed, visitors should look out for the remains of the Great Hall of Berwick Castle, which was demolished in 1847 to make way for the station.

DESTINATION HIGHLIGHTS
12th-century castle and Elizabethan fortified town walls; Berwick Barracks and Gymnasium Art Gallery; tours of old courtroom and jail (Town Hall); floodlit Royal Border Bridge; Riding of the Bounds (1 May); Lowry Trail; Food and Beer Festival (September)

FREQUENCY OF TRAINS
2 per hour

57½ MILES
40 MINUTES

A Voyager diesel train speeds along the East Coast Main Line near Burnmouth.

Diesel trains for the famous seafaring city of Dundee depart westwards from Edinburgh's Waverley station, first heading through the deep cutting below Princes Street Gardens and then burrowing through The Mound and Haymarket Tunnels. At the west end of the latter, busy Haymarket station still features the original building that was opened by the Edinburgh & Glasgow Railway in 1842. As the parallel main line to Glasgow continues westward, Dundee-bound trains on the East Coast Main Line take a northerly route to Dalmeny before crossing the iconic Forth Bridge. The opening of this bridge in 1890 was the final link in the railway between Edinburgh and Aberdeen and it offers passengers panoramic views down the Firth of Forth to the North Sea. Leaving the bridge at North Queensferry, trains call at Inverkeithing before taking the coastal route along the north shore of the Firth of Forth to Kirkcaldy – along this stretch there are fine views across the water to Edinburgh. From Kirkcaldy, the railway heads inland to take a northerly route across Fife countryside through Thornton Junction to call at Markinch.

From Markinch, the railway heads north past the Lomond Hills to Ladybank (junction for the single-track line to Perth) before turning northeast along the valley of the River Eden to reach the market town of Cupar. Continuing down the widening valley, the railway reaches Leuchars, once the junction for lines to Tayport, St Andrews and the Fife Coast. From Leuchars, trains head north to skirt the Ochil Hills before crossing the Firth of Tay on the famous Tay Bridge. Opened in 1887, this was the second bridge to be built, replacing the earlier one that collapsed in 1879. After dramatic views along the Firth to the east and west, trains leave the 2¾-mile-long bridge to enter Dundee's modern station.

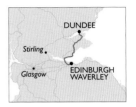

- EDINBURGH WAVERLEY
- HAYMARKET
- SOUTH GYLE
- DALMENY
- NORTH QUEENSFERRY
- INVERKEITHING
- DALGETY BAY
- ABERDOUR
- BURNTISLAND
- KINGHORN
- KIRKCALDY
- MARKINCH
- LADYBANK
- SPRINGFIELD
- CUPAR
- LEUCHARS
- DUNDEE

DESTINATION HIGHLIGHTS
'RRS Discovery' (Captain Scott's ship); 'HMS Unicorn'; North Carr Lightship; walk to top of the Law; Mains Castle (Caird Park); Dudhope Castle; Claypotts Castle (West Ferry); McManuss Galleries; Mills Observatory (Balgay Hill); Verdant Works (jute museum); D'Arcy Thompson Zoology Museum; Tayside Medical History Museum

FREQUENCY OF TRAINS
2 per hour (Mon-Sat)
1+ per hour (Sun)

59¼ MILES
1 HOUR 20 MINUTES

Over 2 miles long, the Tay Railway Bridge was opened in 1887, replacing an earlier bridge that collapsed.

DUNDEE ●
BROUGHTY FERRY ○
BALMOSSIE ○
MONIFIETH ○
BARRY LINKS ○
GOLF STREET ○
CARNOUSTIE ○
ARBROATH ○
MONTROSE ○
LAURENCEKIRK ○
STONEHAVEN ○
PORTLETHEN ○
ABERDEEN ●

This day trip to the Granite City begins at Dundee's modern station, from where diesel trains head east along the north shore of the Tay Estuary through Broughty Ferry to Carnoustie, speeding through two of Britain's least-used stations, Barry Links and Golf Street, en route. From Carnoustie (for the famous golf links), the railway hugs the North Sea coast to Arbroath where Kerr's Miniature Railway can be seen on the approach to the station – the original, attractive station building here was opened by the Dundee & Arbroath railway in 1848. From Arbroath (famous worldwide for its 'smokies'), the railway winds inland for a while before returning to the coast at Lunan Bay, where there are panoramic views of one of Scotland's finest beaches. As the line drops down to Montrose, it becomes single track for a short distance as it crosses the entrance to the tidal Montrose Basin, host to large numbers of wildfowl, waders and migrating geese each year. Uniquely, this stretch of line is the only single-track section on the East Coast Main Line between King's Cross and Aberdeen.

From Montrose, the line passes the site of Kinnaber Junction to head inland up the North Esk Valley before cutting across the fertile farmland of the Howe of Earns, through the recently reopened and restored station at Laurencekirk, to reach the coast again at Stonehaven. Perched high above the town, the station here is approached over the curved 14-span Glenury Viaduct. The rest of the journey closely follows the North Sea coastline along a dramatic cliff-top route through Portlethen to Nigg Bay, where the line loops inland to cross the River Dee and enter Aberdeen station. Opened as Aberdeen Joint Station in 1867, this spacious station has seen many changes, culminating in a major redevelopment with adjacent Union Square which was completed in 2009.

DESTINATION HIGHLIGHTS
Old Aberdeen; Aberdeen Castle; beach and sand dunes; Footdee (ancient fishing village); grand Victorian architecture; Victoria Park and Johnston Gardens (2 of 45 parks and gardens); Art Gallery; Maritime Museum; Provost Skene's House Museum; Gordon Highlanders Museum; Marischal Museum

FREQUENCY OF TRAINS
2 per hour (Mon-Sat)
1+ per hour (Sun)

71¼ MILES
1 HOUR 20 MINUTES

The Granite City – Aberdeen's skyline as seen from the harbour.

Incorporating a trip on a scenic heritage railway, our visit to the 'Whisky Capital' of Dufftown begins at Aberdeen's recently refurbished station, which handles over three million passengers a year. On leaving the station, diesel trains for Keith head northwest, following the Don and Urie valleys for some 25 miles. For the first 32 miles of our journey the mainly single-track line climbs more-or-less continuously as it winds through fertile Aberdeenshire farmland. En route, trains call at the reopened Dyce station, which serves nearby Aberdeen Airport, and continue up the Don Valley to Inverurie, where the original Great North of Scotland Railway station building has been tastefully restored. Departing northwards, trains then pass the site of the GNoSR's locomotive works and continue to climb through an increasingly hilly and forested landscape to reach the small town of Insch. Beyond here, the line is double track to its summit at Kennethmont, 590 ft above sea level.

After passing down Strathbogie, trains call at Huntly before following the heavily forested route down the Deveron and Isla valleys to Keith. Here, passengers for Dufftown disembark for the 20-minute walk to Keith Town station. Diesel trains to Dufftown are operated by the Keith & Dufftown Railway, Britain's most northerly heritage line. Following complete closure in 1991, the 10-mile line was reopened by volunteers in 2001 and now offers visitors a scenic journey up the forested Isla Valley before taking a tour around the Glenfiddich Distillery. Trains depart from the rebuilt Keith Town station and head in a southwesterly direction up the valley through the closed Auchindachy station before calling at Drummuir (for forest walks). On the last part of the journey, the railway drops down a gradient of 1-in-60 to cross Fiddich Viaduct and pass Glenfiddich Distillery before terminating at Dufftown's original Great North of Scotland Railway station.

ABERDEEN
DYCE
INVERURIE
INSCH
HUNTLY
KEITH

KEITH TOWN
DRUMMUIR
DUFFTOWN

DESTINATION HIGHLIGHTS
trip on Keith & Dufftown Railway; ruined Balvenie Castle; tours round Glenfiddich Distillery and Visitor Centre; railway path to Craigellachie

FREQUENCY OF TRAINS
Aberdeen to Keith:
1 every 90 mins (Mon-Sat)
5 per day (Sun)
Keith to Dufftown:
3 per day (Sat-Sun+BHs, Mar-Sept; Fri, June-Aug)

64 MILES
1 HOUR 10 MINUTES +
38 MINUTES

A steam train leaves Dufftown on the scenic Keith & Dufftown Railway.

Having survived several threats of closure, the single-track Kyle Line from Inverness serves many remote stations and rates as one of the most scenic and dramatic railway journeys in Britain. Diesel trains for Kyle of Lochalsh depart northwards from Inverness's terminal station then head west to cross the River Ness and the Caledonian Canal, on the Clachnaharry swing bridge, before running along the southern shore of Beauly Firth. After crossing the Beauly River, the railway reaches Beauly station before turning northwards to Muir of Ord, once the junction for the Fortrose branch. Continuing northwards across the neck of Black Isle, it reaches the Conon Valley before arriving at Dingwall. Set at the western end of Cromarty Firth, Dingwall's spacious station building and its wide platform awning have been tastefully restored and now house a popular tea shop.

While Kyle Line trains head west from here, Dingwall is also the junction for the Far North Line (see page 190) on its long, convoluted route northwards to Wick and Thurso. After passing the site of Fodderty Junction, where the short branch to Strathpeffer once continued west, the railway veers away briefly northwards before starting to climb the long 1-in-50 to Raven Rock Summit. From here, it drops down to the shores of Loch Garve and the line's first station, Garve, from where a railway to Ullapool (for the Western Isles) was mooted in the early 20th century but never built. Continuing westwards on this winding, switchback route, trains follow the north shore of Loch Luichart to remote Lochluichart station before heading up Strath Bran alongside Loch a'Chuilinn and Loch Achanalt to the equally remote Achanalt station.

Continuing westwards through the wild landscape of Strath Bran, the line reaches lonely Achnasheen station where trains normally cross – sadly, the station hotel here, once popular with railway travellers and staff alike, was destroyed in a fire in the 1990s. From here, the railway takes a southwesterly course to Luib Summit (646 ft above sea level) and then down through the forests of Glen Carron, passing Loch Gowan, Loch Sgamhain, tiny Achnashellach station and Loch Dhughaill en route before emerging in the lush valley of the River Carron at Strathcarron station.

From Strathcarron, the railway follows a highly scenic coastal route along the forested south shore of Loch Carron, offering passengers dramatic vistas that culminate in views across the Inner Sound to Skye and the Cuillins. Trains call at Attadale (for Attadale House Gardens), Stromeferry (terminus of the line from 1870 to 1893), tiny Duncraig (complete with octagonal waiting room), Plockton and Duirinish before carving through solid rock to hug the coastline south to Kyle of Lochalsh's terminus station. The station, dramatically located on the shore opposite the Isle of Skye, has seen a welcome upsurge in passenger usage in the last ten years. The restored station building is now home to the Friends of the Kyle line who operate a museum, shop and model railway.

● INVERNESS
○ BEAULY
○ MUIR OF ORD
○ CONON BRIDGE
○ DINGWALL
○ GARVE
○ LOCHLUICHART
○ ACHANALT
○ ACHNASHEEN
○ ACHNASHELLACH
○ STRATHCARRON
○ ATTADALE
○ STROMEFERRY
○ DUNCRAIG
○ PLOCKTON
○ DUIRINISH
● KYLE OF LOCHALSH

DESTINATION HIGHLIGHTS
model railway in restored signal box; Friends of Kyle Line museum, model railway and shop on station platform; bus trip to Skye via Skye Bridge

FREQUENCY OF TRAINS
4 per day (Mon-Sat)
2 per day (Sun)

82¼ MILES
2 HOURS 30 MINUTES

OPPOSITE: With the mountains of Skye in the background, a diesel train heads away from Kyle of Localsh with a service to Inverness.

INVERNESS ●
BEAULY ○
MUIR OF ORD ○
CONON BRIDGE ○
DINGWALL ○
ALNESS ○
INVERGORDON ○
FEARN ○
TAIN ○
ARDGAY ○
CULRAIN ○
INVERSHIN ○
LAIRG ○
ROGART ○
GOLSPIE ○
DUNROBIN CASTLE ●

DESTINATION HIGHLIGHTS
Dunrobin Castle, museum,
gardens and grounds;
restored Arts & Crafts station
and museum

FREQUENCY OF TRAINS
3 per day (Mon-Sat)
1 per day (Sun, April-Oct)

86 MILES
2 HOURS 10 MINUTES

OPPOSITE: *Completed in 1845,
Dunrobin Castle is the family
seat of the Earl of Sutherland
and the Clan Sutherland.*

Although trains only stop at Dunrobin Castle station during the summer months, this day trip allows plenty of time (apart from Sundays) to wander around the stately 'Scottish Baronial'-style home, gardens and grounds of the Duke of Sutherland. As if this wasn't enough, the convoluted railway journey there and back is a treat in its own right. Far North Line trains for Thurso and Wick head north from Inverness's terminus station and follow the same route as the Kyle of Lochalsh day trip (see page 189) as far as Dingwall. From here, they head northeast along the north shore of Cromarty Firth, calling at Alness and Invergordon, a popular deep-water port for visiting cruise liners. After passing the once rail-connected whisky distillery, the line then follows a dead-straight and level route across fertile farmland and alongside Nigg Bay to reach Fearn, where it turns northwest across flat countryside to Tain.

Set on the south shore of the Dornoch Firth, Tain has retained its original Highland Railway station building and attractive latticework footbridge and is also a passing place for trains. Instead of heading north via a bridge across the Dornoch Firth from Tain (as the road now does), the Victorian railway builders took a long inland route via Lairg that adds 20 (very pleasant) miles to the journey. Leaving Tain in a westerly direction, the line hugs the south shore of Dornoch Firth to Ardgay (the termination station for some services from Inverness) then turns north up the Kyle of Sutherland to Culrain, jumping-off point for the youth hostel at nearby Carbisdale Castle. Soon after crossing the Kyle of Sutherland on Invershin Viaduct, trains call at Invershin station before heading north up Strath Shin to reach Lairg. Located some distance from the village it serves, the station is an interchange point for bus services to the far northwest of Scotland and is also a railhead for oil traffic from Grangemouth.

From Lairg, trains head west down Strath Fleet, calling at Rogart station – where two old railway coaches offer self-catering accommodation – before meeting Loch Fleet at the site of The Mound station, former junction for the Dornoch branch. After turning northeast to Golspie – where the original station building built by the Sutherland Railway in 1868 is now a private residence – the line soon reaches Dunrobin Castle station (note that this is a request stop). Built as a private station for the Duke of Sutherland, the timbered Arts & Crafts-style waiting room was constructed in 1902 and has been restored to its former glory. It houses a small museum and a newly restored cloakroom, which was opened by Michael Portillo in 2012. The castle is just a short walk from the station.

PHOTO CREDITS

Jack Boskett: 95

Colour-Rail: front cover, 20 (Jon Bowers); 36, 80, 104, 107 (John Chalcraft); 56 (Gordon Edgar); 69, 88/89, 94 (Paul Chancellor); 83 (P H Wells); 96, 98, 171 (Bob Sweet); 111 (Ian Chancellor); 120; 122 (Derek Cross); 124; 136 (Hugh Ballantyne)

Mike Esau: 40, 44

John Gray: 187

Julian Holland: 23, 29, 39, 77, 91, 93, 170, 172, 174, 180

Image Rail: 17, 18, 22

Milepost 92½: 12, 19, 47, 66, 121, 126, 148, 162, 163

Gavin Morrison: 46, 86, 108, 117, 142, 188

Brian Sharpe: 64, 72/73, 153, 184

Shutterstock: 3 (David Maska); 4/5 (Laurence Gough); 6/7, 157 (Daniel J Rao); 8, 50/51 (Rob van Esch); 9 (J & S Photography); 10/11 (Stephen Rees); 13, 41, 48, 54 (Ian Woolcock); 14 (Kernowphoto); 15, 24, 27 (jennyt); 16 (Jason Ho); 21 (Fotomicar); 25, 37, 45 (Richard Melichar); 26, 79, 82 (Peter R Foster IDMA); 28 (Maisna); 30 (chrisdorney); 31 (BasPhoto); 32/33, 43 (tlorna); 34 (Nick Stubbs); 35, 155 (Jane Rix); 38 (gfdunt); 42 (Mark Castro); 49 (Ron Ellis); 52 (Chris Jenner); 53, 181 (stocker1970); 55 (Standa Riha); 57 (Michael Stokes); 58 (Davis Steele); 59, 102, 140 (i41coc12); 60 (dazgee); 61 (Brians); 62, 63 (Darren Pierse Kelly); 65, 74, 76 (Sue Chillingworth); 67 (Gyrohype); 68 (Mark Burrows Nottingham UK); 70 (Amra Pasic); 71 (Ollie Taylor); 75 (Vicki Anne Nunn); 78 (Becky Stares); 81 (Brian Maudsley); 84, 85 (Graham Taylor); 87 (Photoseeker); 90 (Andy Lidstone); 92 (jamesdavidphoto); 97, 143 (David Hughes); 99, 103, 127, 128, 130, 131, 132, 154 (Gail Johnson); 100 (Luis Santos); 101 (kenny1); 105 (Claudio Divizia); 106 (donsimon); 109 (Jeff Dalton); 110 (Guy Erwood); 112, 137 (Alastair Wallace); 113 (Artur Bogacki); 114/115, 183 (PHB.cz (Richard Semik)); 116 (spectrumblue); 118 (Tim Dobbs); 119 (Pixel Memoirs); 123 (crazychris84); 125 (Tony Brindley); 129 (peresanz); 133 (Ant Clausen); 134/135, 177 (ATGImages); 139 (Phil MacD Photography); 141, 160, 161, 176 (Kevin Eaves); 144 (Steve Heap); 145, 149 (George Green); 146 (Darren Hedges); 147, 156, 159, 164 (Gordon Bell); 150 (Andrew Booley); 151 (Tom Curtis); 158 (Crepesoles); 165 (WDG Photo); 166 (Chris Frost); 167 (Shaiith); 168/169 (Michal Lazor); 173 (Sophie McAuley); 175 (Brendan Howard); 178 (Peter Guess); 179, 191 (Grant Glendinning); 185 (Stephen Finn); 186 (Paula Fisher)

PHOTO CAPTIONS

Front cover:
Restored GWR 'King' Class No. 6024 'King Edward I' heads along the sea wall at Dawlish with a Bristol to Kingswear train.

West Country (p10/11)
Carbis Bay, on the St Ives branch line.

South & Southeast England (p32/33)
The Marshlink Line crosses the River Rother at Rye.

Day Trips from London (p50/51)
Brunel's magnificent Paddington station, the starting point for day trips to Oxford and Bath.

Eastern England (p72/73)
A charter train in Sleaford, Lincolnshire.

Central England (p88/89)
Crossing the River Severn on the Severn Valley Railway.

Wales (p114/115)
A vintage steam train on the narrow-gauge Talyllyn Railway in Wales.

Northern England (p134/135)
Dent Head Viaduct on the Settle to Carlisle line.

Scotland (p168/169)
Remote Corrour station on the West Highland Line.

OTHER BOOKS BY JULIAN HOLLAND

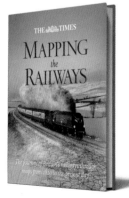

Mapping the Railways
(with David Spaven)
ISBN 978-0-00-743599-9 (HB) £30

Britain's Scenic Railways
(with David Spaven)
ISBN 978-0-00-747879-8 (HB) £30

Exploring Britain's Lost Railways
ISBN 978-0-00-750541-8 (HB) £30